D1385102

CONTEMPORARY Black Biography

ISSN-1058-1316

CONTEMPORARY

Black

Biography

Profiles from the International Black Community

Volume 33

Ashyia N. Henderson, Editor

GALE®

THOMSON

GALE

Detroit • New York • San Diego • San Francisco • Cleveland • New Haven, Conn. • Waterville, Maine • London • Munich

Contemporary Black Biography, Vol. 33

Project Editor
Ashyia N. Henderson

Editorial
Jennifer M. York

Permissions
Maria Franklin, Margaret Chamberlain
Manufacturing
Dorothy Maki, Stacy Melson
Composition and Prepress
Mary Beth Trimper, Gary Leach

Imaging and Multimedia Content
Barbara Yarrow, Dean Dauphinais,
Leitha Etheridge-Sims, David G. Oblender,
Lezlie Light, Randy Bassett, Robert Duncan,
Dan Newell

ISBN 0-7876-5914-2
ISSN 1058-1316

Printed in the United States of America
10 9 8 7 6 5 4 3 2 1

Contemporary Black Biography
Advisory Board

Contents

Introduction ix

Photo Credits xi

Cumulative Nationality Index 183

Cumulative Occupation Index 193

Cumulative Subject Index 211

Cumulative Name Index 255

Introduction

Contemporary Black Biography provides informative biographical profiles of the important and influential persons of African heritage who form the international black community: men and women who have changed today's world and are shaping tomorrow's. *Contemporary Black Biography* covers persons of various nationalities in a wide variety of fields, including architecture, art, business, dance, education, fashion, film, industry, journalism, law, literature, medicine, music, politics and government, publishing, religion, science and technology, social issues, sports, television, theater, and others. In addition to in-depth coverage of names found in today's headlines, *Contemporary Black Biography* provides coverage of selected individuals from earlier in this century whose influence continues to impact on contemporary life. *Contemporary Black Biography* also provides coverage of important and influential persons who are not yet household names and are therefore likely to be ignored by other biographical reference series. Each volume also includes listee updates on names previously appearing in CBB.

Designed for Quick Research and Interesting Reading

- *Attractive page design* incorporates textual subheads, making it easy to find the information you're looking for.

- *Easy-to-locate data sections* provide quick access to vital personal statistics, career informa- tion, major awards, and mailing addresses, when available.

- *Informative biographical essays* trace the subject's personal and professional life with the kind of in-depth analysis you need.

- *To further enhance your appreciation* of the subject, most entries include photographic portraits.

- *Sources for additional information* direct the user to selected books, magazines, and newspapers where more information on the individuals can be obtained.

Helpful Indexes Make It Easy to Find the Information You Need

Contemporary Black Biography includes cumulative Nationality, Occupation, Subject, and Name indexes that make it easy to locate entries in a variety of useful ways.

Available in Electronic Formats

Diskette/Magnetic Tape. *Contemporary Black Biography* is available for licensing on magnetic tape or diskette in a fielded format. Either the complete database or a custom selection of entries may be ordered. The database is available for internal data processing and nonpublishing purposes only. For more information, call (800) 877-GALE. *Online.* *Contemporary Black Biography* is available online through Mead Data Central's NEXIS Service in the NEXIS, PEOPLE and SPORTS Libraries in the GALBIO file.

Disclaimer

Contemporary Black Biography uses and lists websites as Sources and these websites may be obsolete.

We Welcome Your Suggestions

The editors welcome your comments and suggestions for enhancing and improving *Contemporary Black Biography*. If you would like to suggest persons for inclusion in the series, please submit these names to the editors. Mail comments or suggestions to:

The Editor
Contemporary Black Biography
Gale Group
27500 Drake Rd.
Farmington Hills, MI 48331-3535
Phone: (800) 347-4253

Photo Credits

PHOTOGRAPHS AND ILLUSTRATIONS APPEARING IN *CONTEMPORARY BLACK BIOGRAPHY,* VOLUME 33, WERE RECEIVED FROM THE FOLLOWING SOURCES:

All Reproduced by Permission: ***Anderson, Marian,*** photograph. AP/wide World Photos. ***Arthur, Owen,*** pen and ink drawing by Bill Bourne/Bourne Graphics. The Gale Group. ***Bailey, DeFord, Sr.,*** photograph. AP/Wide World Photos. ***Banks, Ernie,*** photograph. AP/Wide World Photos. ***Barnes, Roosevelt Booba,*** photograph. Jack Vartoogian. ***Brooks, Aaron,*** photograph by Andrew J. Cohoon. AP/Wide World Photos. ***Collins, Janet,*** photograph by Sam Faulk. Archive Photos. ***Estes, Sleepy John,*** photograph. Frank Driggs/Archive Photos. bditFutch, Eddie photograph by Dennis Cook. AP/Wide World Photos.***Futrell, Mary Hatwood,*** photograph. AP/Wide World Photos. ***Gibson,, Bob,*** photograph. AP/Wide World Photos. ***Grandmaster Flash,*** photograph by Peter Noble. S.I.N./Corbis. ***Hemphill, Jessie Mae*** photograph. Jack Vartoogian. ***Iman,*** photograph. Mitchell Gerber/Corbis- Bettman. ***Johnson, Rafer,*** photograph. AP/Wide World Photos. ***Lanier, Willie,*** photograph by Joe Raymond. AP/Wide World Photos. ***Lewis, Ray,*** photograph by Doug Mills. AP/Wide World Photos. ***Liston, Sonny,*** photograph. Bettman-Corbis. ***Memphis Minnie,*** photograph by Frank Driggs. Archive Photos, Inc. ***Miller, Reggie*** photograph by Ray Stubblebine. Reuter/Archive Photos. ***Murray, Albert L.,*** photograph by Suzanne Mapes. AP/wide world Photos. ***Nas,*** photograph by Ernest Paniccioli. The Bettman Archive/Newsphotos. ***Ngubane, Ben,*** photograph by Juda Ngwenya. Juda Ngggwenya/Reuter/ Corbis. ***Rainey, Ma,*** photograph. AP/Wide World Photos. ***Ready, Stephanie,*** photograph by Patrick Collard. AP/Wide World Photos. ***The Supremes,*** photograph. AP/Wide World Photos. ***The Temptaions,*** photograph. Corbis/Bettman. ***Thornton, Big Mama,*** photograph. AP/Wide World Photos. ***West, Cornel,*** photograph. Jerry Bauer. ***Williams, Clarence,*** photograph. Frank Driggs/Hulton Archive. ***Zuma, Jacob,*** photograph by Guy Tillum. Reuters/Getty Images.

Kool DJ Red Alert

DJ, producer

The nightclubs, dance parties, and even street corners of Harlem, New York, have long been breeding grounds for innovative musical stylings. The young men "playin' the dozens" under the streetlights and the DJs "mixin' and scratchin'" in the old clubs in the West Bronx gave birth to a distinctive mixture of dance music and rap known as "hip-hop" starting in the early 1980s. As hip-hop gained popularity during that decade, so did the DJs who created the mixes, including one of the originators, Kool DJ Red Alert. His long-running radio shows on New York's WRKS 98.7 KISS FM and WQHT (Hot 97) established him as the premier host of popular mix shows from the 1980s into the 21st century.

Received Hip-Hop Education in Harlem

Red Alert, also known as Fred Krute, began his hip-hop education in Harlem, New York. His mother's Antiguan-born parents raised him, and he received his nickname "Red Alert" while playing basketball at De-Witt Clinton High School. The "Red" referred to the color of his hair, while "Alert" described his style on the basketball court. Although his play earned him a basketball scholarship, basketball was not the driving force behind Red Alert; it was the music.

Red Alert was exposed to the true beginnings of hip-hop during his high school years when he spent his Saturday nights at parties thrown by DJ Kool Herc and MC Coke La Rock, whom Red Alert credits with being the first well-known deejay (DJ) and rapper, respectively. The parties were not only fun and games for Red Alert; they were his classrooms. He studied the songs Kool Herc played and the rhythm he used to mix and

blend the songs one into the other. He also took cues from New York's popular disco DJs of that time, including Grandmaster Flash, who went on to gain fame with Grandmaster Flash and the Furious Five. "I used to watch different eras—the disco, the hip-hop era—and then go on a little turntable and try to emulate that sound," Red Alert told the *Dallas Morning News.* "It was about learning how to hold a record, listening to the grooves."

Soon enough, Red Alert was spinning his own records and perfecting his DJ style with his own equipment. He frequented parties at the Back Door for Grandmaster Flash's shows, as well as the Dixie Club and JHS 123 to catch Afrika Bambaataa. By 1982 he had developed enough as a turntable artist to become a member of Afrika Bambaataa's Zulu nation as one of the DJs.

Became DJ of Rap-Mix Radio Show

The break that launched Red Alert's radio career came in 1983 when New York's WRKS (KISS) FM approached Bambaataa to do a late-night rap show. Bambaataa presented the opportunity to two of his DJs, both of whom turned down the offer because it was a non-paying gig. Red Alert, however, jumped at the chance. "They put me on in October 1983," he told *Billboard.* "That's when I started learning the fundamentals of how to be in and out without playing certain records around the clock."

The show was one of the first rap-mix shows on a commercial station, broadcasting every Friday and Saturday night. As the host, Red Alert did very little talking as he manned two turntables in creating spontaneous dance mixes for his radio audience. Red Alert cultivated that "spontaneity" with careful preparation,

At a Glance . . .

Born Fred Krute.

Career: Began deejaying at block parties and night-clubs, circa 1970s; WRKS 98.7 KISS FM, DJ, 1980s-94, 2001-; WQHT Hot 97, 1994-01; released *Hip-Hop On Wax, Volume 2,* and *We Can Do This,* 1988; *Let's Make It Happen (Part Three),* 1990; *DJ Red Alert's Propmaster Dancehall Show,* 1994; *Kool DJ Red Alert Presents,* 1996; *Beats, Rhymes & Battles, Volume I,* 2001; appeared in over 50 videos.

Awards: Rock & Roll Hall of Fame, exhibit; United Nations, honorary ambassador.

Address: *Website*—http://www.kooldjredalert.com.

often staying overnight at the radio station a day or two before his show just to listen to records. He also scoured New York's vinyl shops in search of new sounds to introduce in his mixes. Red Alert's diverse musical tastes became a trademark of his radio show and one of the cornerstones of his fame. Within a year, Red Alert landed a spot on KISS FM's payroll with his "Dance Mix Party," which would run for the next eleven years.

Meanwhile, Red Alert continued deejaying at clubs in downtown Manhattan like the Roxy and the Area, where he earned a reputation for creating seamless mixes for five or six hours at a time. He also worked as a DJ for various artists during this period; most notably, he became a member of Boogie Down Productions and toured the country with KRS One. In addition to his live performances, Red Alert was active in the studio, producing and managing artists like the Jungle Brothers and A Tribe Called Quest, while producing mix compilation albums of his own. The first was *Hip-Hop On Wax, Volume 2,* followed by *We Can Do This* in 1988. The compilation featured cuts by Boogie Down Productions, The Jungle Brothers, Robe Base & DJ E-Z Roc, and Salt-N-Pepa. *Letapos;s Make It Happen (Part Three)* (1990) featured artists that were part of the Native Tongues movement such as De La Soul, A Tribe Called Quest, and The Jungle Brothers. It also featured female rap artists like Salt-N-Pepa and Queen Latifah. Four years later, Red Alert produced another album, *DJ Red Alert's Propmaster Dancehall Show,* featuring songs by Shabba Ranks and Patra, two very popular Dancehall artists at that time. Red Alert's next compilation release *Kool DJ Red Alert Presents* in 1996 proved to be one of his best, featuring a list of remixes by the top rappers and hip-hop singers at that

time. The release featured Tupac, LL Cool J, Total, Faith Evans, The Junior M.A.F.I.A, and Jay Z and The Lost Boyz.

Changed Radio Stations

In 1994 Red Alert moved his radio mix parties to New York's WQHT Hot 97 radio station to produce two daily mix shows, "The Twelve O'Clock Old School Mix" and "The Five O'Clock Free Ride." At this point, Red Alert was a household name among hip-hop fans all over the United States. In spite of his nation-wide popularity, he resisted requests to syndicate his radio show. "One thing I learned is, the more you get on the inside, as far as doing production and things, the more you lose focus on what's going on on the outside," he explained to *Billboard.* "So if I was making business moves or producing all the time, I'd relate less to my audience." When asked about syndication he re-sponded that "just because your name is popular in one city, it doesn't mean you can hit in every market."

But "popular in every market" would be a valid descrip-tion for the hip-hop pioneer. Over the course of his career, Red Alert appeared in more than 50 music videos, and was honored with his own exhibit at the Rock & Roll Hall of Fame in Cleveland. In addition, he was named an honorary ambassador to the United Nations in recognition of his achievements in music.

After spending more than seven years at Hot 97, Red Alert left the radio station to return to WRKS 98.7 KISS FM in April of 2001. The new show, "DJ Red Alert Kiss Mix at Six," could be heard daily from 6-7 p.m. He also began working on a new release, *Beats, Rhymes & Battles, Volume I.* The *New York Times* described the compilation as "offering a lesson in hip-hop history like a book on tape." The release features some of the classic rap battles that defined hip-hop, and are remembered as the best not just because they stayed on wax. "As we [Red Alert and manager Chris Lighty] talked about the problems with hip-hop right now—all the drama and violence—we had the same idea about taking it back to when it was all about battling on the microphone," Red Alert told *Billboard.* The album includes the Roxanne chronicles, the KRS One/MC Shan battle, and LL Cool J vs. Kool Moe Dee, among others. Each battle is also proceeded with a narrative "history behind the raps" provided by Red Alert to educate the new generation of hip-hop fans unfamiliar with the genre's beginnings. Red Alert has established himself as one of rap, and hip-hop's pioneers.

Selected discography

Hip-Hop on Wax, Volume 2.
We Can Do This, Next Plateau, 1988.
Let's Make It Happen (Part Three), Next Plateau, 1990.

DJ Red Alert's Propmaster Dancehall Show, Next
   Plateau, 1994.
Kool DJ Red Alert Presents, Next Plateau, 1996.
Beats, Rhymes & Battles, Vol. I, Relativity, 2001.

Sources

Periodicals

Billboard, May 21, 1994, pp. 68; April 21, 2001,
   pp.19.
Dallas Morning News, June 26, 1998.
The New York Times, December 7, 2001.

On-line

www.kooldjredalert.com
www.allmusic.com

—Leslie Rochelle

Charles Henry Alston

1907-1977

Painter, muralist

Fusing modern art styles with non-Western influences to create a new and distinctive African-American idiom, Charles Henry Alston was among the most important figures of the Harlem (New York) creative community in the field of the visual arts. Alston was also a pioneering educator whose students included several of the most prominent African-American artists of the twentieth century. All through his long career, Alston remained a student of art himself, responding to contemporary artistic and historical developments and incorporating new approaches into his work.

Alston, nicknamed "Spinky," was born in Charlotte, North Carolina, on November 28, 1907. His father, the Rev. Primus Priss Alston, was born into slavery and attended divinity school after emancipation; he died when Alston was three years old. Alston's mother then married Harry Pierce Bearden, an uncle of the artist Romare Bearden—who later became one of Alston's own students. The family moved to New York in 1913, but the five Alston children (of which Charles Henry was the youngest) often returned to North Carolina to visit relatives. Alston showed artistic ability from a young age, making sculptures out of the red clay found everywhere in North Carolina.

Influenced by Alain Locke

Attending New York's DeWitt Clinton High School, Alston began to find recognition for his talents. He won a school art prize at age 14 and served as art editor of the school magazine. Thus encouraged to study art when he enrolled at Columbia University in New York, Alston graduated in 1929. During his student years he came under the influence of the black philosopher and cultural theorist Alain Locke, who had urged black artists to look to African forms for ways of expressing the African-American experience.

Alston stayed on at Columbia for graduate work and earned an M.A. in 1931. Working for a time with young people in various posts (where, during one stint with the Boys' Clubs organization, he spotted the emerging talent of the later-famous African-American artist Jacob Lawrence), Alston earned a living mostly as an illustrator. Well-acquainted with such Harlem luminaries as poet Langston Hughes and bandleader Duke Ellington, he illustrated publications, record covers, and other items released by the foremost black creative figures of the day. Alston's work was also featured in mainstream commercial publications such as *Redbook* and the *New Yorker*.

In the 1930s, as he worked to apply Locke's ideas, Alston gained recognition as a serious artist. His work was first shown in museums in 1934, as part of a traveling exhibition organized by the Harmon Foundation, and his paintings and sculptures were shown around New York through the 1930s. Such works as the painting *Two Sisters* (1935) were influenced by African masks. Alston was not merely imitating African styles, however, but using their strong geometric orientation to create works that could stand with the latest developments in abstract modernism that were emanating from Europe.

At a Glance . . .

Born on November 28, 1907, in Charlotte, North Carolina; father Primus Priss Alston was a minister; married Myra Logan, a surgeon. died on April 27, 1977. *Education*: Graduated from DeWitt Clinton High School, New York; Columbia College, New York, B.A., 1929; Teachers' College, Columbia University, M.A., 1931; later studied at National Academy of Art, New York, and Pratt Institute, Brooklyn, New York.

Career: Painter, sculptor, and art educator. Worked as magazine illustrator, 1930s and early 1940s; painted major murals for Harlem Hospital, New York, 1936; staff artist, Office of War Information and Public Relations, World War II; became first black instructor, Art Students' League, 1950, teaching there until 1971; became first black instructor, Museum of Modern Art, 1956; professor, City College of New York, 1970-77.

Awards: Arthur Wesley Dow Fellowship, Columbia University, 1929; Rosenwald Fellowships, 1939-40; National Institute of Arts and Letters grant, 1958; named to American Academy of Arts and Letters, 1958.

Encountered Mexican Mural School

Alston also came under another non-Western influence in the 1930s—that of Mexican muralists, including Diego Rivera and Jose Clemente Orozco, who painted enormous, dramatic works of public art that reflected the ferment of political changes that had occurred in their own country. Rivera had worked in the United States in the 1930s, and many art critics embraced his often radical-spirited works as part of a general artistic response to the problems of the Great Depression.

Alston, who also drew inspiration from the classical public art of Michelangelo and others, applied the ambitious dimensions of Mexican murals in a giant pair of murals installed at New York's Harlem Hospital, *Magic and Medicine* and *Modern Medicine*. These works, depicting the whole span of medical practices in African America from African-derived conjure practices to the use of modern hospital technology, were pioneering examples of art works that drew on African-American history. They were funded by the Depression-era Works Progress Administration (WPA) art project, for which Alston served as one of the first African-American supervisors, and were exhibited at the Museum of Modern Art before their permanent installation. Alston married a Harlem Hospital surgeon, Myra Logan.

As World War II broke out, Alston continued to work in the arena of public art. He served in the U.S. Army and was appointed a staff artist for the Office of War Information and Public Relations. After the war, with a growing body of work that included a series of portraits of black southerners, again influenced by the geometric shapes of African art, Alston continued to gain wider recognition. He found his services in demand as a teacher, becoming the first African-American instructor at the Art Students' League in 1950 and again at the Museum of Modern Art in 1956. Galleries in New York and elsewhere began to devote space to solo exhibitions of his work.

Painted Portraits of Black Leaders

Alston continued to change with the times, inflecting his work to match contemporary trends in the art world but never abandoning his personal style. In the 1950s, at the height of the craze for modernist abstraction, he created paintings that contained very little representation of the human form or of recognizable scenes, concentrating on effects achieved by the use of closely related colors. In the 1960s, however, as the civil rights movement gained steam, Alston returned to more accessible styles. He produced startlingly close-up portraits of figures from black history such as Frederick Douglass and the Rev. Martin Luther King Jr. (the latter was exhibited at Detroit's Museum of African American History in 2002), as well as images of more general types (such as a series of blues singers) that used distortions of the face of the painted figure to illuminate or comment upon some aspect of the subject's experience. Alston was a founding member of Spiral, a group of African-American artists who united to promote the cause of racial equality.

Active until the very end of his life, Alston was appointed to the art faculty of the City University of New York in 1970 and became a full professor in 1973. In later life he also coordinated a children's art center at the World's Fair in Brussels, Belgium. Alston died in New York on April 27, 1977. His works are owned by such major institutions as New York's Metropolitan Museum of Art, the Whitney Museum of American Art, and the Detroit Institute of Arts; *Rhapsodies in Black*, a traveling exhibition of the 1990s that formed a major retrospective evaluation of art in Harlem between the world wars, included an overview of his career.

Selected works

Magic and Medicine and *Modern Medicine*, murals, Harlem Hospital, New York, 1926.
Frederick Douglass, portrait, 1967.
Martin Luther King, Jr., portrait, 1967.

Sources

Books

Powell, Richard J., et al., eds., *Rhapsodies in Black: Art of the Harlem Renaissance*, University of California Press, 1997.
St. James Guide to Black Artists, St. James, 1997.

On-line

Afro-American Cultural Center, Charlotte, North Carolina, http://www.aacc- charlotte.org
Inventory of Charles Henry Alston papers, University of North Carolina library, http://www.lib.unc.edu/mss/inv/htm/04931_m.htm

—James M. Manheim

Marian Anderson

1897-1993

Singer

Concert singer Marian Anderson's rich contralto voice, wrote one critic in *People,* "was as perfect as a human instrument can be." The first major black female concert singer of the 20th century, Anderson was lauded by audiences and critics and honored by presidents and kings all over the world both for her phenomenal voice and for her contribution to the struggle for racial equality. As the first permanent African-American member of the Metropolitan Opera Company, Anderson was known for her unfettered delivery—Anderson conveyed the music of Bach, Handel, Tchaikovsky, and many others without any distracting mannerisms. Shunned by racially prejudiced American audiences, Anderson left for Europe, where she was met with overwhelming success. In a field dominated by whites, she was known for maintaining her dignity in the face of the bigotry she was subjected to throughout her career.

While others were marching and making impassioned speeches during the Civil Rights movement, Anderson did not speak out publicly, but was still known as the "voice of the Civil Rights struggle." Because she was forced to pursue her art tenaciously in order to succeed, she challenged the racial barrier in her own courageous and heroic way. "It is my honest belief," Anderson was quoted as saying in *Opera News,* "that to contribute to the betterment of something, one can do it best in the medium through which one expresses one's self most easily." In a PBS documentary of her life, Anderson said, "I did not start out to change the world in any way, because I knew that I couldn't. And whatever I am is the culmination of the … goodwill, the help and understanding of the many people that I have met around the world who have, regardless of anything else, seen me as I am, not trying to be somebody else."

Grew Up Poor, But Not Lacking

Marian Anderson was born February 27, 1897, in Philadelphia, the oldest of three daughters of Annie and John Anderson, a coal and ice salesman. Annie Anderson began taking in laundry to support her children after their father died when Marian was still young. The family lived with Anderson's grandmother in South Philadelphia and she grew up poor, "though never lacking in love and support. My mother always encouraged me to do anything I wanted," she was quoted as saying in *Billboard.* She began singing as a

At a Glance . . .

Born February 27, 1897, in Philadelphia, PA; died April 8, 1996, Portland, OR; daughter of Annie (a laundress) and John Anderson (a coal and ice salesman); married Orpheus H. "King" Fisher (an architect) (d. 1985), 1943. *Education:* Studied with Mary S. Patterson, Agnes Reifsnyder, and Giuseppe Boghetti.

Career: Performed for modest fees as a teen; won first prize New York Philharmonic voice competition and debuted with the Philharmonic at Lewisohn Stadium, 1925; performed at New York's Town Hall; left for Europe on a Rosenwald Fellowship, 1930; debuted in London, 1930; toured Europe, 1930-35; returned to the United States, 1935; took Sol Hurok as her manager; performed at Lincoln Memorial on Easter Sunday, 1939; debuted as the first permanent African-American member of the Metropolitan Opera Company, 1955; left the Met and published her autobiography, *My Lord What a Morning,* 1956; retired from singing, 1965; lecturer.

Awards: Rosenwald Fellowship, 1930; Presidential Medal of Freedom, 1963; Kennedy Center Honors, 1978; Eleanor Roosevelt Human Rights Award of the City of New York, 1984; National Arts Medal, 1986; lifetime achievement Grammy award, 1991; among many others.

toddler and joined the Union Baptist Church junior choir at age six. Though first turned away by a Philadelphia music school because of her color, she studied formally at age 15 with Mary S. Patterson, lessons she scrubbed floors to pay for. Many in her community acknowledged Anderson's exceptional talent, and contributed to her education—the Union Baptist choir raised money to further her training and, later, the black ensemble, the Philadelphia Choral Society, gave benefit performances to raise the funds that allowed her to study with voice coaches Agnes Reifsnyder and Giuseppe Boghetti. She then performed for modest fees, helping to support her mother and sisters. It is a little known fact that Anderson applied to Yale and was accepted, but was unable to raise enough money to cover tuition.

Boghetti entered Anderson into a New York Philharmonic voice competition when she was 28. She won first prize out of 300 competitors, debuted with the

Philharmonic at Lewisohn Stadium that same year, and signed a management contract. A significant concert at New York's Town Hall followed, but Anderson was unable to break any ground in a country as bound by racism as the United States was at the time. Anderson left for Europe on a Rosenwald Fellowship in 1930, in hopes of developing her craft and confidence, perfecting her foreign-language skills, and finding a more accepting audience.

After her 1930 London debut, the singer took Europe by storm. She toured from Italy and Austria to Germany and Scandinavia, where she met composer Jean Sibelius, who was so taken by her "warm, burnished tone and interpretive sensitivity" that he dedicated his song "Solitude" to her, according to *Billboard* critic Susan Elliot. It was on this tour that famed conductor Arturo Toscanini first heard Anderson sing and said, "A voice like yours is heard only once in 100 years," according to *Billboard.*

A Reluctant Return to the States

Anderson returned to the United States in 1935, though very reluctantly, based on her chilly reception there the first time around. After impresario Sol Hurok—who became her manager—heard Anderson sing in Paris, he advised her to return to the States for another appearance at Town Hall. Hurok was right—the concert was to be the turning point in her U.S. career. This time, with the swell of her European success behind her, American audiences and critics paid attention. *New York Times* critic Howard Taubman wrote, "Let it be said from the outset, Marian Anderson has returned to her native land one of the great singers of our time." In 1936 Anderson became the first black to perform in the White House when the Roosevelts invited her, and returned later to sing for the Eisenhowers and the Kennedys.

Anderson's successful return to the States was met with racial prejudice in 1939. Hurok was denied when he attempted to schedule a recital for Anderson at Constitution Hall, which was owned by the Daughters of the Revolution (DAR). Hurok went public with the incident. The incident became a national affair—weeks of debate ensued and many high-profile members, including First Lady Eleanor Roosevelt, immediately resigned from the DAR. Anderson, whose only political statement was her talent, was terribly upset. "Music to me means so much, such beautiful things," she was quoted as saying in *Billboard,* "and it seemed impossible that you could find people who would curb you, stop you, from doing a thing which is beautiful. I wasn't trying to sway anybody into any movements or anything of that sort, you know. I just wanted to sing and share."

The singer became a household name when, after the U.S. government offered her the use of the Lincoln

Memorial for her Easter Sunday recital, 75,000 citizens and political dignitaries descended upon the Washington D.C. site to hear her, and millions more tuned in to the performance on the radio. Her program included "America," Schubert's "Ave Maria" and the spirituals "Gospel Train," "Trampin'," and "My Soul Is Anchored in the Lord." Anderson was bolstered by the nationwide show of support. According to *Jet,* she told the racially mixed audience, "I am so overwhelmed, I just can't talk." The event was the largest public tribute since the one that welcomed Charles Lindbergh back from France ten years earlier. Whether she liked it or not, Anderson had become a symbol in the struggle for Civil Rights. The performance also secured her place among America's outstanding musical talents.

Anderson was best known for her recital repertoire, which ranged from Bach and Handel oratorio arias to the songs of Schubert, Brahms, and Tchaikovsky to spirituals. In all, Anderson's repertoire consisted of more than 200 songs in nine languages and, though labeled a contralto, her voice was effective over three octaves. Spirituals were among the most personal to Anderson. "They are my own music," she was quoted as saying in *Billboard.* "But it is not for that reason that I love to sing them. I love them because they are truly spiritual in quality; they give forth the aura of faith, simplicity, humility, and hope."

Became First Black Met Singer

At the invitation of General Manager Rudolph Bing, Anderson made her debut as the first permanent African-American member of the Metropolitan Opera Company on January 7, 1955, singing Ulrica in Verdi's *Un Ballo In Maschera.* At the age of 57, Anderson's velvety trademark tone was no longer at its peak, and a slight tremelo was audible, but "[h]er style and consistently majestic presence were still very much intact," wrote *Billboard* critic Elliot. A fellow singer remembered the night as an "electric" one where Anderson was met with a ten-minute standing ovation as soon as the curtain rose. After the concert, the contralto revealed she became nervous when the entire house erupted in applause. The audience repeated the ovations after each aria she sung. Anderson left the Met and published her autobiography, *My Lord What a Morning, in 1956.*

Throughout her transition from second-class citizen to opera royalty in the United States, Anderson kept her regal and elegant disposition. She was discriminated against repeatedly in her travels by hotels, restaurants, concert venues, many of which were blatantly closed to blacks until the late 1930s. She rarely spoke publicly about racism, but opened up in an interview in 1960. "Sometimes it's like a hair across your cheek," she said, according to *Jet.* "You can't see it. You can't find it with your fingers but you keep brushing at it because the feel of it is irritating." Anderson was also known to treat anyone who came in contact with her, from the lowest-ranking mailroom worker on up, with the same respect. Though she was presented with the key to Atlantic City, there was not a hotel in the city that would give her a room. Anderson always maintained her dignity, despite the injustices. "You lose a lot of time hating people," she told *People.*

A Rich Life, Rewarded

After she broke opera's color barrier, Anderson was awarded the Presidential Medal of Freedom in 1963, the Kennedy Center Honors in 1978, the Eleanor Roosevelt Human Rights Award of the City of New York in 1984, and the National Arts Medal in 1986. The Marian Anderson Awards, founded in 1943 and resurrected in 1990, have been awarded to such artists as soprano Sylvia McNair and mezzo-soprano Denyce Graves. In 1991 she received a lifetime achievement Grammy award and was the subject of a Public Broadcasting System (PBS) television documentary titled *Marian Anderson.* PBS's *American Playhouse* also developed a drama depicting Anderson's life, the first time an African-American singer's life had been dramatized for television. Anderson did so much for blacks in her field, screen-writer Martin Tahse told *American Visions,* but did so without making a fuss. "She simply said, 'I am black, and I am an artist. I want to sing.'" Many black singers, from Leontyne Price to Jessye Norman and Kathleen Battle, hold Anderson as a role model. As soprano Martina Arroyo, who debuted at the Met in 1961, attested in *American Visions,* "She has been a legend all my life. When I didn't know what opera singing was, I knew her name," adding that it was crucial that Anderson's legacy be kept alive.

Anderson retired in racially turbulent 1965 but continued to give lectures on her life and travels. Quoted in *American Visions,* Vincent Sheean, a correspondent in Europe who covered Anderson's triumphant early years, wrote of the artist at her retirement: "Rain or shine, war or peace, she has been before us now for 30 years as a living part of the national consciousness, the voice of the American soul. She came at a moment when a great Negro personality, which the whole nation could admire, esteem and love, had become very early an historical imperative, and in that mysterious way which destiny takes for its working, when she was needed, there she was."

After her retirement, Anderson lived on her farm, called Marianna Farms, in Danbury, Connecticut, to work with her "hands and heart and soul," she was quoted as saying in *American Visions.* A Steinway grand piano sat in the rural farmhouse, atop which sat signed photos of the Roosevelts, the Kennedys, the Carters, and Richard Nixon, next to her congressional gold medal, and various other medals, awards, and keys to a slough of cities worldwide. In 1992, her health failing at age 95, she moved to Portland, Oregon, to live with her nephew, conductor James DePreist. She died of congestive heart failure at home in Portland on April 8, 1993, one month after she had suffered a stroke. Her husband, architect Orpheus H. "King" Fisher, whom she married in 1943, died in 1985, and Anderson is survived only by DePreist. By the time of her death, Anderson told *People,* one of her greatest dreams, though bittersweet, had come true: "Other Negroes," she said, "will have the career I dreamed of." Though very few recordings of Anderson exist, the Metropolitan Opera Guild released a disc of the artist's songs, spirituals, oratorio, and opera after her death.

Sources

Books

Anderson, Marian, *My Lord, What a Morning,* Viking Press, 1956.
New Grove Dictionary of Opera, Second Edition, Volume One, Macmillan Publishers, 2001.
Sadie, Stanley, ed., *New Grove Dictionary of Opera,* Macmillan Press, 1992.

Periodicals

American Visions, December-January 1992, p. 44.
Billboard, April 24, 1993, p. 8.
Jet, April 26, 1993, p. 14.
Opera News, July 1993, p. 54.
People, April 26, 1993, p. 126.

—Brenna Sanchez

Owen Arthur

1949—

Prime Minister of Barbados

Owen Arthur, elected prime minister of the Caribbean nation of Barbados in 1994, is perhaps the most visible representative of a new breed of Caribbean leader that emerged at the end of the 20th century. Nationalistic without being leftist-oriented, professionally trained as an economist, and wary of but not hostile toward the United States and other First World countries, Arthur gained popularity with the ordinary folk of Barbados. He implemented changes in the country's economy that resulted in a notable increase in prosperity; indeed, it is his stated aim that his tiny Windward Island country should join the ranks of developed nations in the 21st century.

A native of Barbados and the son of working-class parents, Arthur was born on October 17, 1949. He did well at school, and soon it was clear that he was destined for higher education and a professional career. Unlike earlier Caribbean politicians who went to England for some portion of their studies, Arthur acquired his entire education in the Caribbean. He attended the University of the West Indies, receiving a bachelor's degree in economics in 1971, and then won a scholarship for graduate study at the university's main campus in Kingston, Jamaica.

Worked as Jamaican Government Planner

After a stint as a research assistant in the university's social science department, Arthur began his career in Jamaica as an assistant in the government's planning department. He rose quickly, becoming Jamaica's chief economic planner within five years and then serving as director of economics for the Jamaican Bauxite Institute from 1979 to 1981. While in Jamaica, Arthur represented the country at various international conclaves but also came under the influence of Jamaica's charismatic socialist leader of the day, Michael Manley. Thus, when he returned home to Barbados in 1981, he possessed a unique combination of familiarity with the world of international high finance and commitment to a stake for ordinary citizens in governmental affairs.

Arthur took a job as a project analyst with the Barbadian Ministry of Finance, but it did not take the leadership of the ruling Barbados Labor Party (BLP) long to realize that he was a natural for electoral politics. Encouraged to run for the Barbados House of Assembly by party leader Tom Adams, Arthur was given the added advantage of running in a district that had been receiving heavy government aid after recent

At a Glance . . .

Born October 17, 1949, in Barbados. Married. *Education*: University of the West Indies, B.A. in economics and history, 1971; University of the West Indies, M.Sc. in economics, 1974.

Career: Prime Minister of Barbados. Assistant economic planner and then chief economic planner, National Planning Agency, Jamaica, 1974-81; economics director, Jamaica Bauxite Institute, 1979-81; chief project analyst, Ministry of Finance and Planning, Barbados, 1981; elected to Barbados House of Assembly, 1984; taught at University of the West Indies, late 1980s; became leader of opposition Barbados Labor Party, 1993; became prime minister when party returned to power, 1994; strong re-election victory, 1999.

Addresses: *Office*—Office of the Prime Minister, Government Headquarters, Bay Street, St. Michael, Barbados.

floods. Nevertheless, the newcomer lost a 1984 election by one vote. Arthur, with what the *Times* of London called "the terrier-like determination that would characterise his future career," appealed the resulting recounts to the Barbados High Court, roughly equivalent to the U.S. Supreme Court. The court mandated a new election, which Arthur won.

In 1986 Arthur's fortunes took a turn for the worse when the BLP was defeated in national elections. Arthur briefly returned to academia as an economics lecturer at the University of the West Indies, and, in a televised speech, threatened to leave the political arena altogether. But he was already emerging as a spokesman for the BLP, having combined his education in economics with his newfound political experience. When the Barbadian economy hit the skids in the early 1990s as its twin pillars of tourism and sugar took strong hits as a result of an international slowdown, Arthur was able to frame critiques of government economic policy in a language accessible to ordinary Barbadians.

Became Prime Minister

Named BLP party leader in 1993, Arthur was a heartbeat away from becoming prime minister—in the Barbados electoral system, modeled on that of Britain, the leader of the party that wins the most seats in the country's legislature becomes the national leader. After

the BLP recaptured its majority in 1994 elections, Arthur was sworn in as the country's fifth prime minister on September 7, 1994; he was also the first Caribbean head of state who was also a trained economist. From the start, he pursued policies that reflected both the populist and the technocratic aspects of his background.

Early in his term, for example, Arthur impressed observers by appearing on a radio talk show—common enough in U.S. politics but a novelty in the Caribbean. Promising increases in education spending aimed at bringing universal schooling to Barbados, he also courted international investment, pitching Barbados as a promising location for foreign information and financial services firms and thus attempting to diversify the island's economy. His government took some criticism early on for passing a constitutional amendment that shielded the salaries of government employees from future cuts, and for refusing to devalue the weakened Barbadian dollar. Soon enough, however, the island's economy began to turn around, with the stability engendered by Arthur's personal popularity helping to create an environment conducive to growth. "No country can ever truly develop," Arthur was quoted as saying in *Current Leaders of Nations*, "unless it finds the means of engrossing everyone in the task of nation building, whatever their class, creed, color or political persuasion." Arthur wrangled with international financial agencies over what he identified as an unfair double standard shown in the pressure applied to Barbados to reform its money-laundering laws; wealthy European countries such as Switzerland and Luxembourg, which had long served as financial havens, were given more time than hard-pressed Barbados. But such disputes did little to stand in the way of a Barbadian recovery.

Unemployment Slashed

The country's unemployment rate, which had stood at a ruinous 22 percent in 1994, fell to 15.9 percent by 1997. The employment statistics were bolstered by strong increases in agricultural production and tourism, as new hotels and other tourist facilities sprouted on the island. Arthur and the BLP retained power in a landslide victory in 1999, winning 26 of the national assembly's 28 seats. Arthur's leadership was endorsed even by members of opposition parties.

Arthur's government announced ambitious plans in its second term, including the implementation of a national minimum wage and massive new spending on education. Arthur moved to strengthen trade ties with the United States while at the same time curtailing the ability of U.S. counter-narcotics ships to operate in Barbados in an unrestricted manner. At the end of the century, Arthur set in motion a proposed confederation of eight small Eastern Caribbean countries that would coordinate government services including judicial systems, aviation, telecommunications, shipping, education, health, and disaster response, among others.

"The move is a logical process in facing up to the inevitable economic and political changes in preparation for the challenges of a new world order in the 21st century," Arthur was quoted as saying in the *Financial Times*. One of those challenges that faced Barbados was a decline in tourism due to the U.S. terrorist attacks of September 11, 2001, and to the general slowdown in the world economy. Yet, as a result in part of Owen Arthur's efforts, Barbados faced these challenges fortified by solid economic fundamentals and new possibilities of cooperation with its immediate neighbors.

Sources

Periodicals

Financial Times (London, England), September 28, 1994, p. 5; April 26, 1995, p. 36; March 27, 1998, p. 5.

The Guardian (London, England), March 3, 2001, p. 24.

International Money Marketing, December 2001, p. 25.

Journal of Commerce, October 11, 1994, p. A1.

Los Angeles Times, January 23, 1999, p. A2.

Ottawa Citizen, January 24, 1999, p. A8.

St. Louis Post-Dispatch, August 2, 1998, p. A3.

The Times (London, England), November 13, 2000, Features section.

On-line

Current Leaders of Nations, Gale Group, 1999. Reproduced in *Biography Resource Center*, Gale, 2001, http://www.galenet.com/servlet/BioRC.

—James M. Manheim

DeFord Bailey

1899-1982

Musician

The son of a tenant farmer, DeFord Bailey was born on December 14, 1899, in Smith County, Tennessee. His mother, Mary Reedy Bailey chose the name DeFord in honor of two of her teachers—Mr. DeBerry and Mrs. Stella Ford. Bailey was not raised by his parents, since his father, John Henry Bailey, moved away and remarried, and his mother died within a year of his birth. His father's younger sister, Barbara Lou Bailey, and the man she married, Chuck Odum, took charge of the child.

Musical talent existed within each branch of Bailey's family, and, indeed, Bailey once claimed that, as a child, he was given a mouth harp instead of a rattle. His paternal grandfather, Lewis Bailey, was considered the best musician in Smith County. Bailey's father and other family members sometimes performed in a popular string band. Yet, despite the prevalence of music in his life, Bailey was expected to become a farm worker like the other men in his family.

In 1904 Bailey was stricken by polio and he could not walk for a year. This disease also affected his physical development, and he remained small. At age 12, he was the size of a nine- year-old, and, as an adult, he stood four feet ten inches tall. He was also slightly crippled from the polio, and weighed less than 100 pounds.

Learned to Play the Harmonica

It was during his recovery from polio that Bailey began playing the harmonica and the guitar. His size, which made him ill-suited for heavy farm work, enabled him to continue on with his music. Bailey also learned to play the mandolin and, to a lesser extent, the fiddle. Many of his instruments were homemade, including banjos and wash tub bass fiddles. He also used beef ribs to make bones, a percussion instrument.

Bailey's foster family moved to a farm near Newsom's Station in 1908. Now just ten miles from Nashville, where his father lived, Bailey rode the train for the first time to visit his father. The family moved to another farm around 1914, this time south of Nashville in Williamson County. It was in Williamson County that Bailey first came into contact with black musicians outside of his family. There, too, he received most of his schooling. He learned enough arithmetic to handle money and also learned how to sign his name. However, he refused to learn to read. Then in about 1916

At a Glance . . .

Born born on December 14, 1899, in Smith County, TN; died on July 2, 1982; son of John Henry Bailey (a tenant farmer) and Mary Reedy Bailey; married Ida Lee Jones, 1929 (divorced); children: DeFord Jr., Dezoral Lee, Christine Lamb.

Career: Musician. Worked at odd jobs, 1920-25; WSM, Nashville, TN, appeared on radio programs, 1925-41; recorded 11 singles, 1927-28; opened shoe shine shop, 1933; operated barbeque stand, 1933-41; performed in two segments of a syndicated film series entitled *Grand Ole Opry*, 1967; appeared on local television programs, 1950s; syndicated television appearances, 1960s.

Awards: June 23, 1983 proclaimed "DeFord Bailey Day" by mayor of Nashville.

the family moved to yet another farm seven miles south of Franklin, Tennessee. In about 1917 a white shopkeeper, Gus Watson, asked Bailey to live with him and his wife. Bailey helped out in Watson's general store and also played for the customers.

Bailey's father died in July of 1918. That fall, Odum decided to move his family to Nashville, and Bailey decided follow. Odum had found a job as groundskeeper for Mr. and Mrs. J. C. Bradford, one of Nashville's wealthiest families. The Bradfords also hired Bailey as a houseboy, but he later played the harmonica to entertain the Bradfords and their guests. After leaving the Bradford family, Bailey followed Odum to work for another family.

From 1920 to 1925 Bailey worked in a variety of odd jobs, including: a shoe shine person, a delivery person, a car washer, and an elevator operator. During breaks in work, he would play his harmonica. Bailey's family began to drift apart after the death of Barbara Lou Odum in 1923. Clark Odum rented a house in Nashville for the children and traveled to Detroit where he found work and was able to send money back to the family.

Began Radio Career

Bailey was working as an elevator operator when radio came to Nashville in the spring of 1925. Bailey entered a contest sponsored by WDAD, the first station on the air in Nashville. Though Bailey was the superior musician, the contest promoter only awarded him second prize. WSM, Nashville's second radio station, went on the air in the fall of 1925. That December WSM began a series of broadcasts featuring country music—these programs were later named *The Barn Dance*. Bailey appeared on the program in early 1926, and his set was so successful that he was given two dollars and asked to perform again the following week.

In the fall of 1927, Bailey was the first country musician introduced on a program following a network classical music presentation from Chicago. After Bailey played one of his famous train songs, "The Pan American Blues," according to David C. Morton and Charles K. Wolf, authors of *DeFord Bailey*, the program host, Judge Hay, asserted, "For the past hour, we have been listening to music largely from Grand Opera, but from now on, we will present 'The Grand Ole Opry.'" By December the program's official name became *The Grand Ole Opry*.

Bailey became a program favorite, and, between mid-1926 and April of 1927, he appeared on *The Grand Ole Opry* more than any other performer. In 1928 he appeared on 49 of the program's 52 shows. Bailey continued to appear on the program throughout the 1930s, often performing two sets in one night.

Bailey spent 18 weeks in 1927-1928 recording some 11 singles. Although some of the recordings had modest success, Bailey received very little money for them. He made no further attempts to record, but remained a popular radio performer. Three of his songs were especially popular with audiences: "The Fox Chase," "The Pan American Blues," and "Dixie Flyer."

Dissatisfied with the fact that white performers made more money, Bailey tried to break away from Nashville in 1928. He worked briefly in Knoxville and considered moving to California. However, a pay raise—from $7 a show to $20 per show—persuaded him to return to WSM.

Bailey married Ida Lee Jones in 1929. The marriage ended in divorce, but not before the couple had three children: DeFord, Jr., Dezoral Lee, and Christine Lamb. In about 1930, Bailey attempted to earn more money to support his growing family by opening a barbecue stand, which remained in operation for eight years. In 1933 he, along with his uncle, opened a shoe shine shop. To cash in on his fame as a radio performer and to earn more money, Bailey also went on tour.

WSM organized the Artists' Service Bureau in 1933, and many aspiring country music singers used Bailey's popularity in audiences for their own music. On this tour, Bailey often had difficulty getting the promoters to pay him, so WSM demanded that Bailey be paid a fee of $5 a performance. However, this arrangement did not always work to Bailey's advantage, since Bailey could often have earned more if he had shared the standard percentage of the gate.

Fired from the Opry

Around 1940 contract negotiations between the American Society of Composers, Authors, and Publishers (ASCAP) and the radio networks broke down. ASCAP had set a deadline of January 1, 1941, for a new contract with the radio networks, but the networks resisted and boycotted ASCAP-copyrighted music. This meant radio performers had to write new material, rather than perform ASCAP-copyrighted songs. Many of the songs that Bailey performed were traditional, but they nonetheless had ASCAP copyrights. Bailey did not like the idea of composing music for his program, and his refusal to write new material may have led to his release from the Opry in late May of 1941. Since Bailey remained extremely popular with audiences, WSM continued to pay him three dollars a week just to be present and visible at shows for several weeks.

After his dismissal from WSM, Bailey decided never to work for anyone else again. He expanded his shoe shine business to include several more shops in the black Edgehill section of Nashville. The majority of his clientele was black, but he also attracted business from large numbers of whites, some of whom even mailed their footwear to him from out of town. Bailey became a father figure to many of the neighborhood's young blacks, and he bought every gun that was offered to him, just to get them out of circulation.

Bailey still performed occasionally during these years, but his relationship with the Opry worsened after he found out that, while he had received only $50 for appearing in a wartime propaganda film featuring Opry performers, other performers earned $1000. In 1967 Bailey performed in two segments of a syndicated film series entitled *Grand Ole Opry*, and these segments were later included on the 1988 videotape, *Legends of the Grand Ole Opry*. In the 1950s he became a regular guest on a local television program, and occasionally sang gospel music with his children in local churches.

Appeared on Television Shows

In the 1960s Bailey appeared several times on the syndicated television show *Night Train*. These appearances allowed a new generation of folk music fans to discovered him. Bailey appeared for the first time in ten years when he played on the last show in the Ryman Auditorium in 1974. Although he could have performed more often during the time, Bailey turned down many offers because he suspected that he would still be exploited. Bailey once asserted, according to Morton and Wolfe, "They say I don't like white people. They got me wrong. I'm just like white people. I just want my money.... I don't want more than anyone else, but I want the same as they get."

Bailey's health was generally good until shortly before his death. He died on July 2, 1982. Nashville's mayor declared June 23, 1983, "DeFord Bailey Day," and the mayor, along with Bailey's family and friends, gathered at his grave for a ceremony marking the unveiling of a monument. The monument's inscription read: "Harmonica Wizard, Musician, Composer, Entertainer, Early Star of Grand Ole Opry."

Sources

Books

The Comprehensive Country Music Encyclopedia. Times Books/Random House, 1994.
Guralnick, Peter. *Lost Highway: Journeys &Arrivals of American Musicians.* Boston: Godine, 1979.
Notable Black American Men, Gale Research, 1998.
Morton, David C., with Charles K. Wolfe. *DeFord Bailey.* University of Tennessee Press, 1991.

Periodicals

Nashville Tennessean, Weekend, February 10, 1991.

On-line

Biography Resource Center, Gale, 2001, http://www.galenet.com/servlet/BioRC.

—Robert L. Johns and Jennifer M. York

Ernie Banks

1931—

Baseball shortstop

The first African-American player to take the field for professional baseball's Chicago Cubs, Ernie Banks amassed a legendary record as a player over 19 seasons with the team. He hit a franchise record 512 home runs, was twice chosen the National League's Most Valuable Player, and played in 13 All-Star games. Yet as important as his exploits on the field was Banks's status as a positive-thinking and reliably comic icon of the long-suffering Cubs team. By the time Banks retired in 1971 he was known as "Mr. Cub," and in 1977 he was named to baseball's Hall of Fame in his first year of eligibility.

Ernest Banks was born in Dallas, Texas, on January 31, 1931, the second child and first boy of 12 children. "He never prowled, helped with the chores, went to Sunday School and church, and was a blessing to us all," his mother, Essie, was quoted as saying in the *Washington Post*. Banks's legendary outgoing personality—he often invites autograph seekers to join him at his table in restaurants—did not develop until adulthood. "I came from a family of 12 …" Banks told the *Chicago Sun-Times*. "I did not have self-esteem. I know that sometimes all it takes is one person to say something or do something that just sets it off."

Played Other Sports in School

Banks's father was a pitcher and catcher with the Dallas Green Monarchs and the Black Giants, two teams of the all-black Negro League circuit that flourished before the major leagues were integrated in 1947, and he often brought his son along to serve as a batboy. Nevertheless, though naturally athletic, he rarely played baseball as a youngster. Attending Booker T. Washington High School in Dallas he notched a basketball average of 20 points per game and excelled as a track star (he could clear five feet, eleven inches in the high jump). Baseball wasn't a school sport at the time, and Banks knew little of the world beyond Dallas except for the cotton farms where he worked the fields for $1.75 a day. "It was a small universe," he told the *Dallas Morning News*. "I was never exposed to anything outside of my neighborhood."

But playing softball one day in 1947, Banks was spotted hitting home runs nearly at will by a local baseball scout and newspaper publisher, Bill Blair, who had once pitched for the Negro Leagues' Indianapolis Clowns. That led to a room-and-board gig with a small all-black club called the Amarillo Colts, playing around

At a Glance . . .

Born Ernest Banks in Dallas, TX, January 31, 1931; Divorced;children: Eddie B. *Education*: Graduated from Booker T. Washington High School, Dallas, 1950; attended Northwestern University. *Military service*: U.S. Army, 1951-53.

Career: Professional baseball player. Played for Kansas City Monarchs, Negro Leagues, 1950, 1953; signed to Chicago Cubs, 1953; became first black player on the field for Cubs, September, 1953; played for Cubs, 1953-71; retired in 1971 with 512 home runs, 1,636 RBIs; worked for Cubs as coach, consultant, and spokesman after retirement; became spokesman and consultant, New World Van Lines, 1984; founder and president, Ernie Banks International, a sports marketing firm.

Selected awards: Named Most Valuable Player, National League, 1958 and 1959; member of National League All-Star Team 13 times between 1957 and 1970; inducted into Baseball Hall of Fame, 1977.

Addresses: *Office*—Ernie Banks International, Inc., 520 Washington Blvd., Suite 284, Marina Del Rey, CA 90292-5442.

Texas and the Southwest. Banks, who was still in high school, played only in the summer. Though he was new to baseball, his skills developed rapidly. "You had to show Ernest everything one time, and he learned it," Blair told the *St. Louis Post- Dispatch*. "The talent was all natural."

Soon Banks moved up to the Kansas City Monarchs, a top-level team that had featured the talents of major-league pioneer Jackie Robinson and quotable pitcher Satchel Paige. After graduating from high school, Banks joined the Monarchs in 1950. "It was a new beginning in my life," Banks told the *Post-Dispatch*. "I was really traveling. I was meeting people from all over. I was seeing other cities. My eyes were opened." At that point, however, he joined the U.S. Army for two years, and when he returned to baseball the Negro Leagues were in a tailspin—in the wake of Robinson's breaking of the color barrier in previously all-white major- league baseball, many of the top black stars had been signed to major-league teams.

First Black Player for Cubs

Discouraged by his prospects, Banks briefly returned to Dallas. But he was persuaded to return to the Monarchs by manager Buck O'Neil, who had gotten wind of interest the major-league Chicago Cubs had expressed in his talented young player. Banks, who received a signing bonus of $2,000, joined the Cubs on September 17, 1953; though another black player, Gene Baker, had signed a contract a few days earlier, Banks was the first black player seen on the bases at the Cubs' Wrigley Field. His top salary with the Cubs was $65,000 a year.

With the number of black major-league players growing, Banks encountered little outright discrimination, but he recalled that white Cubs players mixed little with him and Baker at the start. Nevertheless, Banks soon became an indispensable part of the Cubs' lineup at his starting position of shortstop. Rarely missing a game between 1954 and 1969, he started strong in 1954, his first full season, with a .275 batting average and 19 home runs. Thereafter he improved consistently, slamming 44 home runs in 1955. Banks hit more home runs than any other player between 1955 and 1960, including such better-known sluggers as Hank Aaron and Willie Mays.

The high point of Banks's career came in the 1958 and 1959 seasons, in which he hit 47 and 45 home runs respectively, batting over .300 in both seasons. He was named the National League's Most Valuable Player for both years. After that Banks's pace slackened somewhat, but he remained a consistent player through the 1960s with batting averages in the .260 and .270 range and between 20 and 40 home runs in most seasons. His trademark phrase, "Let's play two," was first uttered on a torrid 100-degree day in 1969 when Banks attempted to lighten the mood of his depressed teammates. By that time Banks had become beloved by Cubs fans for his sportsmanship and unfailingly pleasant outlook. A Chicago alderman once suggested replacing a large Picasso sculpture that stands in the city's downtown with one of Banks instead.

Among Top Sluggers in History

On May 12, 1970 Banks joined a select group in baseball when, with one and the same swing, he hit his 500th home run and notched his 1,600th run batted in. By the time he retired the following year due to the effects of arthritis, he had 512 home runs, good for 12th place at the time on the list of all-time top home-run sluggers. His lifetime batting average was .274, and he also ranked among the top 15 in RBIs. When Banks became eligible for induction into the Baseball Hall of Fame in 1977, he was chosen for the honor in his first year—a feat only eight other players had achieved at the time. Banks in retirement might serve as a model for other players, as he has carved out goals and interests of his own independent from the world of baseball. For a time he worked as a Cubs coach and served in the team's front office, but, he told *People*, "I felt trapped. No one looked at me as a human being. I couldn't get on with my life." With the help of a psychologist, Banks decided that he wanted to become more than "a cigar store wooden Indian."

He continues to be associated with the Cubs as an occasional goodwill ambassador, but in the 1990s organized and headed a sports marketing firm of his own, Ernie Banks International. Banks has also established the Ernie Banks Live Above and Beyond Foundation, a nonprofit group that assists children and senior citizens in building self-esteem. He is the author, with Jim Enright, of an autobiography, *Mr. Cub*.

Sources

Periodicals

Chicago Sun-Times, February 9, 1992, p. 20; March 8, 1996, p. 116.
Jet, September 13, 1993, p. 48.
New York Times, September 28, 1984, p. A29.
People, April 11, 1983, p. 67.
St. Louis Post-Dispatch, October 5, 1997, p. F7.
USA Today, July 9, 1990, p. E4.
Washington Post, January 20, 1977, p. C4.

—James M. Manheim

Roosevelt "Booba" Barnes

1936-1996

Blues harmonica player, guitarist

Roosevelt "Booba" Barnes made only one full-length record in his life, *The Heartbroken Man*, but the harmonica and guitar player was a legend in the Mississippi Delta long before anyone heard the album. Known for his outrageous on- stage persona, Barnes was brought up in the blues clubs and bars of Greenville, Mississippi, by blues legend Howlin' Wolf, and made no bones about imitating him. However, he was praised on his own merits as "one of the toughest postwar bluesmen" of the Delta.

Played on the Plantation

Roosevelt Melvin Barnes was born September 25, 1936, on a plantation in the town of Longwood, Mississippi, about 20 miles outside Greenville. Barnes's family worked in local cotton fields and raised hogs for a living. Barnes lost part of a finger in a childhood encounter with a hog; as he and his father wrangled the beast in order to put a ring through its nose, it bit him. Barnes was still a child when he first began playing harmonicas that his older brother, a Negro League baseball player, sent him from the road. He became infatuated with the instrument, and soon became dis-

tracted from his work on the plantation. Often, Barnes could be found playing his harmonica and dancing between the rows of cotton instead of working. He earned his nickname, "Booba," when his brother declared him "worse than a booby trap," according to a *Blues Notes* article reprinted online at the Cascade Blues Association's website.

As a young teen, Barnes ventured out into the streets of nearby Greenville and Belzoni, intrigued by the local blues musicians there. The aspiring harmonica player caught the attention of fellow harpists and local legends Little Walter and Sonny Boy Williamson, as well as guitarist Elmore James. During his formative years, Barnes attempted to imitate Williamson's style. It was during this time that the teen met and became friends with legendary bluesman Howlin' Wolf, and Wolf took him under his wing. Wolf nicknamed Barnes "Little Wolf," because when the young man sang, his voice was indistinguishable from his mentor's. "They say I sound more like the Wolf than Wolf did," Barnes was quoted as saying in *Guitar Player*.

After a few years, Barnes began to play on his own in the blues bars on Greenville's famed Nelson Street. At

At a Glance . . .

Born Roosevelt Melvin Barnes on September 25, 1936, Longwood, MS; died on April 3, 1996, Chicago, IL.

Career: Started playing harmonica on a plantation at age 7; played in blues clubs as a teen in Greenville, MS; started to learn guitar in 1960; formed his own band the Playboys, 1957-58; moved to Chicago, IL, 1963; returned to Greenville, MS, 1971; opened Playboy Club in Mississippi, 1982; released *The Heartbroken Man* on Rooster Blues and moved to Chicago, 1990.

age 17, he was sitting in with the local bands, playing with Charlie Booker, Bill Wallace, and the Jones Brothers, who were led by Barnes's brother-in-law, Little Jerry Jones. The groups typically played songs by B.B. King, whose music was the rage in the South at the time. Barnes also began building his stage persona, acting crazy and swinging from the rafters in clubs while wearing outrageously colored suits.

Developed Rambunctious On-Stage Persona

Barnes followed his older brother, then playing baseball for the St. Louis Cardinals, and moved to St. Louis. The St. Louis blues scene was ruled by Albert King and Little Milton, both of whom requested the young musician to sit in with them from time to time. Frustrated that he could not find a guitarist who could play the patterns he envisioned, Barnes decided to take matters into his own hands, and learned to play the guitar.

Careful not to come off as imitating the style of any other guitarist of the time, Barnes added on-stage acrobatic antics to his guitar act—leaping and duck-walking around the stage; he also played his guitar between his legs, behind his head, while lying down, and with his teeth. Barnes revealed his on-stage secret to *Guitar Player*: First, he said, "I play from my heart." He would play a few fast songs at the start of his set, to get the crowd dancing and drinking, then would shift to hard blues as the crowd became more intoxicated. "Round about 12 o'clock they ready for it, see. Put it on 'em."

Barnes's time in St. Louis was dynamic but short-lived. He returned to Greenville in the early 1960s, and the harmonica became his focus once again. He played with guitarist Smokey Wilson and eventually formed his own group, the Swinging Gold Coasters. Over the years, Barnes tried several times to make it big in Chicago, a blues-music capital. When he first went there in 1963, he recorded with the Jones Brothers, but this material was never released. After an introduction by Little Jerry Jones, Barnes's childhood idol Little Walter befriended him, and even called him "son." He finally broke up the Swinging Gold Coasters in 1968 to move to Chicago, where he worked at a steel mill and played wherever and whenever he could.

Heartbroken, but Famous

Three years later, in 1971, Barnes returned to Greenville. He picked up where he left off, playing in clubs with such artists as T-Model Ford. In 1982, Barnes converted a used furniture store at 928 Nelson Street in Greenville into his own blues bar, which became one of the hottest spots in the Mississippi Delta. Barnes was king of the Playboy Club, as he called it, and presided over the marathon, freestyle jam sessions that took place there. One such session was captured on film in the 1991 documentary *Deep Blues*, directed by Robert Mugge and written by blues journalist Robert Palmer. Barnes also led the bar's house band, the Playboys, who became well-known beyond Nelson Street and performed throughout the United States, in the South and Midwest, and on the East Coast. Barnes's big-screen career also included an appearance as himself in the documentary about Robert Johnson called *Hellhounds On My Trail: The Afterlife of Robert Johnson*, which was also directed by Mugge.

Barnes's first and only full-length recording, *The Heartbroken Man*, was released in 1990 on the independent, start-up Rooster Blues record label. The recording was uncannily similar to Howlin' Wolf at times, wrote Jas Obrecht in *Guitar Player*. Barnes was the first Mississippi-blues artist to record for the label, and the album gave Barnes widespread popular and critical success, and he and the Playboys toured the United States and Europe to support it.

Barnes responded to increased demand for his performances in Chicago by moving back to the city in the early 1990s, following in the footsteps of Howlin' Wolf. After a year-long battle with lung cancer, the bluesman died April 3, 1996, in a Chicago nursing home. Barnes played his last show at the Rock &Roll Hall of Fame in Cleveland shortly before his death.

Sources

Books

Erlewine, Michael, Vladimir Bogdanov, Chris Woodstra, and Cub Koda, editors, *All Music Guide to the Blues*, Miller Freeman Books, 1996.
Larkin, Colin, editor, *Encyclopedia of Popular Music*, Muze UK Ltd., 1998.

Periodicals

Guitar Player, August 1996, p. 24.

On-line

Cascade Blues Association, http://www.cascade blues.org/history/rooseveltbarnes.htm (January 7, 2002).

Bluespeak, http://www.bluespeak.com/feature/96/05/960531.html (January 7, 2002).

—Brenna Sanchez

John Biggers

1924-2001

Artist and educator

As a painter, muralist, illustrator, and sculptor, John Biggers has made innumerable contributions to American art and culture. In the 1950s he became one of the first African-American artists to travel to Africa, and to integrate African motifs and symbolism into his artwork. His pioneering achievements have influenced generations of artists in the United States and abroad.

Biggers also influenced thousands of young artists directly, as a professor of art at Texas Southern University. In 1949 he was recruited by the newly founded university to establish its art department. Biggers taught at Texas Southern for more than thirty years, winning several prestigious awards for his teaching.

In 1995 a retrospective exhibition of Biggers's work, titled *The Art of John Biggers: View from the Upper Room*, was organized by Houston's Museum of Fine Arts. The show also traveled to five cities in the South and Northeast. "He is someone who has retained, over 50 years, an emphasis on African-American culture," Alvia J. Wardlaw, curator of the exhibition, told the magazine *American Visions*. "He was one of the first African-American artists to study and live in West Africa and to bring back to us, in the late 1950s, images of African culture that were positive and personal—and accurate. And I think that is probably his greatest gift to American culture," Wardlaw continued.

"John Biggers is a poet, philosopher, teacher, draughtsman, painter, sculptor, muralist, and, above all, an inspirational leader," wrote Peter C. Marzio, director of Houston's Museum of Fine Arts, in the

exhibition catalog, also titled *The Art of John Biggers: View from the Upper Room*. "He leads us with his powerful imagery, his impassioned discourse, his intense energy, and his all-consuming belief in the human community and its mystical interaction with the natural world," he added.

Created Afrocentric Artwork

John Thomas Biggers was born April 13, 1924, in the small town of Gastonia, North Carolina. He was the seventh and youngest child of Paul and Cora Biggers. His father was the principal of the local black school, owner of a shoe shop, and a minister. His mother helped to run the family farm, taking in laundry for extra income. Biggers was raised in an extended family, part of a close-knit black community in the segregated town.

As a child, Biggers enjoyed copying drawings from his father's Bible. More importantly, however, he was an insightful observer of his surroundings. The people, landscape, and everyday objects of Biggers's rural Southern childhood would become important themes in his later work.

After Paul Biggers died of diabetes in 1937, Cora Biggers accepted a job at an orphanage in Oxford, North Carolina. Young John was sent to board at Lincoln Academy, a private school initially founded to teach former slaves, in nearby Kings Mountain, North Carolina. To help pay for his tuition, Biggers worked as

At a Glance . . .

Born John Thomas Biggers on April 13, 1924, in Gastonia, NC; died on January 25, 2001, Houston, TX; son of Paul Biggers, a school principal, shoe store owner and minister, and Cora Finger Biggers, a laundrywoman; married Hazel Hales, 1948. *Education*: Hampton Institute, Hampton, VA, 1941-43, 1946; Pennsylvania State University, BA, MA in art education, 1948, PhD in art education, 1954. *Military Service*: U.S. Navy, 1943-45.

Career: Painter, muralist, illustrator, sculptor, 1941-01; Alabama State Teachers College, instructor, 1949; Texas State University, associate professor and department head, department of art, 1949-54; author, *Ananse: The Web of Life in Africa*, 1962; Univ. of Wisconsin, Madison, visiting professor, 1965-66; co-author, *Black Art in Houston*, 1978; Texas State Univ., full professor, 1954-83.

Awards: Teaching Fellow, Pennsylvania State Univ., 1948; Purchase Prize, The Museum of Fine Arts, Houston, 1950; Schlumberger Prize, Museum of Fine Arts, Houston, 1951; Purchase Prize for Prints and Sculpture, Atlanta Univ., 1952; UNESCO Fellowship, 1957; Excellence in Design Award for *Ananse*, 1963; Minnie Stevens-Piper Foundation Professor Award for Outstanding Scholarly and Academic Achievement, 1964; Danforth Foundation E. Harris Harbison Award for Distinguished Teaching, 1968; Distinguished Alumnus Award, Pennsylvania State Univ., 1971; Mayor's Award for Outstanding Contributions as Visual Artist, Houston, 1980; Texas Artist of the Year, The Art League of Houston, 1988; Award for Achievement, Metropolitan Arts Foundation, 1988; Honorary Doctor of Human Letters, Hampton Univ., 1990; Texas Medal of Arts, 2001.

a janitor, and was in charge of keeping the fires lit at the school. During the hours he spent in the school's boiler room, he continued to draw, copying engravings from old issues of the *New York Times Book Review*.

In 1941, after graduating from Lincoln, Biggers enrolled at Hampton Institute (later Hampton University), an historically black college in Hampton, Virginia; among its distinguished alumni was Booker T. Washington. The following year, Biggers met Hazel Hales,

an accounting major at Hampton. The couple married in 1948.

Initially Biggers planned to become a plumber, but soon began to take art classes with Professor Viktor Lowenfeld, a Jewish refugee from Germany. Lowenfeld, who would become Biggers's mentor, encouraged his students to learn about their African cultural and artistic heritage. "He told us, 'You don't want to draw like a European, you want to speak out of your heart,'" Biggers was quoted as saying in *Emerge*.

In 1943 Biggers had the opportunity to show his work in the exhibition *Young Negro Art*, organized by Lowenfeld and shown at the Museum of Modern Art in New York. It was unprecedented for a major museum to take such interest in student artwork, let alone work by African-American students. In reviews of the exhibition, however, Biggers's mural, "Dying Soldier," was singled out for criticism. Despite the discouraging response, he continued to dedicate himself to his work as a painter, sculptor, and muralist.

That same year, Biggers's studies were interrupted when he was drafted into the Navy. After basic training, he was sent back to the Navy training school that had been established at Hampton, where he created two murals. However, Biggers was outraged at having to serve in a segregated military, and became deeply depressed. When the war ended, he spent a month in the naval hospital in Philadelphia before being given an honorable discharge.

In 1946 Biggers enrolled at Pennsylvania State University, where Lowenfeld had accepted a teaching position. During his years at Penn State, Biggers first began to achieve some recognition for his work. Two of the murals that Biggers had completed during his studies at Hampton—including "Dying Soldier"—were acquired by a transportation union for its headquarters in Chicago. He also completed three murals for Penn State, before earning both a bachelor's and a master's degree in art education in 1948.

Established Art Department at TSU

After graduating, Biggers taught briefly at Penn State and then Alabama State University. The following year, 1949, he was asked to establish an art department at Texas Southern University, a black college that had been founded just two years earlier. Biggers accepted the position as head of the art department, and taught at Texas Southern for more than 30 years. As an art professor, Biggers followed Lowenfeld's example, encouraging his students to look to their own communities and their African heritage for artistic inspiration.

During the 1950s Biggers continued to build his reputation, accepting several mural commissions in Houston's black community. One such mural was "The Contribution of Negro Women to American Life and

Education," which he created for the YWCA in Houston. The mural, which portrayed African-American women as symbols of heroic struggle and survival, established a theme that Biggers would explore again and again in his work. "Africa has a female sensibility" Biggers was quoted as saying in *Emerge*. "The woman was so powerful in African culture," he continued. According to Wardlaw, writing in *The Art of John Biggers*, "The mural established the foundation for all of his images of black women and their communities that Biggers would create during the next forty years." Biggers later based his doctoral thesis on the research he had done for the project, receiving a doctorate in art education from Penn State in 1954.

In the early 1950s Biggers also won purchase prizes in competitions sponsored by the Dallas Museum of Art and the Museum of Fine Arts in Houston—despite the fact that both institutions were segregated at the time. Neither museum had expected an African-American artist to enter their competitions, let alone win, and Biggers's success was deeply embarrassing. At the Dallas Museum of Art, a reception planned for him was mysteriously cancelled. At the Museum of Fine Arts in Houston, Biggers could not attend the awards reception, because it fell on a day when the museum was closed to blacks. A few months later, the MFA in Houston changed its segregation policy; four decades later, it would organize the traveling retrospective of Biggers's work.

Traveled to Africa

In 1957 Biggers made a trip to Ghana that would change his entire philosophy of life and art. Before this journey, Biggers later wrote in his book *Ananse: The Web of Life in Africa*, "I felt cut off from my heritage, which I suspected was estimable and something to be embraced, not an ignobility to be scorned. I believed that many of my American brothers, in their flight from the stereotyped concepts of our race, had also flown from their real selves" Funded by a fellowship from the United Nations Educational, Scientific, and Cultural Organization (UNESCO), Biggers and his wife traveled to Ghana, Togo, Dahomey (now the Republic of Benin), and Nigeria.

At the time, very few African-American artists had traveled to Africa to study. And although Biggers had spent months researching Africa's history and culture, he realized, once he arrived, that most of his ideas about the continent were completely inaccurate. Nevertheless, the people they met welcomed them like long-lost family members. The story of one particular village's reaction was typical. "We didn't speak the language, and we wore Western clothes. The drums announced that two 'Europeans' had arrived," Biggers told Rosalyn Story of *Emerge*. On meeting the couple, however, the chieftain turned to the crowd of villagers and announced, "For the first time the drums have

made a mistake. These are your brothers who have returned after 400 years," Biggers recounted.

Over the years, Biggers had developed a system of visual icons, imbuing them with mythical meanings. As Wardlaw explained in *The Art of John Biggers*, "The washpot represents the womb, the source of spiritual waters and rebirth; the scrub board represents a ladder, a symbol of ascension; the anvil represents community organization, and the transformation of natural resources (metals) into tools and weapons." In Africa, Biggers expanded his vocabulary of symbols to include African motifs, including combs, drums, and masks.

Biggers's portrayal of human subjects also altered dramatically. As his wife, Hazel, told *Emerge*, "Before, his paintings showed people who were depressed, and poor—sad. But in Africa, the women walked and danced with a certain joy. And even though they might be doing common labor, there was a certain dignity that the people had. They didn't seem to feel beaten down."

For Biggers, the process of assimilating what he had seen in Africa into his artistic practice was extremely difficult. "The impact of Africa almost paralyzed my creative efforts; the drama and the poetic beauty were devastating," he wrote in *Ananse: The Web of Life in Africa*, a journal about the trip that included more than 80 drawings of African life. *Ananse* was published in 1962, just as the civil rights movement in the United States was gathering momentum, and black Americans were beginning to take pride in their African heritage. The book, reissued in 1967, made an invaluable contribution to the growing consciousness of African history and culture.

Became Subject of Retrospective Exhibition

Throughout the 1960s and 1970s, Biggers continued to teach at Texas Southern, participated in solo and group exhibitions, and created murals, including several on the Texas Southern campus. Many of the murals he painted in Houston can still be seen today: "The walls of Houston have in large part preserved the brilliant range of Biggers's mural oeuvre," wrote Alison de Lima Greene in *The Art of John Biggers*.

Biggers retired from teaching at Texas Southern in 1983, having received numerous awards for his teaching and academic achievement. As the 1980s progressed, Biggers began to receive more recognition for his work. In 1988 he was named Texas Artist of the Year by the Art League of Houston. The following year, his paintings were featured in the exhibition *Black Art, Ancestral Legacy: The African Impulse in African American Art*. The show, curated by Wardlaw, a professor of art history at Texas Southern, initially opened at the Dallas Museum of Art and then traveled to Atlanta; Milwaukee, Wisconsin; and Richmond, Virginia.

In 1995 Wardlaw put together a solo retrospective of Biggers's work, entitled *The Art of John Biggers: View from the Upper Room*. The exhibition, sponsored by Houston's Museum of Fine Arts, encompassed 120 paintings, drawings, murals, and sculptures. The show later traveled to Raleigh, North Carolina; Hartford, Connecticut; Hampton, Virginia; and Boston.

In the early 1990s, Biggers was asked to create several murals for Hampton University, where he had studied almost 50 years prior. The process of creating the murals at Hampton was documented in an independent video called *John Biggers: Journeys (A Romance)*. Several of his paintings also hang in the university's museum.

Biggers's work has been collected by the Dallas Museum of Art, the Museum of Fine Arts in Houston, and by many private collectors, including the poet Maya Angelou. "John Biggers, one of America's most important artists, leads us through his expressions into the discovery of ourselves at our most intimate level," Angelou wrote in *The Art of John Biggers*.

"Biggers's career is without equal in our time," wrote de Lima Greene, a curator at Houston's Museum of Fine Arts, also in *The Art of John Biggers*. "No other artist of his generation has left us so vivid a record of African-American community life in the rural and urban South. Biggers's lifelong career as an educator is eloquently recorded in his paintings; they not only reflect the changing self-identity of African Americans, but invite all viewers to share in their transcendental passion," she concluded.

In 1999, at the unveiling of his mural, "Nubia," at Texas Southern University, Biggers was asked if he considered himself an artist, first, or a storyteller. He replied, "It's hard for me to separate the two things. Mural painting has to do with wall design and storytelling has to do with content. I try to blend both." "Nubia" depicted the development of civilization in the East African area that is now Egypt and Sudan, and the symbolic importance that gold had during that time. The mural was also inspired by two African-American spirituals, "Two Wings," and "I Stood on the Banks of Jordan."

Biggers died on January 25, 2001, at his home in Houston. He was 76 years old. About one year after his death, the city of Minneapolis made the difficult decision to tear down Biggers's landmark mural, "Celebration of Life," despite an outcry from the neighborhood. Radio show host, Travis Lee, called the decision "sacrilegious" but the mural needed to be removed to make way for the redevelopment of Heritage Park, a large housing project. A new work of art was commissioned to honor the work and life of John Biggers.

Sources

Books

Biggers, John. *Ananse: The Web of Life in Africa*, University of Texas Press, 1962.
Warlaw, Alvia J. *The Art of John Biggers: View from the Upper Room*, Harry N. Abrams, Inc., 1995.

Periodicals

American Visions, December/January 1996, p. 20; April/May 1995, p. 12.
Booklist, May 15, 1995, p. 1625.
Emerge, October 1997, p. 58.
Parabola, Spring 1995, p. 16.
Star Tribune, December 30, 2001, p. O3B.
The Houston Chronicle, September 22, 1999, p. 38; January 27, 2001, p. 1.

—Carrie Golus and Christine Miner Minderovic

Aaron Brooks

1976—

Professional football player

"My whole life has been about turning you into a believer," New Orleans Saints quarterback Aaron Brooks told the *Hartford Courant* early in the 2001 season, his first full year as a starting quarterback in the National Football League. "Trust me, sooner or later I am going to make you believe in Aaron Brooks." Blessed with tremendous natural ability, Brooks had to overcome obstacles all his life—and usually did so by applying himself in lengthy stretches of sheer hard work. Brooks had already made believers of Saints fans with a strong finish in the 2000 season, in which he came off the bench to lead the Saints to their first NFL divisional championship since 1992 and to the team's first playoff victory ever.

The obstacles Brooks faced began with his home environment. Born March 24, 1976, in Newport News, Virginia, Brooks grew up poor as the youngest of three children in a single-parent household. Brooks is a cousin of Atlanta Falcons quarterback Michael Vick, and in an interview with the *St. Louis Post-Dispatch* he recalled how the deck was stacked against the two young athletes. "Where we come from, it's a slim-to-none chance of getting out of there," Brooks said. "There's so much negativity going around, you

don't really have any type of aspiration or people or role models to look up to. And we just really had to work at what we were doing and stay with it, and it was a break for both of us."

Showdown With Iverson

Emerging as a star at Ferguson High School in Newport News, Brooks became quarterback of the football team and lettered in three sports altogether. In what became a recurring motif in his career, however, Brooks's accomplishments were somewhat overshadowed by the feats of a rival quarterback in nearby Hampton, Virginia—future NBA star Allen Iverson. When one long-awaited showdown between the two quarterbacks came along, Brooks dominated, amassing almost 400 yards in completed passes.

Iverson ended up focusing his efforts in basketball instead. But when Brooks enrolled at the University of Virginia, the same story repeated itself. Brooks spent two years on the bench in the shadow of better-known players and another year off the field entirely; he was "red-shirted," or held back a year so that the team could make use of his talents in his fifth year of college.

At a Glance . . .

Born in Newport News, Virginia, March 24, 1976; youngest of three children; cousin of Atlanta Falcons quarterback Michael Vick. *Education*: University of Virginia, Charlottesville, VA, degree in anthropology, 1998.

Career:New Orleans Saints quarterback. Excelled as starting quarterback for Virginia, 1997 and 1998; signed to Green Bay Packers in fourth round of 1999 NFL draft; traded to New Orleans Saints for 2000 season; replaced injured Saints quarterback Jeff Blake, September, 2000; led Saints to division championship and wildcard playoff victory, 2000; named Saints starting quarterback, 2001; set team records in several categories.

Addresses: *Office*—c/o New Orleans Saints, 5800 Airline Dr., Metairie, LA 70003.

Brooks made good use of the time by declaring and eventually completing a challenging major in anthropology, a far cry from the minimally academic coursework often undertaken by powerhouse-program college athletes.

When he assumed the mantle of starting quarterback for Virginia in 1997, Brooks was ready to show the world what he could do. Though the attention of the national press corps was focused upon Georgia Tech quarterback Joe Hamilton, Brooks excelled by any standard; over two years he notched six games with over 300 passing yards, and ended up in the all-time top five of all of the venerable Virginia team's career passing statistics categories. He was named team captain in his senior year and won the school's Ben Wilson Award, given to the team's outstanding offensive player.

Stellar 1999 Quarterback Class

The 1999 NFL draft once again put Brooks in the position of having to make himself stand out from a crowd, as the nation's college programs produced a bumper crop of top quarterbacks that year. Faced with competition from the likes of Daunte Culpepper, Tim Couch, and Donovan McNabb, Brooks was not even invited for a private tryout with an NFL team—a blow to the sometimes self-doubting player. Brooks found the NFL's "scouting combine," a mass tryout attended by hundreds of players, to be a degrading experience. "You stand there wearing next to nothing and they

measure everything on you, even your kneecaps," Brooks told *Sports Illustrated*. "Then doctors pull on you, grab each place you've been injured. It's horrible."

Finally drafted by the Green Bay Packers in the fourth round, Brooks ended up as the team's number-three quarterback. Far from discouraged, he set out to learn the ways of the NFL in his chilly new home and sought special help from veteran Packers starter Brett Favre; he asked Favre to name the best game he had ever played and then watched films of that game over and over. Though Brooks logged no playing time in 1999, he impressed Favre and the Packers management, who began to market him as a potential star to teams in need of help at the quarterback position.

Brooks was traded to the New Orleans Saints in 2000 and began the year in continued obscurity. His breakthrough came in the 11th week of the season when Saints starter Jeff Blake suffered a foot injury that kept him out for the rest of the season. Journalists wrote the Saints off, but Brooks passed for 1,514 yards and nine touchdowns in the last six games of the season, with a Saints record 441 yards passing in a game against the Denver Broncos. A threat as a rusher as well—he ran for 108 yards the following week against the San Francisco 49ers—Brooks reminded some observers of the similarly rangy star quarterback John Elway (Brooks stands six feet, four inches tall).

Won Wildcard Playoff

Under Brooks, the Saints won the NFC West division championship, their first title in nine years, and went on to win their first-ever playoff game in a wild-card contest against the St. Louis Rams. Saints fans took to the young quarterback, with his Number 2 jersey becoming a strong seller at shops that carried Saints gear. In the spring of 2001, with Blake on the mend, Brooks logged marathon eight-hour practice sessions in preparation for the 2001 season.

Named the Saints' starting quarterback by coach Jim Haslett, Brooks faced new problems during the 2001 season. He took criticism after television cameras caught him smiling after an incomplete pass during a game in which the Saints were trounced by the Tampa Bay Buccaneers; Brooks maintained to the New Orleans *Times-Picayune* that "I wasn't out there laughing it off," and that his reaction stemmed from frustration at a game in which nothing seemed to go right. As the Saints' playoff hopes fell apart in a four-game losing streak at the end of the season (during which Brooks was sacked 15 times), some observers questioned what they saw as a chip on the young quarterback's shoulder. Once again Brooks found himself overshadowed—this time by Vick, who was the NFL's top draft pick and pulled down a multimillion-dollar annual salary in comparison with Brooks's $275,000.

Nevertheless, Brooks had already demonstrated impressive statistics for a first- year starter. On track near the end of the season to set team records in passing yards, total yards, and touchdown passes, Brooks harmonized well with the rest of the Saints' offense. With fans beginning to notice his resemblance to television star Jimmie Walker of "Good Times" situation-comedy fame, Brooks became more comfortable in the spotlight, although he remained shy about press attention. A generous man who has given more than perfunctory support to New Orleans area charitable endeavors, Aaron Brooks still had obstacles to conquer but seemed on track to become one of the NFL's great quarterbacks.

Sources

Periodicals

Chicago Sun-Times, July 1, 2001, p. 102.
Hartford Courant, September 28, 2001, p. C3

Houston Chronicle, January 4, 2001, p. Sports-1.
Sports Illustrated, December 25, 2000, p. 70.
St. Louis Post-Dispatch, April 22, 2001, p. D3; October 21, 2001, p. E2.
St. Petersburg Times, December 22, 2001, p. C1.
Times-Picayune (New Orleans, Louisiana), November 25, 2000, p. Sports-1; December 3, 2000, p. Sports-6; December 22, 2001, p. Sports-1; January 3, 2002, p. Sports-1.
USA Today, December 29, 2000, p. C1.
Washington Post, August 26, 1999, p. D4.

On-line

http://www.neworleanssaints.com
http://www.nfl.com

—James M. Manheim

Cora M. Brown

1914-1972

Social worker, lawyer, politician

With her 1952 election to the Michigan State Senate, Cora Brown became the first woman—and the first black woman—elected to a state senate. Furthermore, she was the first female to be elected, rather than appointed to fulfill an unexpired term. A political pioneer, Brown also worked as a social worker and a lawyer.

Brown, the only child of Richard and Alice Brown, was born on April 16, 1914, in Bessemer, Alabama. When Brown was seven years old, her family moved to Detroit, where her father opened a tailor's shop. In 1931 Brown graduated from Detroit's Cass Technical High School and enrolled in Nashville's Fisk University.

During her college years, Brown attempted to help pay expenses by working at a Detroit Urban League summer camp for underprivileged children. Additionally, her mother accepted a job as a cook for a family. Despite these efforts to generate additional income, sometimes Brown had to wear the same dress to her classes and had to wear the same evening gown to all the dances. However, *The Negro Politician* author Edward T. Clayton characterized Brown's years at Fisk by her ability to remain "diligent in her pursuit of an education." Clayton also noted her willingness to battle injustice. After the 1933 lynching in Columbia, Tennessee of a young African American who was accused of attempted rape, Brown participated in a demonstration on the Fisk campus. Members of the community and Fisk faculty attempted unsuccessfully to discourage the demonstration. The *Detroit Free Press* noted in 1956 that Brown's involvement in the demonstration marked the debut of her lifelong campaign against "injustice and inhumanity."

Brown earned her degree in sociology from Fisk in 1935. She then returned to Detroit, where she worked as a social worker for the Old Age Assistance Bureau, the Children's Aid Society, and the Works Progress Administration (WPA). From 1941 to 1946 Brown worked as a policewoman in the Women's Division. Here, such assignments as the preparation of legal cases inspired Brown to study law. Brown enrolled in Wayne State University in 1946, receiving a law degree in 1948. She passed the bar examination within two weeks of graduation. She entered the firm of Morris and Brown where she practiced general law and maintained an interest in criminal law. Geraldine Bledsoe, a friend of Brown's, summarized Brown's nonpolitical years in the *Michigan Chronicle* in 1972: "She gave wise counsel, guidance and defense to those continuing to be caught in the confusing maze of the system."

Brown began her political career by becoming involved in district activities. In 1950 she ran for the state senate in Detroit's Second District, losing the election by 600 votes. When A. J. Wilkowski was denied his state senate seat in 1951, a special election was called, and Brown campaigned again, only to be defeated by a disc jockey. Then, when Brown ran for the same position again in 1952, she won the Democratic nomination from a field of eight opponents in the primary. She found that during the primary, as she told the *Detroit News* in 1952, "It wasn't too hard to sell the women on voting for me. I found there is a little loyalty in our sex.

At a Glance . . .

Born on April 16, 1914, in Bessemer, AL; daughter of Richard and Alice Brown; died on December 17, 1972, in Detroit, MI. *Education*: Fisk University, sociology degree, 1935; Wayne State University, law degree, 1948.

Career: Old Age Assistance Bureau, social worker; Children's Aid Society, social worker; Works Progress Administration (WPA), social worker; Women's Division, policewoman, 1941-46; Morris and Brown law firm, lawyer; Second District, Detroit MI, state senator, 1953-57; U.S. Post Office, special associate general counsel, 1957-60; opened law office in Los Angeles; Michigan Employment Security Commission, 1970-72.

Memberships: National Council of Negro Women, Detroit chapter; NAACP; YWCA; Alpha Kappa Alpha Sorority; Order of the Eastern Star; Improved Benevolent Order of Elks of the World; New Calvary Baptist Church.

Awards: Outstanding Woman Legislator, 1956.

The men were a little more stand-offish." Brown's opponent in the general election was a black man—an assistant city corporation counsel. In November of 1952, Brown's third bid for a state senate seat was successful. After analyzing the election results, she commented on the role that women voters played in the election to the *Detroit News*: "These women voters have awakened and they expect their views to be properly represented. Women have always been able to bring sound and humane reasoning into everyday life. I believe they are the hope of the country."

Before assuming office, Brown stated, as reported by Clayton in *The Negro Politician*, "I don't expect much opposition because I am a woman. I haven't found that too difficult a 'handicap' to overcome." Brown even received several letters from other state senators expressing their delight at the prospect of working with her. During her first term, however, the *Detroit News* found Brown "seated in lonely feminine determination" among 32 senators. Then, after her second term in office, Brown voiced a different opinion in the *Michigan Chronicle*, saying in 1958, "I have found sex a greater handicap than ever."

Brown served two terms in the Michigan state senate, leaving office in 1957. *Ebony* magazine regarded Brown as an "energetic and able" senator. Brown had

no fear of controversy, and she would openly disagree with other blacks. Regardless, the *Detroit Free Press* noted Brown's reputation as a "champion of the underprivileged," and a 1972 issue of the newspaper called her the Michigan Democratic Party's "perennial thorn in the conscience."

Throughout her political career, Brown focused on such issues as civil rights, community, education, health, and labor. In 1956 Brown co-introduced a bill with a Republican senator that would revoke or suspend all state and local licenses held by businesses that discriminated on the basis of race. The bill was passed in February of 1956. That same month, Brown, who was selected as the Outstanding Woman Legislator of 1956, accused the First Congressional District incumbent of favoring his Polish constituents at the expense of his black constituents. She then announced her own candidacy for the First District's Democratic nomination for Congress.

Brown lacked the support of the Democratic Party in her effort to become the United States' first black congresswoman, and she lost the August election by 6,491 votes. In October she shocked her Democratic colleagues when she endorsed Republican Dwight D. Eisenhower's bid for reelection. Brown asserted that her decision was based on civil rights issues. She opposed Adlai Stevenson, the Democratic candidate, because of his support from pro-segregationists. Brown, along with black New York congressman Adam Clayton Powell, urged blacks to vote for Democratic local and state candidates, but for the Republican president.

Eisenhower was reelected, and, according to Clayton in *The Negro Politician*, "Having relinquished her senatorial post to make a bid for Congress, then defying party leadership to support Eisenhower, she [Brown] now found herself without political office or favor."

However, the Republicans rewarded her in August of 1957, when Brown was appointed special associate general counsel of the United States Post Office. She was the first black woman to serve on the post office's legal staff. Brown held the position until 1960, when John F. Kennedy's election to the presidency returned the Democrats to power.

Next Brown moved to Los Angeles, where she opened a law office. Nearly ten years later, Brown returned to Detroit in 1970. She was appointed to the Michigan Employment Security Commission, becoming the first black woman referee in 35 years. Brown died on December 17, 1972, at Grace Central Hospital in Detroit.

Sources

Books

Clayton, Edward T. *The Negro Politician, His Success and Failure*. Johnson Publishing Co., 1964.

Notable Black American Women, Book 2. Gale Research, 1996.

Periodicals

Detroit Free Press, February 25, 1956; December 19, 1972.
*Detroit News,*August 10, 1952; November 6, 1952.
Ebony, August 11,1956, pp. 81-84; September 22, 1967, pp. 27-34.
Michigan Chronicle, December 11, 1958; December 30, 1972.

On-line

Biography Resource Center, Gale Group, 2001, http://www.galenet.com/servlet/BioRC

—Linda M. Carter and Jennifer M. York

Blanche Kelso Bruce

1849-1898

Politician, educator

Blanche Kelso Bruce, a Republican senator from Mississippi, was the first African American to serve a full term in the U.S. Senate. Bruce may be remembered best for his participation in the investigation into the collapse of the Freedmen's Savings and Trust Company. Before entering politics, Bruce was a successful educator.

Bruce was born on March 1, 1841, on a plantation in Farmville, Prince Edward County, Virginia. His mother, Polly, was a slave, and his father was probably Polly's master, Pettus Perkinson. Polly named her 11th child Blanche Bruce, but Bruce added the middle name Kelso as an adult. Various accounts of Bruce's childhood all acknowledged that he had more advantages than many other slave children. Bruce learned to read and demonstrated an eagerness for learning. Bruce's mother encouraged her children to take advantage of learning opportunities.

During the early years of the Civil War, Bruce fled from Missouri to Laurence, Kansas. When the fugitive slave returned to Missouri in 1864, the state was forced to recognize him as a free man. Bruce then founded a school for black children in Hannibal, Missouri. Some accounts of his life suggest that Bruce attended Oberlin College, however, this has never been established by Oberlin. By 1868 Bruce had begun working as a cotton farmer in Mississippi.

Bruce was now ready to take advantage of all of the opportunities available to an ambitious, emancipated black man in the post-Civil War South. Literate, articulate, ambitious, and light-skinned, Bruce was well-advantaged. David S. Barry, a contemporary of Bruce's, said, as quoted in *Aristocrats of Color: The Black Elite 1880-1920*, that Bruce was of "high moral, mental, and physical standards ... a handsome man, well- built, with a finely shaped head covered with curly black hair." These characteristics, combined with his ability to recognize and seize opportunities, made Bruce an ideal politician.

In January of 1870 Bruce was elected sergeant-at-arms of the Mississippi Senate. The following year he became the sheriff and tax assessor of Bolivar County. In 1880 Bruce, a Republican, became the first black man to lead the Republican National Convention. According to Howard N. Rabinowitz, author of *Black Leaders*, white planters who dominated the politics of the area considered Bruce, who had offended no local whites, "safe—a dignified and educated mulatto who did not identify himself with threatening issues." Bruce was also a landowner—he had turned 640 acres of swampy land into a plantation—which made him even more appealing to white voters

In 1873 Bruce declined an offer to run for lieutenant governor. He had his eye one a senatorial seat instead. Most Republicans wanted Bruce in the Senate, especially James Hill, Mississippi's most influential black leader. According to John W. Cromwell in *The Negro in American History*, Hill had once told Bruce, "I can and will put you there [in a Senate seat]; no one can defeat you."

Bruce announced his candidacy for a U.S. Senate seat in 1874. Bruce defeated two white carpetbaggers and was elected, becoming the second black man from Mississippi to serve in that position. During the next six years, Bruce maintained a secure reputation, often presiding over the Senate. Bruce was considered a moderate in his political views. Like Booker T. Washington, Bruce wanted civil rights for blacks, though not necessarily social equality. Bruce argued for the desegregation of the U.S. Army.

Bruce chaired the investigation into the Freedmen's Savings and Trust scandal. Since its inception, after the federal government's 1865 authorization of a bank for blacks that would help former slaves become economically stable, mismanagement and corruption had plagued Freedmen's Savings and Trust. By 1874, the bank had collapsed.

Following the end of his term in Senate, Bruce had become one of the most influential men of the black middle class and had formed strong alliances with white Republican leaders. Using his reputation and status as

a gentleman farmer, politician, and educator, Bruce was able to secure positions after he left office. In 1881 he became the first black Register of the Treasury under President James Garfield. President Benjamin Harrison appointed Bruce as Recorder of Deeds of the District of Columbia in 1889, and he remained in this post until 1894. In 1895, under President William McKinley, Bruce held an appointed post of Register of the Treasury for three months until an illness forced him to leave the position. Bruce operated a successful business in Washington, D.C., handling investments, claims, insurance, and real estate. He also served on the Board of Trustees of Howard University from 1894 to 1898, receiving an honorary degree from the school in 1893. Regarded by some historians as the most successful black politician of the Reconstruction period, Bruce died from diabetic complications in March of 1898, in Washington, D.C. He was 57 years old.

Sources

Books

Bruce, H. C. *The New Man: Twenty-nine Years As a Slave, Twenty-nine Years a Free Man; Recollections of H. C. Bruce.* 1895. Reprint, Miami: Mnemosyne Publishing Co., 1969.

Cromwell, John W. *The Negro in American History.* The American Negro Academy, 1914.

Gatewood, Willard B. *Aristocrats of Color: The Black Elite 1880-1920.* Indiana University Press, 1990.

Johnson, Allen, ed. *Dictionary of American Biography.* Charles Scribner's Sons, 1953.

Litwack, Leon, and August Meier, eds. *Black Leaders of the Nineteenth Century.* University of Illinois Press, 1988.

Logan, Rayford W., and Michael R. Winston, eds. *Dictionary of American Negro Biography.* Norton, 1982.

Lynch, John R. *The Facts of Reconstruction.* Neale Pub. Co., 1913.

Notable Black American Men. Gale Research, 1998.

Notable Black American Women . Gale Research, 1992.

Stamp, Kenneth M. *The Era of Reconstruction, 1865-1877.* Random House, 1975.

On-line

Biography Resource Center Gale, 2001, http://www.galenet.com/servlet/BioRC

—Grace E. Collins and Jennifer M. York

Francis L. Cardozo

1837-1903

Educator, politician, minister

Francis L. Cardozo contributed to the development of two important black educational institutions: the Avery Institute in Charleston, South Carolina, and Paul Laurence Dunbar High School in Washington, D.C. Although, noted for his achievements in education, Cardozo was also active in politics. He was elected first as South Carolina's secretary of state, but also served as the state's treasurer.

The son of Jacob N. Cardozo, a white journalist, and a free woman of mixed African and Native American ancestry, Cardozo was born on February 1, 1837, in Charleston, South Carolina. Cardozo and his siblings, Thomas W. Cardozo and Mrs. C. L. McKinney, all appear to have been educated in illegal—though tolerated—schools for free black children. Cardozo was apprenticed to a carpenter at age 12. He completed five years as an apprentice and four years as a journeyman. A member of the Second Presbyterian Church, Cardozo received a letter of recommendation from the church's pastor and, in about 1848, left to study in Great Britain. He spent four years at the University of Glasgow, and then spent the next three years attending Presbyterian seminaries in Edinburgh and London.

Cardozo returned to the United States in 1864. He spent a year as pastor of the Temple Street Congregational Church in New Haven, Connecticut. He married Catherine Romena Howell and the couple had six children: four sons and two daughters. At least one daughter died in infancy. Rather than work as a minister, Cardozo aimed at becoming an educator. He asked the American Missionary Association (AMA) to

send him south where he would establish a school to train black teachers. The assignment the AMA gave him, however, was to go to Charleston, South Carolina and investigate rumors about the conduct of his brother, Thomas.

Before heading the AMA school in Charleston, Thomas Cardozo had taught school in Flushing, New York. Thomas, a married man, had either seduced one of his students in Flushing, or been seduced by her, and she was blackmailing him. Although Thomas confessed to his brother and promised to change his ways, the AMA fired Thomas and appointed Francis head of the Charleston school in August of 1865.

In his new position, Cardozo directed an integrated staff which included white teachers from the North and black teachers from both the North and South. He often requested that more northern teachers be hired, but these requests were sometimes viewed as indicative of a lack of confidence in black instructors. Cardozo responded, however, by explaining that he wanted northern teachers of both races because of the superior training available in the North. Cardozo was also accused of favoring light-skinned black students, and, in response, he pointed out that many of those students had been free black before the Civil War and had obtained a head start in education.

As southerners reclaimed property confiscated in the Civil War, Cardozo was required to find a new location for the school. Cardozo learned that the Charles Avery estate planned to contribute $10,000 to establish a

At a Glance . . .

Born on February 1, 1837, in Charleston, SC; died on July 22, 1903.;son of Jacob N. Cardozo (a white journalist) and a free woman of mixed African- and Native-American ancestry; married Catherine Romena Howell; children: four sons and two daughters; *Education*: University of Glasgow, Scotland; studied for 3 years at Presbyterian seminaries in Edinburgh, Scotland and London, England.

Career: Carpenter's apprentice, five years; journeyman, four years; Temple Street Congregational Church, New Haven, CT, pastor; American Missionary Association school, Charleston, SC, principal, 1865-68; served on a board advising South Carolina's military commander about voter registration regulations, 1866; elected to the state constitutional convention, 1868; Union League, president, 1868; SC secretary of state; 1868-72; Howard University, Latin teacher, 1871-72; SC state treasurer, 1872-76; U.S. Treasury Department, 1877; Colored Preparatory High School, Washington, D.C., principal.

school in Atlanta. Cardozo hoped to be granted a similar sum from the trustees of the estate, but first he needed to win the backing of the governor and the mayor of Charleston. Cardozo called on his contacts in the black community and obtained the backing of the white establishment. In addition to monies granted by the Avery estate, Cardozo also received money from the Freedmen's Bureau. In April of 1867 Cardozo and his teachers moved to Bull Street and an elegant new building was built on the lot next door. The school was renamed the Avery Institute. A normal school, the Avery Institute retained a primary department mainly for the purpose of teacher training. The school became a very successful teacher education school and, later, a bastion of Charleston's black elite. In April of 1868 Cardozo handed over the reins of the school.

Cardozo began his political activities the spring of 1866, when he served on a board advising the military commander of South Carolina about voter registration regulations. In the spring of 1868 he was elected to the state constitutional convention held in Charleston. Although he still served as principal of the AMA school while he attended the convention, he had to give up teaching classes. While principal, Cardozo also drew up plans for state-supported public education. His plans allowed but did not require separate schools for blacks and whites. In 1868 Cardozo served as president of the Union League, which worked to ensure a Republican

victory in the elections. The only black candidate on the state-wide Republican ticket, Cardoza was then elected South Carolina's secretary of state. He resigned his school position on May 1, just days before Avery Institute was formally dedicated.

As secretary of state Cardozo fought against the fraud he found in the state's Land Commission, reorganizing the Commission in 1872. He was reelected secretary of state in 1870, and there was some support for him as a possible candidate to the U.S. Senate. During this time, he also worked as a teacher of Latin at Howard University in Washington, D.C. Cardozo was next elected as state treasurer, a position he held until 1876. He supported efforts of reform by the Republicans to lower taxes and do away with corruption.

In 1877 Cardozo left South Carolina, accepting a post in the U.S. Treasury Department in Washington, D.C. During this time, South Carolina Democrats launched a smear campaign against all Republicans, and Cardozo was charged with eight counts of fraud. In 1879 a political deal resulted in a pardon and the dismissal of the remaining charges.

Next Cardozo became principal of Washington D.C.'s Colored Preparatory High School. The school became best known by its later name, Paul Laurence Dunbar High School. Between 1884 and 1896 Cardozo effectively built the high school into the country's leading black preparatory school. A commercial department was formed in 1884, and in 1887 Cardozo introduced a two-year non-college preparatory course in business. However, William Calvin Chase of the *Washington Bee* led a long campaign to oust Cardozo, and Cardozo's departure may not have been entirely not voluntary. Cardozo died on July 22, 1903.

Sources

Books

Drago, Edmund L. *Initiative, Paternalism, and Race Relations: Charleston's Avery Normal Institute*. University of Georgia Press, 1990.

Greenwood, Willard B. *Aristocrats of Color*. University of Indiana Press, 1990.

Holt, Thomas. *Black over White*. Urbana: University of Illinois Press, 1977.

Logan, Rayford W., and Michael R. Winston, eds. *Dictionary of American Negro Biography*. Norton, 1982.

Notable Black American Men. Gale Research, 1998.

Richardson, Joe M. *Christian Reconstruction*. University of Georgia Press, 1986.

Simmons, William J. *Men of Mark*. Geo. M. Rewell, 1887.

Williamson, Joel. *After Slavery*. University of North Carolina Press, 1965.

Periodicals

Journal of Negro Education, Winter 1979, pp. 73-83.

Journal of Negro History, July 1917, pp. 252-66.

Negro History Bulletin, November 1956, pp. 45-46

On-line

Biography Resource Center, Gale, 2001, http://www.galenet.com/servlet/BioRC

—Robert L. Johns and Jennifer M. York

Janet Collins

1917—

Dancer, choreographer, teacher

Janet Collins broke the color barrier in classical ballet when she became the first black prima ballerina to dance at New York's Metropolitan Opera House as a permanent member of the Metropolitan Opera. The sensational and exquisite dancer found as a teen there was no room for blacks in ballet, but was judged for her talent alone when she joined the Met in 1951. She performed with the Met and on her own for years before dedicating herself to teaching, and ultimately to religious painting. Collins fascinated critics and balletomanes alike with her exquisite sense of movement, both in her own dancing and through her choreography. "You could show Janet a movement, and immediately it became something that nobody else could do. But she did not alter it," former partner Loren Hightower recalled in *Dance* magazine. "It was as if Janet looked inward, and a strange power that she had seemed to come from there … it was magic, hypnotic. It was totally intuitive, and when anything is that unadornedly genuine, it's absolutely compelling."

Painting was Open to Blacks; Dance Was Not

Janet Faye Collins was born in New Orleans on March 2, 1917, one of six children of a hardworking tailor and seamstress. She moved with her family to Los Angeles in 1921, where at the age of ten she began to study dance. Some reports claim she was unable to enroll in regular classes—reserved for white dancers—so was forced to study with a private teacher. Others suggest she enrolled at the Catholic Community Center where her mother agreed to sew costumes for the center in exchange for her daughter's classes.

Collins was also a talented visual artist, and her family encouraged her to forgo dance for painting which, at the time, offered more opportunities to blacks. She studied art at Los Angeles City College and the Los Angeles Art Center School. Though an art-major student on a scholarship, Collins continued to study dance with Adolph Bolm, Carmelita Maracci, and Mia Slavenska, among others.

Most of Collins' training had been classical, but she found a cool reception in the world of professional ballet. Collins auditioned for Leonide Massine, then director of the Ballet Russe de Monte Carlo, when the company performed in Los Angeles during its American tour. As the girls were called by Massine to audition

At a Glance . . .

Born on March 2, 1917 in New Orleans, LA. *Education*: Los Angeles City College and Los Angeles Art Center School, studied painting; studied ballet with Adolph Bolm, Carmelita Maracci, Mia Slavenska, and Madam Toscanini; San Francisco School of Ballet, attended, 1954; studied Hebrew music with composer Ernest Bloch; studied modern dance under Lester Horton; studied Spanish dance with Angel Casino; studied choreography under Doris Humphrey and Hanya Holm.

Career: Dancer, performed as a teen in vaudeville shows; Los Angeles Musical Productions, principal dancer, 1940-41; Katherine Dunham and Lester Horn dance companies, princ. dancer c. 1941; formed duo with Talley Beatty; performed in film *Thrill of Brazil*, 1946; first solo recital, Las Palmas Theater, Los Angeles, 1947; New York debut, 92nd Street "Y," 1949; Cole Porter's *Out of This World*, princ. dancer, 1950; Metropolitan Opera, prima ballerina, 1951-54; Columbia Artists Management, choreographer, solo performer, 1952-55. Choreographer, 1947-74; Teacher: Modern Dance School of American Ballet, 1949-52; Saint Joseph School for the Deaf, 1959-61; Marymount Manhattan College, 1959-69; Manhattanville College of Sacred Heart, 1961-65; Mother Butler Memorial High School, 1966; Scripps College and Mafundi Institute, c. 1970. Religious painter, 1974-.

Awards: Julius Rosenwald Fellowship, 1945; named The Most Outstanding Debutante of the Season, *Dance* magazine, 1949; Merit Award, 1950; Young Woman of the Year, *Mademoiselle* magazine, 1950; Donaldson Award for best dancer on Broadway, 1951; The Committee for the Negro in the Arts, honoree, 1950; guest of honor and keynote speaker, Eighth International Conference of Blacks in Dance, 1995.

one by one, a hush fell over the dancers when Collins took her turn. Massine saw talent in Collins, but could not get past the budding dancer's skin color. He offered her a place in the company—on the condition that she paint her skin white for performances. Collins was crushed. She declined and cried all the way home. "I thought talent mattered, not color," Collins was quoted as saying by *U.S. News & World Report*. When she arrived home, Collins' Aunt Adele told her to keep practicing. "Don't try to be good," Collins quoted her as saying in *U.S. News & World Report*, "be excellent." The Collins family was extremely proud of their background, according to Collins in *U.S. News & World Report*. Far from having any feelings of inferiority, she said, "they were arrogant. I had to overcome arrogance."

Studied Her Craft Intensively

Other popular forms of dance were more open to Collins and her talent. While a teen, she performed as an adagio dancer in vaudeville shows. In 1940 she became the principal dancer for the Los Angeles musical theater productions of *Run Little Chillun* and *The Mikado in Swing*. She performed as a dancer for Columbia Studios in *The Thrill of Brazil*, a film choreographed by Jack Cole, that featured her in the "Rendezvous in Rio" macumba. Modern dance also welcomed blacks, and Collins performed with the notable companies of Lester Horton and Katherine Dunham. Though the companies were open, the practice space was not—Collins and her dance partner still had to sneak into the dance studios before hours to rehearse, as the space was closed to blacks.

Collins studied at the San Francisco School of Ballet after receiving a Julius Rosenwald Fellowship of $1,800 in 1945. Here, she began to develop her own talents as a choreographer. She was intrigued by liturgical dance, and also studied in Oregon with composer Ernest Bloch, a Hebrew music expert. She began to produce a diverse repertory, with several works that explored her French as well as her black heritage—as well as dances created to spirituals; Collins based other routines on life in New Orleans. Her dance *Blackamoor* was choreographed to music by Bach, and told the story of life in Louis XIV's court from the perspective of a young black page. After Collins's first solo concert, she was unable to escape critical praise for her dance, as well as for her costumes, which she had designed. Her one-night performance at the Las Palmas Theater in Los Angeles earned her a scholarship to study composition under Doris Humphrey in New York City. The concert was a hit, but was not as successful financially, and Collins paid her own way to New York.

New York opened its arms to Collins after her debut there in 1949. Her audition for a showcase of young dancers at the Young Men's and Young Women's Hebrew Association on 92nd Street (also known as the 92nd Street "Y") was telling. "Janet did a dance to a Mozart rondo," Muriel Stuart, a member of the audition committee, recalled in *Dance*. "When she finished, there was applause. I mean spontaneous applause. I mean we clapped, we shouted, we stamped our feet." Collins performed two solos in the show on February 20, 1949, stunning New York critics just as she had those in Los Angeles. *Herald Tribune* critic Walter Terry, wrote that "it took no more (and probably less) than eight measures of movement in the opening dance to establish her claim to dance distinction…She could, and probably would stop a Broadway show in its tracks." After another Y showcase and a solo performance there, Collins was named "The Most Outstanding Debutante of the Season" in the May 1949 issue of *Dance* magazine.

Judged Solely on Talent at the Met

As Terry had predicted, Collins soon was dancing on Broadway. She was cast as the principal dancer Cole Porter's *Out of This World*, which opened on December 21, 1950. Again, the critics were generous with their praise—in many reviews, she earned more print space than the production's theatrical leads. "Janet Collins dances with something of the speed of light," *Compass* critic Arthur Pollack wrote, "seeming to touch the floor only occasionally with affectionate feet, caressing it as if she loved it and, loving, wanted to calm any fears it might have that in her flight she would leave it and never come back." Later that year she was named "Young Woman of the Year" by *Mademoiselle* magazine. She also appeared on television, on variety shows such as *The Admiral Broadway Review*, *This is Show Business*, and the *Paul Draper* and *Jack Haley* shows. She received scholarships to study ballet under Madam Toscanini, daughter of celebrated Italian conductor Arturo Toscanini, and modern dance with Hanya Holm, who choreographed Collins's part in *Out of This World*. She also was recognized by the black community. The Committee for the Negro in the Arts praised Collins "for outstanding contributions as an artist to the cultural life of the United States and to the struggles of the Negro people and their artists for full equality and freedom," according to *Dance* magazine. In 1951 she earned the Donaldson Award for the best dancer on Broadway.

Zachary Solov, the new ballet master of the Metropolitan Opera, first saw Collins in *Out of This World*. "She walked across the stage," he recalled in *Dance*, "pulling a chiffon curtain, and it was electric. The body just spoke." Solov instantly set his sights on her for a new production of *Aida* he was choreographing. Solov told Rudolf Bing, the Metropolitan Opera's general manager, that Collins was "wonderful," according to *Dance*, and Bing made the decision to hire her as the first black prima ballerina of the Met, in 1951. Though the Met had previously engaged blacks to play specialty roles, Collins was the company's first full-time black dancer.

Solov used Collins's own movement to choreograph her part in *Aida*, which firmly established Collins as a "dancing sensation," according to *Dance* writer Yael Lewin. Collins remained with the Met until 1954, inspiring Solov in three new productions. She appeared in *Carmen* as a gypsy in 1952; in *La Gioconda* in 1952 as the Queen of the Night in the "Dance of the Hours," notably the only time she performed at the Met on pointe; and in *Samson et Dalila* in 1953. While Collins's dressing room at the Met was located on the first floor, where all the stars' dressing rooms were assigned, she often lost her star status when the company left New York City on tour. When the company performed in Memphis and Atlanta, Collins was replaced by understudies. Bing and Solov threatened not to return unless blacks were permitted to perform and allowed a room in any hotel, with the rest of the company. Collins even encountered discrimination in Canada. Once in Toronto, Collins and her dance partner were told by the man at the door of an obviously open restaurant that the place was closed. According to her partner, Collins told the man that it was pity because she had heard so many good things about his restaurant, and asked if he might suggest another one open nearby. Collins "behaved like a queen," her partner, Loren Hightower, told *Dance*.

Dedicated Herself to Teaching

While with the Met, Collins also kept up a rigorous solo touring schedule, performing her own choreography for Columbia Artists Management. She also taught modern dance at the School of American Ballet from 1949 to 1952, and she began to volunteer her time for charity. In 1957, she taught dance at St. Joseph's School for the Deaf in the Bronx. Because "dance is a mute and living art form," Collins wrote in an article, according to *Dance*, it is an ideal tool for deaf children, whom she claimed displayed a natural ability of for pantomime, while many speaking, hearing people are immobile.

Collins began to bind her teaching with her increasing commitment to Roman Catholicism. She ignored North American and European tour offers to teach full time and to develop her own troupe. She was known as a demanding teacher who required her students to study human anatomy and undergo extensive physical training—in short, she expected no more of them than she would of herself. She took concurrent positions at Manhattanville College of the Sacred Heart at Purchase, New York, Mother Butler Memorial High School, and Marymount Manhattan College where, in 1965, she premiered *Genesis*, a dance she had been working on for more than ten years. In 1970, already relocated to California, Collins returned to the opera world one last time as choreographer of *Nabucco* for the San Francisco Opera. She also taught at Scripps College and the Mafundi Institute. Her final New York City premiere was *Canticle of the Elements*, which she choreographed for the Alvin Ailey Dance Company in 1974. The company continues to perform Collins's *Spirituals*, a work she first danced and choreographed in 1947. "The movement radiated from a central axis onstage and kept returning to it" *Dance* critic Doris Hering wrote of *Spirituals* in 1949. "The whole body was constantly, ripplingly, in motion, and yet there was a ... calm about the whole conception."

Collins donated her professional archives to the New York Public Library for the Performing Arts at Lincoln Center, but the documentation ceased at 1974. It took more than twenty years for the always elusive Collins to resurface, when she appeared in Philadelphia as the keynote speaker at the Eighth International Conference of Blacks in Dance in 1995. The great dancer revealed that she had returned to her other creative talent, painting, and was painting religious subjects exclusively. The living room in her Seattle home was her studio. 2001 marked the 50th anniversary of her debut with the Met, and she was living and still painting in Fort Worth, Texas.

Selected works

(as dancer)

Run Little Chillun, 1940.
The Mikado in Swing, 1940.

(at the Met)

Aida.
Carmen.
La Gioconda.
Samson et Dalila.

(as choreographer)

Blackamoor, 1947.
Eine Kleine Nachtmusik, 1947.

Spirituals, 1947.
Protest, 1947.
Aprés le Mardi Gras, 1947.
Juba, 1949.
Three Psalms of David, 1949.
Moi L'Aimé Toi, 1951.
Chére, 1951.
The Satin Slipper, 1960.
Genesis, 1965.
Cockfight, 1972.
Birds of Peace and Pride, 1973.
Song, 1973.
Fire Weaver, 1973.
Sunday and Sister Jones, 1973.
Canticle of the Elements, 1974.

Sources

Books

Complete Marquis Who's Who, Marquis Who's Who, 2001.
Smith, Jessie Carney, editor, *Notable Black American Women*, Book I, Gale Research, 1992.

Periodicals

Dance, February 1997, p. 66.
Jet, November 19, 2001, p. 26.

—Brenna Sanchez

Barry Cooper

1956—

Journalist, CEO

Creating communities, presenting job opportunities, providing a wide variety of retail options and keeping in touch are just some of the things that Barry Cooper has worked toward in the African-American cyber community. Cooper has provided a venue for these services through Blackvoices.com, a website that African-American web surfers can "call home," according to Cooper in a conversation with Cara Beardi for *Advertising Age*. "They go online to look for and hook up with friends," he explained. "And to find our what's the buzz around Black America. And while they're there, they hear or see about employment opportunities." With Blackvoices.com, Cooper has basically created the leading recruitment site/virtual community for African Americans.

As a young man, Cooper dreamed of becoming a professional athlete. Although he drifted away from the idea as he got older, Cooper remained connected to the sports realm by becoming a sports writer and eventually producing a syndicated sports column. Even as a sports writer, Cooper proved to be a "chronicler of African American affairs," according to a write-up on him at Blackvoices.com. He has more than twenty years of experience as a writer and columnist, and earned a Pulitzer Prize nomination in 1983 for a series he composed on disadvantaged athletes. That writing experience propelled Cooper into the position of becoming the first editor of the *Orlando Sentinel* online, the paper's first attempt at web publishing.

While he was editing the *Sentinel* online, the blueprint for Cooper's virtual city came into being. Cooper had noticed a lack of content of specific interest for African Americans and felt that a destination where ideas and information could be exchanged was what African Americans that were online were looking for. During the mid-1990s, the field was wide open for sites out to serve a community of minorities largely unrecognized by the World Wide Web.

Cooper's vision was born in the form of a simple click at the *Sentinel*'s site. "The focus was entirely on creating audience and eyeballs," Cooper said to *Advertising Age*, and in December of 1995, Blackvoices.com was launched as part of the *Orlando Sentinel*'s site on America Online (AOL). Under Cooper's direction, his website was able to create an interest and, seemingly, a need among African Americans for news on the web while also providing other features, including chat rooms.

The site quickly caught the attention of African Americans in the Orlando, Florida region and eventually acquired a national following. According to the Blackvoices.com site, their users quickly came to represent close to one-third of all usage at the *Tribune*'s Digital City sites on AOL. Due to this popularity and demand, Cooper was able to move into his own domain by April of 1997. Within the first three days of launch, nearly 15,000 users signed up for the ride. Content featured on the site includes news and entertainment, sports features, career advice and job opportunities, clubs, contests, chat rooms and member photos.

"It is absolutely essential that we have full participation on the Internet, that we have all ethnic groups represented," Cooper explained in a conversation with Soo Hi Ji for *Crain's Chicago Business.* Creating the destinations and content of interest is one half of the puzzle in initiating full participation by ethnic groups previously ignored in cyber space. "In the minority communities," he continued, "we have a great opportunity … to harness the great power of the Net. I think that the Internet really makes our world smaller."

By 1999 the *Tribune* committed to expanding Blackvoices.com. By this time, the site had become the nation's number one online community and job- recruitment service for African Americans. *PR Newswire* reported that the *Tribune* invested $5 million to expand the recruitment service of the site. Cooper, along with Blackvoices.com's headquarters, also relocated to Chicago and became a division of Tribune Interactive Inc. President of Tribune Interactive, Jack W. Davis described Blackvoices.com as one of their trend-setting sites. "Black Voices is an innovative site that continues to break new ground in the highly competitive Internet market," Davis told *PR Newswire.* "It's exciting to develop a successful business, but it's even more exciting and rewarding when it's a business that was the brainchild of an employee," he continued.

The end of the twentieth century proved very positive for Cooper and Blackvoices.com. They partnered with the Thurgood Marshall Scholarship Fund and the Tom Joyner Foundation to host the first Black College Virtual Job Fair, as well as with Cars.com to provide exclusive automotive content to the website. Cooper expressed to *PR Newswire* that African-American consumers would have "the most complete information and resources needed to make knowledgeable choices in the automotive market place," with the addition of Cars.com to the website.

In July of 1999 the website had upwards of 400,000 registered members and according to *PR Newswire,* more than 14 million page views. In November of 1999, Cooper's website launched Soko.com, an online retail store that featured African-inspired merchandise. *Black Enterprise* magazine had already crowned Cooper a leader of the "Black Digerati," the group of African Americans setting trends in cyber space. And as the new millennium rushed in, he was presented with MOBE awards at the MOBE-IT Conferences held in 1999 and 2000. The symposiums were organized by Yvette Moyo and her husband Kofi to recognize African Americans making strides in cyberspace.

Cooper also set his sights on new partnerships in the new millennium. By October of 2000, he announced a three-year marketing partnership with the General Motors Corporation (GM). *PR Newswire* reported that GM was seeking online relationships with African Americans. They would sponsor features on the website that included Automotive information, including "GM Spotlight on Excellence" that would showcase African Americans leading the way in their professions and the community, and a sports channel that paid special attention to Historically Black Colleges and Universities.

According to Cooper, Blackvoices.com was excited with the partnership, "We're thrilled about the many opportunities that we can leverage in alliance with GM, including delivering great content to the African American Community," he explained to *PR Newswire.* "GM is the leader in the automotive industry. The company's commitment to Blackvoices.com underscores the strength of our business and effectiveness in reaching consumers nationwide."

Partnerships such as the one that Cooper formed with GM proved very effective towards the end of 2000 when many internet start‐up companies targeting the general population plummeted in stock value and folded, and several highly regarded websites focusing on the African-American community either folded or put expansion plans on hold. *Black Enterprise* reported the demise of BlackFamilies.com and Onelevel.com, while HBO delayed the launch of Volume.com and Russell Simmons formed a partnership with BET.com to keep 360hiphop.com afloat. The GM deal also made the continuation of Cooper's vision to go beyond the web possible because it included sponsorship of the off-line publication, *BVQ,* and scholarships.

In spite of the digital shakeups, Cooper still felt a strong future was ahead for Blackvoices.com and for cyber cities and commerce in general. "About 40% of all African Americans have some access to the Internet, be it at home or work," Cooper told *Advertising Age.* "That number is going to grow, we think, over time." With Black Enterprise reporting more that 500,000 registered users for Blackvoices.com, the growth Cooper predicts has become evident over the years.

Ultimately, Cooper has a grand vision for Blackvoices.com. He laid out plans to seek approximately $25 million from private investors in the site. "We want Blackvoices to spin off and ready itself for an IPO 18 to 24 months down the road," he said to *Advertising Age*. "We have a chance to create a large, multi-media company. We see a day when the Blackvoices brand will extend beyond the Internet into broadcast and print."

Sources

Periodicals

Advertising Age, November 1, 1999, p. 48.
Black Enterprise, October 2000; Dec. 20, 2000.
Business Wire, May 8, 2000.
Crain's Chicago Business, November 27, 2000.
Editor &Publisher, December 18, 1999.
PR Newswire, April 28, 1999; August 2, 1999; August 30, 1990; November 15, 1999; October 3, 2000.

On-line

Blackvoices.com

—Leslie Rochelle

Chuck Davis

1937—

Dancer, choreographer, director

At the end of a DanceAfrica Festival, all of the dance troupes and musicians who have participated come together to perform on stage in an energetic finale. Chuck Davis, founder of the festival and a dancer himself, can be seen at the center of the swirling figures, a tall, joyous man. Founder of the Dance Africa Festivals and the principal of the African-American Dance Ensemble, Davis has played a major role in introducing Americans to African and African-influenced dance.

Davis was born on New Year's Day in 1937 to Tony and Ethel Davis in Raleigh, North Carolina. He attended Ligon High School before enrolling in a special high school program with the U.S. Navy which combined his last two years of high school with four years of active and reserve service. In the Navy he was trained as a medical assistant. When he completed the program in 1957, he went to work in the Washington D. C. area for a local hospital. His career goal was to get a nursing degree and eventually teach nursing.

In the evenings, after his shift had ended, he would go to the clubs in D.C. and dance to the music of performers like Roland Kave and the Latin-American All-Stars, a Afro-Cuban group. Dancing became a passion. He began taking dance classes at a local dance studio, a small basement studio that barely contained his six-foot six-inch height. When Davis raised his hands in fifth position, they would touch the ceiling of the studio. Davis struggled to compensate for his height until he met Jeffrey Holder, a professional dancer who taught a master dance at a local studio. At 6'8", Holder

was taller than Davis by 2 inches. Holder encouraged Davis not to shrink into himself when he danced, but to use his long arms and legs to his advantage.

Another encounter that had an impact on Davis was when, at the 1964 World's Fair in New York, he saw a performance of the Sierre Leone National Dance Company. He became interested in African dance and, he resolved that he would visit Africa one day. Also, around this time, Davis met Owen Dodson, director of the Theater Department at Howard University. Dodson encouraged him to enroll in the Theater and Dance Program at Howard. Davis's career goals began to shift: he started to consider a career in dance as an alternate to a career in medicine. In his view, dancing was an affirmation of life, if not life itself. He told *Contemporary Black Biography* that he began to see the study of medicine as the study of healing and to see the study of dance as the study of health.

Trained in New York

While studying dance in Washington D.C., Davis formed a dance trio with two other dancers, and they performed at local clubs. On the day of the March on Washington, his trio was performing at the Crow's Toe, and Babatunde Olatunji, an African drummer who garnered an international reputation in the 1960s, saw Davis's trio perform and invited Davis to join his African dance troupe. Davis moved to New York to work with Olatunji. He delivered sandwiches during the day in the garment district to earn money to live on, and spent the rest of his time performing and taking dance classes. Some of his friends were students at Julliard, and he would slip in to take dance classes with them.

Soon Davis began performing with Eleo Pomare's dance company. Pomare was a Panamanian known for his highly political choreography. By 1968 Davis was teaching dance classes at Bernice Johnson's dance studio and the South Bronx Community Center. One of the directors at the South Bronx Community Center urged him to start his own dance company, and he gathered 25 dancers and musicians to form the Chuck Davis Dance Company in 1968. The troupe's focus was "dance from the Diaspora," including modern, jazz, tap, African, and African-American dance.

The troupe started slowly. At their first concerts, performers were paid $1.25 apiece. But in the next 10 years, their repertoire expanded and their popularity grew, until in 1977 they were selected to represent the Eastern United States at an international dance festival in Africa called FESTAC. The dates of the tour con-

flicted with a workshop engagement the troupe had, so Davis ended up leading a workshop in Texas while his dance troupe traveled to Africa without him. The troupe was well received at FESTAC; in fact, many of the African dancers at the festival couldn't believe that the troupe was American and not African.

Inaugurated DanceAfrica

The same year that the troupe traveled to FESTAC, the company was invited to perform at the Brooklyn Academy of Music. Davis suggested that instead of just featuring his troupe, the musical directors consider hosting several troupes in a celebration of African-related dance. The festival, called DanceAfrica, included a concert featuring several dance troupes, dance classes, and an African Marketplace. It became a tradition, and expanded. In the next two decades, in addition to an annual Brooklyn appearance, DanceAfrica festivals were held in major cities around the country, including Chicago, Washington, D.C., Hartford, Connecticut, Minneapolis, Los Angeles, Philadelphia, and Miami. Troupes performing at DanceAfrica festivals have included traditional troupes from Africa, newly formed hip-hop troupes, and African-Brazilian troupes.

Each year, all the dance performances are woven together with a storyline. Davis, dressed in traditional African robes, often takes the role of griot, the storyteller who presents the story that weaves all the dances together. The finale is always a celebration of dance and culture, with all the troupes performing on stage together and involving the audience as well. DanceAfrica festivals have been a major vehicle for educating Americans about African and African-American dance, and the culture and traditions they embody. In 2002, the festival celebrated its twenty-fifth anniversary, having brought African and African-American dance to hundreds of thousands.

In the early 1980s Davis become involved with the American Dance Festival, then associated with Connecticut College. When the American Dance Festival relocated to North Carolina, Davis began a series of summer residencies with them in North Carolina. He developed what he called "community in-reach" programs, in which he would take dance into the community. He discovered some talented young dancers, and, the American Dance Festival gave him support in working with them. In order to develop them further, he formed a new dance troupe in 1983 called the African-American Dance Ensemble. Several of the principals he had worked with soon followed Davis to North Carolina, including the principal musician of the Chuck Davis Dance Troupe, Khalid Saleem.

Created the African American Dance Ensemble

Within a few years, the African American Dance Ensemble had performed several complete concerts, and was becoming a showcase for Davis's choreography, including "Saturday Night, Sunday Morning" and "Drought," both of which premiered at the 1985 concert. Meanwhile, his first troupe, the Chuck Davis Dance Company, based in New York, was continuing as a separate entity under different leadership. It eventually disbanded, although company members continued to gather for reunions.

The mission of the African American Dance Ensemble from its inception was to preserve and share the traditions of African and African-American dance. The dances in its repertoire include traditional African dance, contemporary African-American dance and modern dance numbers. When it presents concerts and workshops, the troupe also educates the audience through commentaries on the history and culture that gave birth to the dances they are performing. Inspired by the troupe's motto, "peace, love, and respect for everybody," Davis has long viewed his ensemble as an agent for social change as well as a showcase for African and African-influenced dance. It is his belief that dance allows one to understand the human condition, and encourages us to counteract the negatives and reinforce the positive aspects of it.

Starting in the 1980s, Davis began leading annual trips to Africa, bringing musicians, dancers, and others to study the traditional dance and music forms of the different countries of Africa. Davis's choreographic work has been heavily influenced by these cultural explorations. A prolific choreographer, Davis has created over 30 works. Many of them are traditional African dances. One piece, "N'Tore," which premiered in 1986, is a dance of Watutsi warriors which pays homage to the Tutsi tribe of Burundi. The idea for the piece began in 1963 when he met some Watutsi dancers at the World's Fair in New York. The dance is written for tall male dancers and has become a signa-

ture piece for Davis. Another piece of his, inspired by Nina Simone's song, "Four Women" is an example of his work in the jazz and blues mode.

When Davis creates a dance, he selects a style that he feels is best suited to the story he wants to tell or the message he wishes to convey. In his interview with *CBB* he stated, "I choreograph for the non-dancer. I want that person to look at it, understand it, and be motivated by it." Through his choreography and his leadership in Dance Africa and the African-American Dance Ensemble, Davis has had a significant impact on the arts landscape in the United States.

Sources

Periodicals

Dance Magazine, September, 1995, p. 87.
New York Times, May 20, 2001, Sec. 2, p. 31; May 29, 2001, Sec. E, p. 5.

On-line

Biography Resource Center, http://galenet.gale group.com
African American Dance Ensemble Website, http:// users.vnet.net/aade

Other

Additional information for this profile was obtained from a promotional packet from African American Dance Ensemble, Inc., and a personal interview with *Contemporary Black Biography*, on January 13, 2002.

—Rory Donnelly

Wilhelmina R. Delco

1929—

Politician, educator

Elected to a school board seat, Wilhelmina Ruth Delco was the first African American elected to the school board of Travis County, Texas. She spent twenty years serving in the Texas state legislature. After leaving the legislature, she accepted a position as adjunct professor of education at the University of Texas.

Delco was born on July 16, 1929, in Chicago, Illinois. She was the first of five children born to Juanita Fitzgerald Watson and William P. Fitzgerald, Sr. Her mother was a probation officer, while her father was a court deputy to a Chicago judge. Delco was very close to her mother, who was her role model. Her mother stressed the importance of education. Delco told the *Austin American-Statesman*, "My mother felt that education was the only thing nobody could take away from you."

As a Wendell Phillips High School student, Delco was active in student government organizations. She served as president of her senior class and graduated salutatorian. Delco continued her education at Fisk University in Nashville, Tennessee, where she was involved in dramatics and sociology projects. She was a student during the early tenure of Fisk's first black president, Charles Spurgeon Johnson, an internationally renowned sociologist. In 1950 Delco received her B.A., majoring in sociology and minoring in economics and business administration.

While at Fisk Delco met Exalton Alfonso Delco, Jr., a native of Houston, Texas. The couple married in 1952, and moved to Austin in 1957. The Delcos eventually had four children: Deborah, Exalton Alfonso III, Loretta, and Cheryl. An involved parent, Delco served as president of an elementary school Parent-Teachers Association (PTA), a junior high school PTA, and a county PTA council. A life member of the Texas Congress PTA, Delco was also the first black elected to the school board of Travis County, Texas.

Delco has been involved with numerous civic organizations. Among her involvements with educational committees and boards, Delco has held membership on the Education Commission of the State's Task Force on Education for Economic Growth; served as a board member of the Southern Education Foundation; and was chairman of the Educational Testing Service Board in Princeton, New Jersey.

From 1974 to 1995, Delco served as a Democrat in the Texas House of Representatives, representing, District Fifty, Travis County. She was the first black legislator from District Fifty. Her commitment to education resounded through her legislative committee appointments. She served at least five consecutive legislative sessions as chairman of the House Higher Education Committee. She also served on the State, Federal, and International Relations committees.

Delco has received much recognition for her work in the Texas state legislature. The *Texas Observer* cited her as one of the "brightest spots in the House" and "a dedicated and forthright leader." She was named Distinguished Professional Woman for 1987 by the Committee on the Status of Women at the University of Texas Health Science Center at Houston.

At a Glance . . .

Born July 16, 1928, in Chicago, IL; daughter of Juanita Heath Watson (a probation officer) and William P. Fitzgerald (a court deputy); married Dr. Exalton A. Delco, Jr., 1952; children: Deborah, Exalton III, Loretta, Cheryl. *Education*: Fisk University, B.A., 1950. *Politics*: Democrat.

Career: Texas House of Representatives, 1974-95; University of Texas, adjunct professor.

Memberships: Texas Congress PTA, life member; first black elected to the Travis County, TX, school board; Austin League of Women Voters; Education Commission, State's Task Force on Education for Economic Growth; Southern Education Foundation; and Educational Testing Service Board, Princeton, NJ, former chair; Vision Village, head.

Awards: Texas Women's Hall of Fame in Austin, inducted, 1986; Distinguished Professional Woman, Committee on the Status of Women, University of Texas Health Science Center, 1987; building named in her honor, Prairie A&M University, 1996; Legends of Texas Award, 1999; honorary degrees from St. Edward University, Lee College, Southwestern University, Houston-Tillotson College, and Wiley College; numerous other awards.

Addresses: *Office*—University of Texas, Department of Education Administration, Room SZB 310, Austin, TX 78712. (512) 471-7551.

In 1986 Delco was inducted into the Texas Women's Hall of Fame. At that time, she chaired the state legislative committee on higher education and was recognized for providing permanent funding to public state universities. To further attest to her recognition as a champion for higher education, Delco has received honorary degrees from St. Edward University, Lee College, Southwestern University, Houston-Tillotson College, and Wiley College.

After leaving the Texas state legislature in 1995, Delco remained active in community affairs. She served as chair of the National Advisory Committee on Institutional Equality and Integrity for then U.S. Education Secretary Richard Rile. Delco co-founded and headed Vision Village, a non-profit group. The organization worked toward building a neighborhood which would house unwed mothers, the elderly, and a school for students who were at risk of dropping out. Also, when then-governor George W. Bush signed a bill abolishing Capital Metro's board of directors in 1997, Delco was named to the transit agency's interim board. She has also taken a position as adjunct professor of education at the University of Texas.

Sources

Books

Notable Black American Women, Book One. Gale Research, 1992.
Who's Who Among African Americans, 14th edition. Gale, 2001.
Who's Who Among Black Americans, 6th ed. Gale Research, 1990.

Periodicals

Austin American-Statesman, August 13, 1996, p. E1; August 24, 1996, p. A1; May 24, 1997, p. A1; January 28, 1999, p. B4.
Fisk News, Winter 1989, pp. 19-20.
Houston Chronicle, February 19, 1996, p. 23.
Informer (Texas), October 10, 1987.

On-line

Biography Resource Center, Gale, 2001, http://www.galenet.com/servlet/BioRC
Texas State Legislature, http://www.lrl.state.tx.us/legis/women.htm (February 19, 2002).
University of Texas, http://www.utexas.edu (February 19, 2002).

Other

Additional materials for this profile include: Wilhelmina Delco's resume, 1988; Edelen Communications News Release, September 23, 1986; and an interview with Mrs. Delco, conducted by Mavis Donnelly, February 27, 1990.

—Joan Adams Bahner and Jennifer M. York

Sleepy John Estes

1899-1977

Blues vocalist, guitarist

A highly distinctive voice within the tradition of southern country blues, Sleepy John Estes was among the most popular blues artists who recorded during the 1920s and 1930s. He enjoyed a second flowering of his career as a result of the folk and blues revivals of the 1960s. While not a guitar virtuoso or a master of rhythmic tension like some of his contemporaries, Estes stands out in the history of early blues for a number of reasons. Mostly it was the resonant melancholy of his voice; for the unusually specific pictures painted by the lyrics of some of his songs; and for the mixture of blues and jug band music heard on many of his recordings.

John Adam Estes was born in Ripley in western Tennessee on January 25, 1899; he was one of sixteen children of sharecropper parents and grew up doing farm work. As a child Estes was blinded in one eye by a stone that hit his face during a baseball game. According to some accounts his nickname "Sleepy John" referred to the droopy eye that resulted from this accident, while others attribute it to occasional narcolepsy-like blackouts caused by a recurrent blood-pressure disorder. As an adult Estes was known to fall asleep on the bandstand during performances.

Worked on Railroad Gang

As a young man Estes received a musical education from two sources: from his father, who was a guitarist, and from his experiences on a railroad work crew. He had been picked for the railroad job because his piercing voice was well-suited to leading his co-workers in work songs. By his teenage years Estes was playing house parties and fish fries around Brownsville, Tennessee, where his family had moved in 1915.

The country blues is sometimes thought of as a solo music, but Estes worked mostly with small ensembles, continuing to perform with the same musicians for years after he had first made a connection with them. An integral part of his sound was the mandolin playing of James "Yank" Rachell, whom he met around 1920. Later Estes joined forces with harmonica player Hammie Nixon, who also played the jug—a liquor jug that was the centerpiece of the "jug band," a streetcorner ensemble that was popular in the nearby big city of Memphis. Sometimes in combination with guitarist Son Bonds or jug player Jab Jones, Estes made annual trips to Memphis during the cash-rich fall harvest period, performing for white audiences as well as black.

At a Glance . . .

Born John Adam Estes in Ripley, Tennessee, January 25, 1904; died June 5, 1977. Married; five children.

Career: Blues guitarist, vocalist, and composer. Played for parties in and around Brownsville, 1910s; worked with mandolinist "Yank" Rachell, harmonica player Hammie Nixon; performed and recorded with Three Js Jug Band, ca. 1928; recorded for Victor with Rachell and Nixon, 1929; numerous recordings of original material for Decca and Bluebird labels, late 1930s and early 1940s; pioneered blues lyric style that depicted actual persons and events; rediscovered, 1962; appeared at Newport Folk Festival, 1964; toured Europe; enjoyed 15-year career during blues revival until his death.

In 1929 Estes, together with Rachell on mandolin and Jones on piano, made his first recordings; the Victor label is said to have paid them the unusually generous sum of $300 per musician, which would suggest how popular Estes had become in the Memphis area. These recordings showed how Estes created a unique sound balanced between country and city. Estes himself, with his predominantly rhythmic guitar style and his powerful holler-like vocals, drew on early blues traditions and on the field hollers and work songs that underlay them. But the music of the group as a whole often had a relaxed swing feel that served as a foil for Estes's lowdown sound.

Wrote Vivid Lyrics

The Depression kept Estes out of the recording studio for a time, but he recorded again, this time for the Decca label, in 1934. These sessions included the blues standard "Drop Down Mama" and other songs that became well known to the musicians in whose hands the new Chicago blues style was taking shape. Estes himself moved to Chicago that year and remained there for much of the 1930s. He claimed to have performed for the gangster Al Capone.

In the late 1930s Estes added an even more distinctive element to his music: the proportion of original compositions in his output increased, and with it came a new kind of blues song. Whereas the majority of blues songs speak of trouble, love, or fun in an abstract way, many of the most famous Sleepy John Estes recordings, such as "Lawyer Clark Blues," contain vivid images of actual individuals that Estes knew in Browns-

ville. Other recordings, such as "Stone Blind" (Estes lost sight in his other eye as he got older), drew on the musician's own life. Such songs are powerful documents of life in a poor small-town black community; they recorded wider social developments, such as the mechanization of southern agriculture that forced sharecroppers to look for work in the factories of the North.

In the early 1940s Estes temporarily retired from music due to a combination of factors. The curtailing of recording activity during World War II put an end to his recording career, and the brash, electronic sounds of Chicago blues were replacing the more personal southern country style. Completely blind by 1950, Estes slipped deeper into poverty. He appeared on a few recordings made by Hammie Nixon and may have had contact with the Sun label helmed by Memphis producer Sam Phillips, but for 20 years there was no musical niche that he could fit into.

Rediscovered Living in Poverty

That changed in 1962, thanks to a revival of traditional folk and blues music which had taken root on college campuses and spread to a wider public. After a search through the back roads of the South, filmmaker David Blumenthal found Estes scratching out a living on a deserted farm with his wife and five children. Estes spoke about his experiences in Blumenthal's documentary, *Citizen South, Citizen North,* made that year. Blues enthusiasts were shocked at the conditions in which Estes was living, but his fortunes took a turn for the better as he began to appear at blues and folk festivals. The most famous of these was the Newport Folk Festival, held in Rhode Island in 1964; that appearance made Estes an icon of the blues revival and placed his music before many aspiring young rock musicians.

These appearances also led to a modest revival of Estes's own recording career; still working with Nixon and Yank Rachell, he recorded several albums for Chicago's Delmark label beginning with *The Legend of Sleepy John Estes* in 1962. Estes toured until the end of his life, traveling to Europe in 1964 and 1968 and to Japan (the first American blues performer to do so) in 1974. Sleepy John Estes died on June 5, 1977, in Brownsville. The money he had made during the second wind of his career probably prolonged his old age but never made him well-off; he died in a shotgun shack, and blues enthusiasts had to take up a collection to pay for his funeral.

Selected discography

The Legend of Sleepy John Estes, Delmark, 1962.
Broke and Hungry, Delmark, 1963.
In Europe, Delmark, 1966.
Brownsville Blues, Delmark, 1969.

Down South Blues, MCA, 1970 (compilation of 1930s material).

Complete Works, vols. 1 & 2, Document (Austria), 1990.

I Ain't Gonna Be Worried No More: Sleepy John Estes, 1929-1940, Yazoo, 1992.

The Essential Sleepy John Estes, Classic Blues, 2001.

Sources

Books

Contemporary Musicians, volume 25, Gale Group, 1999.

Erlewine, Michael, et al., eds., *The All Music Guide to the Blues,* 2nd ed., Matrix Software, 1999.

Harris, Sheldon, *Blues Who's Who,* Arlington, 1979.

Oliver, Paul, Max Harrison, and William Bolcom, *The New Grove Gospel, Blues, and Jazz,* Macmillan, 1986.

On-line

http://www.blueflamecafe.com

http://www.eyeneer.com/America/Genre/Blues/Profiles/estes.html

—James M. Manheim

Grandmaster Flash

1958—

DJ

Known as one of the founding fathers of hip-hop, Grandmaster Flash was one of rap's earliest technical pioneers. The deejay (DJ) innovative turntable techniques he experimented with in the 1970s have become synonymous with rap and hip-hop today. Flash and his group, the Furious Five, became one of the best-known rap acts of the early 1980s, with popular singles such as "The Message," "The Adventures of Grandmaster Flash on the Wheels of Steel," and "White Lines (Don't Do It)." Flash split from the Furious Five and went on to record on his own, but faded from mainstream popularity in the 1980s. Flash came back into view in the 1990s as an elder statesman of the genre, revived and celebrated by contemporary hip-hop groups and media.

Turntable Antics Became Hip-Hop Legend

Grandmaster Flash was born Joseph Saddler on January 1, 1958, in Barbados, West Indies, but was raised in the Bronx, New York. Recognizing her boy's fascination with electronics, Saddler's mother sent him to Samuel Gompers Vocational High School. His musical tastes were shaped by what he snuck from his father's and sister's record collections—he plucked Glenn Miller, Louis Armstrong, Miles Davis, Ella Fitzgerald, Dinah Washington, and Stan Kenton from his father; his sister's collection exposed him to Michael Jackson, Tito Puente, Eddie Palmieri, James Brown, Joe Corba, and Sly and the Family Stone, among others. He attended early DJ parties thrown by DJ Flowers, Ma-Boya, and Peter "DJ" Jones as a teen. Jones took an interest in the young Saddler, and the upstart DJ began to engineer his own turntable style.

Flash was not the first person to experiment with two turntables, but his discoveries are among the most known in contemporary hip-hop. Among the innovative turntable techniques Flash is credited with developing are "cutting" and "scratching" (pushing the record back and forth on the turntable)," phasing" (manipulating turntable speeds), and repeating the drum beat or climatic part of a record, called the "break." He developed a way to segue between records without missing a beat, using a mixer. He also was known for his technical tricks, mixing records behind his back or under tables, and manipulating mixing faders with his

At a Glance . . .

Born Joseph Saddler on January 1, 1958, in Barbados, West Indies, raised in the Bronx, New York.

Career: Began spinning records at block parties in the South Bronx in the early 1970s; formed Grandmaster Flash and the Furious Five with MCs Cowboy, Kid Creole, Melle Mel, Rahiem, and Scorpio; group made recording debut with single "Super Rappin'," Enjoy Records, 1979; Sugarhill Records bought out contract, 1980; released platinum-selling "The Message," 1982; Flash left the group and signed with Elektra Records, 1983; released solo debut album, *They Said It Couldn't Be Done*, 1985; released two more solo albums on Elektra, 1986-87; group reunited for a charity concert, 1987, and again in 1994; co-produced Terminator X's solo record, *Super Bad*; was musical director and DJ for HBO's *Chris Rock Show*, late 1990s; recorded *The Official Story*, 2001.

Addresses: *Office*—853 Broadway, Ste. 1516, New York, NY 10003. *Website*—http://www.grandmaster flash.com.

feet. In the late 1980s, he was the first DJ to design andmarket his own DJ device, the Flashformer.

After nearly a year spent practicing in his 167th Street apartment, Saddler started spinning records at free block parties and parks in the Bronx, often illegally pilfering power for his sound system from intercepted power mains until being shut down by police. He soon earned the nickname "Flash" for his rapid hand movements and general dexterity on the decks. Not completely satisfied that his wily turntable tricks were enough in themselves to completely entertain an audience, Flash invited friend and vocalist Keith Wiggins, later known as Cowboy, to share the stage with him. Wiggins would become one of rap's first "MCs," rapping lyrics over Flash's beats.

Was Paid to DJ

Until he was approached by promoter Raymond Chandler, Flash performed in the style of the times—for free. Chandler was among the first to see the commercial viability, and Flash agreed to let Chandler promote him and charge entrance fees, though Flash could not believe anyone would pay to see him spin records.

In the mid-1970s, friends Grandmaster Melle Mel (Melvin Glover) and Kid Creole (Nathaniel Glover) joined

with Flash and Wiggins to form Grandmaster Flash and the Three MCs. Two more rappers, Kurtis Blow (Kurt Walker) and Duke Bootee (Ed Fletcher) joined and were later replaced by Rahiem (Guy Todd Williams) and Scorpio (Eddie Norris, aka Mr. Ness) and the sextet became known as Grandmaster Flash and the Furious Five, which became one of rap's first groups. The crew was known for its choreography, studded leather stage wear, and solid rapping skills. According to GrandmasterFlash.com, Furious Five MC Cowboy pioneered phrases like "Throw your hands in the air, and wave 'em like ya just don't care!," "Clap your hands to the beat!," and "Everybody say, ho!" which are echoed tirelessly in contemporary hip-hop. The early days of live rap fostered head-to-head rapping competitions between rival MCs, often competing for their competitor's equipment in lieu of prize money.

Flash and the group recorded a number of singles for the Enjoy label, the first of which, "Super Rappin'," was released in 1976. Though an underground hit, the song went mostly unnoticed, as did the subsequent singles "We Rap Mellow," and "Flash to the Beat." Joe Robinson Jr. bought out Flash's Enjoy contract for his Sugarhill record label, and one of the most legendary artist-label teams was born. Robinson's wife, Sylvia, began writing songs for the group, and they released "Freedom," which was pushed to gold-selling status by the first major tour in rap history. The single "Birthday Party" followed, but the revolutionary "Grandmaster Flash on the Wheels of Steel" was released soon after and became a smash hit. The first song to incorporate samples, "Grandmaster Flash on the Wheels of Steel" dramatically showcased Flash's singular talent and changed the way music was recorded.

Got "The Message"

Co-written by Sylvia Robinson, 1982's "The Message" was decidedly darker and more focused on urban issues than the group's previous party anthems and, though Flash and the Five recorded it reluctantly, the record became a platinum-selling hit within a month of its release. During recording of the anti-cocaine single "White Lines (Don't Do It)," Flash and Mel had a falling out. Also, despite the group's success, Flash had not seen much in the way of profits, so he left Sugarhill Records and took Kid Creole and Rahiem with him to sign a deal with Elektra Records. The rest of the group stayed as Melle Mel and the Furious Five, and achieved nearly instant success with the single "White Lines." The popular anthem was ironic, as Flash himself had become a freebase cocaine addict. Flash and Mel later appeared together on a 1995 cover of the song by Duran Duran.

Flash drifted out of mainstream culture for much of the 1980s. His solo record, 1985's *They Said it Couldn't be Done*, met with low critical response. Songs like "Alternate Groove" and "Larry's Dance Theme," critic

Ralph Novak wrote in *People*, were fun, enjoyable, and incorporated the lyrical phrasing and turntable and synthesizer manipulations that Flash was famous for. But those two strong songs were lost in the sea of "homogenized pop" that dominated the record, Novak continued. Novak declared Flash could not "be forgiven for forsaking the rhythmic rapping that made him" a hip-hop star. 1986's *The Source* noted that the album was a bitter and boastful declaration that alleged all other rappers had only copied Flash and his style. The record's strong point, noted *People* critic David Hiltbrand, was Flash's "feverish…turntable scratching technique" on what he considered the "best tracks," "Fastest Man Alive," and "Style," but those skills were hidden throughout most of the record.

Grandmaster Flash and the Furious Five reunited onstage for a charity concert hosted by Paul Simon in 1987, but a proper reunion did not occur until 1994, for a rap-oldies show that also featured Kurtis Blow, Whodini, and Run-DMC. Flash returned to mainstream consciousness in the 1990s, celebrated by hip-hop culture and media as an elder statesman of hip-hop. He co-produced Public Enemy DJ Terminator X's solo record, Super Bad, and hosted a call-in radio show that showcased hopeful MCs. A slough of greatest hits records were released in the late 1990s, and Flash worked as musical director and DJ of HBO's *Chris Rock Show*.

At the end of 2001 Flash was busy at work on a new solo project built around the sounds he experimented with at the South Bronx block parties of the late 1970s. *The Official Adventures of Grandmaster Flash* was set for release in January of 2002, and included cuts from original block party tapes, and exclusive interview footage with Flash himself. Flash also prepared a 28-page booklet to be included with the release, featuring rare photographs from the period and a detailed history of the era.

Selected discography

They Said It Couldn't Be Done, Elektra, 1985.
The Source, Elektra, 1986.
Ba Dop Boom Bang, Elektra, 1987.
On the Strength, Elektra, 1988.
Greatest Messages, Sugarhill, 1983.

Grandmaster Flash Vs. the Sugarhill Gang, Recall, 1997.
Greatest Mixes, Deep Beats, 1998.
Adventures on the Wheels of Steel, Sugarhill, 1999.
Official Adventures Of Grandmaster Flash, Strut, 2002.

With Melle Mel/Furious Five

The Message, Sugarhill, 1982.
Work Party, Sugarhill, 1984.
Stepping Off, 1985.
On The Strength, 1988.
Greatest Hits, Sugarhill, 1989.
Message from Beat Street: The Best of Grandmaster Flash, Melle Mel &the Furious Five, Rhino, 1994.
More Hits from Grandmaster Flash &the Furious Five, Vol. 2, Deep Beats, 1996.
Adventures of Grandmaster Flash, Melle Mel &The Furious Five: More of the Best, Rhino, 1996.
Right Now, Str8 Game, 1997.

Sources

Books

Larkin, Colin, editor, *Encyclopedia of Popular Music*, Muze UK Ltd., 1998.
Rolling Stone Encyclopedia of Rock & Roll, Third ed., Fireside/Rolling Stone Press, 2001.

Periodicals

Entertainment Weekly, June 24, 1994, p. 14.
People, March 25, 1985, p. 22; June 23, 1986, p. 18.

On‐Line

All Music Guide, http://www.allmusic.com (March 21, 2002).
Rolling Stone online, http://www.rollingstone.com (January 7, 2002).
http://www.grandmasterflash.com (January 7, 2002).
New Musical Express online, http://www.nme.com (January 7, 2002).

—Brenna Sanchez

Vivian L. Fuller

1954—

Athletic director

In a time that preceded the WNBA, women's professional boxing, and women's Olympic soccer teams, there was a woman who dared to prove she could do anything a man could do. Though Vivian L. Fuller is not known as an athlete, she broke ground as a pioneer in sports. Fuller shook up the sporting world as the first African-American woman to become an athletic director at a National Collegiate Athletic Association (NCAA) Division I school with a football team. Her success did not come without controversy, though; but when life threw her a curve ball, she proved that there was power in her swing.

Born October 17, 1954 in Chapel Hill, North Carolina, Fuller enjoyed participating in recreational sports like softball and volleyball. Fuller, who was also a runner, told *Contemporary Black Biography* that one of her biggest accomplishments was running in Nashville's Music City Marathon. It was no wonder that she decided to pursue a Bachelor of Science degree in physical education at Fayetteville State University in her home state of North Carolina. After graduating, Fuller decided to continue the pursuit of education—a decision that was likely driven by the motivation of her mother. "Education was the forefront of discussions and made a priority in my household," Fuller told *CBB*. After earning a Master's degree in Education and a doctorate in higher education administration, she put her degrees and knowledge to the test.

Started Career as Director of Intramurals

In 1978 Fuller began her career at Bennett College, an institution for women in Greensboro, North Carolina. She played a dual role as Bennett's director of intramurals and a physical education instructor. In 1984 she moved on to North Carolina Agricultural &Technical State (A&T) University to become the school's assistant director of athletics, as well as the women's volleyball and softball coach. Three years later, Fuller packed her bags and left for Pennsylvania, after accepting a position as associate director of intercollegiate athletics at the Indiana University of Pennsylvania. She told *CBB* that Frank Cignetti, who hired her for the position, inspired her to accomplish even more through his belief in her capabilities.

As her career developed, Fuller demonstrated a genuine concern for student athletes and programs. She often voiced the needs of women's athletics to educate college administrators and coaches. Climbing the ladder of success meant that her eyes were glued to positions that were traditionally held by men. As a result, she was often met with opposition and even curiosity by people who wondered why she chose that path. "I felt that I always had to justify why I was there," she was quoted as saying on www.momentummedia-.com. Fuller's determination pushed her above the questions and doubt raised by her peers and observers. In fact, it appeared that the negative inquiries may have turned out to be nothing less than motivating.

In 1992 Fuller joined the ranks of a select few when she took over the role of director of intercollegiate athletics at Northeastern Illinois University in Chicago. According to *Athletic Management,* she became "one of

At a Glance . . .

Born on October 17, 1954 in Chapel Hill, NC. *Education:* Fayetteville State University, BS in physical education, 1977; University of Idaho, Masters' of Education, 1978; Iowa State University, 1985.

Career: Bennett College, 1978-84; North Carolina A&T University, 1984-87; Indiana University of Pennsylvania, 1987-92; Northeastern Illinois University, 1992-97; Tennessee State University, 1997-99; University of Maryland-Eastern Shore, 2000-.

Awards: Atalanta Award, Athletic Management, 1995.

Member: National Collegiate Athletics Association (NCAA), National Association of Collegiate Directors of Athletics, Delta Sigma Theta Sorority, Inc., Princess Anne and Salisbury Chamber of Commerce.

Address: University of Maryland-Eastern Shore, William P. Hytche Athletic Center, Physical Education Department, Princess Anne, MD 21853.

eight women in the country [to] hold the title of Athletic Director at a school where the majority of sports compete at the NCAA Division I level." *Athletic Management* noted that having the opportunity to head a program with a football team was very important to Fuller. "Women are always being told that it's something we can't do, that we don't know enough about football," she was quoted as saying.

A member of the NCAA Gender Equity Task Force, the NCAA Council, and the National Youth Sports Program, for which she served as chairperson, Fuller stayed in the forefront of sports issues. In 1995 she was recognized for her efforts when she received *Athletic Management*'s Atalanta Award in the category of Role Models. Fuller pointed to her mother as her inspiration. " ... I always told people if there was a person I'd like to be like, it would be her," she was quoted as saying on www.momentummedia.com.

Hired at TSU

Two years later, Fuller won the biggest fight of her blossoming career. The woman who was known for speaking out on topics like gender equality and women in management placed her name in the hat for the athletic director position at Tennessee State University (TSU). At the age of 41, she beat three other candidates for the position, becoming the first African-American woman to hold this position at a Division I school with a football team. "I don't think gender makes a difference in how you do your job, so I'm going to be coming in here to evaluate this program and see what it takes to move into the next millennium," Fuller was quoted as saying in *The Commercial Appeal*. She took the bull by the horns, and in her first full season with TSU, the Tigers football team finished the season 9-3 and walked away as winners of the Ohio Valley Conference (OVU) championship—an accomplishment that, according to *Athletic Management*, had not been achieved since the mid-1980s. Unbeknownst to Fuller, her fervor would be short-lived.

On January 29, 1997, nearly 15 months after the *Onnidan Online News* quoted him as stating "Dr. Fuller brings to us remarkable organizational ability, excellent marketing skills, and a broad base of experience," university president James Hefner abruptly fired Fuller. The firing shocked many. The decision was met with plenty of "controversy and speculation"—so much so that it prompted Tennessee Board of Regents Chancellor Charles Smith to request a letter of explanation for Fuller's release.

According to the *Commercial Appeal*, Hefner adhered to the request, citing 24 reasons for firing Fuller. Among those reasons were accusations that Fuller cost the school more than $1,500 in penalties for missing a state tax filing date and that she failed to respond to student requests for scholarship reinstatements. Hefner stated that Fuller caused additional loss of funds by failing to schedule games in the Tennessee Oilers' new stadium—an agreement that was reached between the university and the state to help fund the arena. The letter accused Fuller of reprimanding an assistant coach for filing a complaint with the government's Office of Equal Opportunity and Affirmative Action and he claimed—in contradiction to Hefner's earlier statement in the *Onnidan Online News*—that Fuller lacked organizational skills.

Sued TSU for Wrongful Termination

Fuller sued the university. According to *Jet*, Fuller claimed she was fired without explanation, and that Hefner and other university officials "obstructed her efforts to help women's teams and 'ignored and diminished' the contributions" she made to the university. The case was settled, but the details were not disseminated to the public. On www.thepost.mindspring.com, Fuller was quoted as saying that she was often "second guessed" by her co-workers and that she faced "backstabbing" in her position at Tennessee State. She did however, tell *Athletic Management* that she had "no ill feelings against TSU," and wished the university "the best in their future."

In an interview with *Athletic Management*, Fuller revealed that some soul searching was required to determine the next step in her career. She realized that she had been doing what was in her heart, and in June of 2000, she stepped back up the plate. Soon she accepted the athletic director position at University of Maryland-Eastern Shore—another Division I school.

According to *Athletic Management*, her recent concentrations have been on providing opportunities for underrepresented athletes, advancing women's programs, improving recruitment programs, and finding more role models for females in sports. Despite the fact that Maryland-Eastern Shore does not have a football team, Fuller felt right at home. "I feel like this is the place where I'm supposed to be," she told *Athletic Management*. "University of Maryland-Eastern shore has given me a second chance." Her second chance is one that she hoped would encourage other women to strive for their goals, despite roadblocks. She told *Athletic Management* that she hoped the story of her life featured "... A woman who was dynamic and quite accomplished, who all of a sudden fell off her horse and then rebounded....I'm very positive about the situation. I can live with it. I've learned from it. I've grown from it. And I'm a better person. Although, two years ago, I never thought you would hear me say that."

Sources

Periodicals

Athletic Management, October/November 2000.
Jet, September 20, 1999, p.8.
The Commercial Appeal, October 2, 1997, p. D5; February 18, 1999 p. D5.

On-Line

Biography Resource Center, Gale Group.
www.educ.iastate.edu/awards/alumni/1996/fuller. html
www.momentummedia.com
www.nashville.bcentral.com/nashville/stories/1998/ 11/30/story1.html
www.onnidan.com
www.tennessean.com
www.thepost.mindspring.com
www.umes.edu

Other

Additional information for this profile was obtained through a personal interview with *Contemporary Black Biography* on January 9, 2001.

—Shellie M. Saunders

Eddie Futch

1911-2001

Boxing trainer

Eddie Futch spent 66 years in boxing, and during that time, he earned the respect and trust of most people in the sport because of his integrity. He received several awards from the Boxing Writers Association of America over the years, and before his death was to be honored at his 90th birthday with a star-studded gala event at Caesar's Palace. He trained thousands of amateurs and 21 champions; six of those champions were heavyweights: Joe Frazier, Ken Norton, Trevor Berbick, Riddick Bowe, Larry Holmes, and Michael Spinks. It was his desire to help others through boxing. Two of his fighters, Joe Frazier and Ken Norton, were the only ones to defeat Muhammad Ali during his prime years. He was quoted as saying by *Sports Illustrated,* "Boxing enabled me to create a life for myself out of the ghetto. It has been my passion for the last six decades to help other young men make something of themselves."

Sparred with Joe Louis

Eddie Futch was born in Hillsboro, Mississippi on August 9, 1911. He was the son of a sharecropper, and when he was eight years old, the family moved to Detroit, Michigan, where he grew up in the Black Bottom section of the city. The young Futch played basketball and, according to heavyweight champion Joe Frazier in his autobiography, *Smokin' Joe,* became a star who was good enough to play against semi-pro teams. But at seventeen, Futch was married and in need of a job. He worked as a waiter at a local hotel. Later he became interested in boxing but had no interest in it as a career; he simply wanted to hit the speed bag and skip rope. But soon Futch tried some sparring, and he joined the Detroit Athletic Association at the Brewster Community Center.

Futch had gotten a late start in the sport compared to most fighters, but he had several of the center's boxers teaching him. He began competing as an amateur and in 1932 won the Detroit Athletic Association Lightweight championship. A year later he won the Detroit Golden Gloves lightweight title.

One of the boxers he sparred with was Joe Louis, who was still an amateur but fast becoming known in boxing circles. Louis would go on to become the heavyweight champion of the world in 1937, holding the title until 1948. He was considered by many boxing insiders and

At a Glance . . .

Born August 9, 1911, in Hillsboro, MS; died October 10, 2001 in Las Vegas, NV; wife's name Eva; children: four. *Education:* Attended high school.

Career: Boxer; road laborer; welder; sheetmetal worker; postal worker. Detroit Athletic Association Lightweight championship, 1932; Detroit Golden Gloves, 1933. Boxing trainer and manager until death in 2001.

Awards: Boxing Writers Association of America, Manager of the Year, 1975, Long and Meritorious Service, 1982, Trainer of the Year, 1991, 1992, James A. Farley Award for honesty and integrity in boxing, 1996. International Boxing Hall of Fame, Canastota, NY, 1994; World Boxing Hall of Fame, Los Angeles.

fans to be the finest heavyweight champion of all time. Louis broke barriers and became admired around the world.

When Futch met Louis at the Brewster Community Center, he was " ... not too impressed. I expected something more flashy. I didn't know enough to realize he was a real gem," Futch said in *Smokin' Joe.* Louis asked Futch to spar, but Futch told him to go after the middleweights, that they were fast enough for him. Louis insisted on sparring with Futch because he was so fast. Futch decided that he would study the technique of the larger fighter so that he would not get hurt in sparring with him. It was then that he laid the groundwork for his years as a successful trainer. "By studying Joe, that's when I first found that if you look, you can see things. Studying him, I picked up some things that maybe nobody else ever thought about. Things I've used working with fighters ever since," he told author Dave Anderson for *In The Corner.* Futch and Louis became friends. But during sparring sessions it was all business, and Futch noted that Louis once knocked him through the two top ropes of the ring and out onto the floor. Futch was stopped from turning pro when a physical discovered a heart murmur.

During his post-boxing years, Futch tried other work: road laborer, welder, sheetmetal worker, post office worker. But he returned to boxing, this time as a trainer of amateurs. He used his watchful, analytical style to first learn his boxer's skill levels and technique, and then he used it to bring out their strengths. Emanuel Steward, head of the Kronk Gym and himself a trainer of many world champions, would later say of Futch in the *Detroit News,* "The thing about Eddie, he was not a trainer, he was a teacher. He really got control over his fighter's mind like no one I've ever seen. He had that personal one-on-one contact with fighters."

Turned Boxers Into Champions

While Futch trained amateurs and worked at other jobs, he developed his teaching style. That style included not changing a fighter. Trainer Freddie Roach was trained by Futch, first as a fighter, and then as a trainer. Roach later told Steve Kim for MaxBoxing.com, "I see a lot of fighters become trainers and they try to make fighters fight like they did. They try to change a fighter. [Futch] told me to take a person's natural ability and work on that. Don't change a fighter, because as soon as the bell rings, they'll go back to what comes naturally to them." Futch had plenty of practice, noting in *In The Corner,* that he had worked with 2,000 amateur fighters by 1955. Futch's teaching methods and other factors, such as desire and willingness to learn, all came together in 1958 when his fighter Don Jordan won the welterweight championship in 1958.

Futch did not know Joe Frazier, nor his trainer and manager Yank Durham, when he was brought into the Frazier "camp" in 1966, but they already knew Futch by reputation. The three hit it off. Futch said in *In The Corner,* "It was like we'd known each other forever." Futch would later say that Joe Frazier was the easiest boxer to work with that he had ever trained. Frazier was the Olympic champion when Futch began working with him, but Durham remained his prime trainer. Futch gave advice when asked, and was responsible for Frazier's bob and weave style. Futch took over completely when Yank Durham died of a stroke. By 1970 Frazier had racked up enough wins to be considered the heavyweight champion by the World Boxing Association, a title that Muhammad Ali had held until he was exiled from boxing for his refusal to be inducted into the Army during the Vietnam war. They fought for the championship in March of 1971. Frazier won by unanimous decision.

The two fighters faced each other two more times, and Futch is perhaps best known for his decision to stop the Ali-Frazier fight, the "Thrilla in Manilla" in 1975. The bout was considered the best of the three classic fights in which Frazier and Ali faced each other, and one of which Ali would later refer to as "the closest thing to death." Frazier could not see the punches coming because his eyes, especially the left, were badly swollen. Although he was eager to get up and finish the fight, with just one more round to go, Futch threw in the towel. He told Frazier in words that became as well known as the fight, "Sit down, son. No one will ever forget what you did here today." Futch later said in the *Las Vegas Review-Journal* that although he had thought about stopping the fight in the 13th round when Ali knocked Frazier's mouthpiece into the crowd, "I decided to give him one more round." Futch remained Frazier's manager until the boxer retired.

Futch worked with many more amateurs and champions. Some were kids just wanting to box, and many were amateurs who dreamed of becoming professional boxers and title holders. One such fighter was Freddie Roach. Futch trained Roach for ten years and finally advised him to hang up his gloves. Roach had begun training with Futch at eighteen years of age. When he stopped boxing, Futch later hired him as an assistant trainer. Roach worked for Futch for five years before going on to train 25 champions himself. Futch's training helped several of his fighters to win their titles, while others had already become champions when he stepped in. One such fighter was Larry Holmes. Holmes followed Muhammad Ali as the heavyweight champion, and was always compared to him. He held the title for seven years after winning it in 1978.

Retired from Boxing

Eddie Futch retired in January of 1998. At the time he was working with light heavyweight Montell Griffin. Griffin won the title in 1997 by disqualification of his opponent, Roy Jones. After a disagreement with Griffin's management team, Futch made the decision to retire. At the time, he wasn't very happy with boxing. He was quoted as saying in *Sports Illustrated,* "These days, with the proliferation of weight classes and titles and the emphasis on money, boxing is getting worse. Quality is disappearing from the sport." By the time he retired, Futch had been in the sport for 65 years and had trained 22 world champions. It was his wish to spend more time with his family. When he died, he had begun traveling with his wife, Eva. The sport of boxing was left without a highly respected and positive influence. Emanuel Steward, trainer of 25 world champions including heavyweight Tommy Hearns, told Steve Kim of Max Boxing.com, "He was a man of dignity. He always believed in respect, principles."

In 1999 Futch was a member of a five-man panel for the Associated Press to select the Fighter of the Century and the top fighters in ten weight classes. The voting came down to two: Muhammad Ali and Joe Louis. The vote that Futch would cast would make the decision. It was thought that he would automatically vote for Louis because they had been friends. Instead, Futch examined the records of both fighters, compared them, and watched a tape of a 1941 fight between Joe Louis and Billy Conn. He chose Muhammad Ali, based on his speed.

Futch died on October 10, 2001. His 90th birthday celebration had been scheduled for September 29th but was canceled because of the terrorist attacks in the United States on September 11th. The service was conducted by minister Richard Steele, who had been trained by Futch as a fighter and who had been a boxing referee. The eulogy was delivered by Motown records founder Berry Gordy, who had also been trained by Futch as an amateur boxer in Detroit, at age 15. Gordy, quoted in the *Las Vegas Review-Journal,* described Futch as having the "mind of a warrior and the heart of a poet" and as a "gentle giant." He called Futch boxing's "statesman, strategist, philosopher and ambassador."

Sources

Books

Anderson, Dave, *In The Corner,* William Morrow and Company, Inc., 1991, pp. 225-255.
Frazier, Joe, *Smokin' Joe,* Macmillan, 1996, pp. 141-142.

Periodicals

Associated Press, October 18, 2001.
Detroit News, October 14, 2001.
Las Vegas Review-Journal, October 11, 2001; October 17, 2001.
Sports Illustrated, January 26, 1998, p. 28.

On-line

BBC Sport, http://news.bbc.co.uk
Black Athlete Sports Network, www.blackathlete.com
Caesars Palace press release, http://biz.yahoo.com
CNN Sports Illustrated, http://sportsillustrated.cnn.com
The Detroit News, http://www.detnews.com
Guardian Unlimited, http://sport.guardian.co.uk
International Boxing Hall of Fame, www.ibhof.com
Las Vegas Review-Journal, www.lvrj.com
MaxBoxing, www.maxboxing.com
Sports.com, http://ft.sports.com
Sportserver, www.sportserver.com

—Sandy J. Stiefer

Mary Hatwood Futrell

1940—

Educator

Considered an influential figure in American education, Mary Hatwood Futrell has served as president of the leading teachers' union in United States for many years, a position which prompted *People* magazine to deem her "one of the most powerful black women in America" in 1983. A tireless labor activist, charity board member, and public education reformer, Futrell is dean of the Graduate School of Education and Human Development at George Washington University in Washington, D.C.

Futrell was born in 1940 in Altavista, Virginia, one of four daughters. She was four years old when her father, a construction worker, died of kidney disease. The family was left with large hospital bills that took eight years to pay in full. Her mother, Josephine Hatwood, was a domestic worker who held three jobs to make ends meet. "She'd be gone before we'd wake up for breakfast," Futrell recalled in an interview with *People*, "and still not come home by dark."

Despite their financial hardships, and undeterred by the fact that she herself only had a sixth grade education, Futrell's mother encouraged her daughters to read, and tried to stimulate their minds in a variety of ways. "My

mother always read to me and my sister, had spelling contests with us, checked our report cards, and came to school any time it was necessary," Futrell recalled in an interview with Mark F. Goldberg for *Phi Delta Kappan*, "even though it might mean changing buses two or three times."

The schools Futrell and her sisters attended were segregated institutions in the Lynchburg school district. Though her teachers at Dunbar High School knew Futrell was bright, they shunted her into a vocational curriculum in high school, aware that her family would never be able to send her to college. Nevertheless, she did extremely well in school and was eventually switched to a more demanding, college-track program at Dunbar halfway through. At her high school graduation, Futrell's teachers presented her with an envelope containing an informal scholarship fund: they had collected $1,500 from local businesses, churches, and individuals to help her pay her college costs. Futrell began her undergraduate education at Virginia State College (now University), which was an all-black school in Petersburg at the time. There she studied business and education.

After graduating in 1962, Futrell became a business education teacher at an all-black high school in Alex-

At a Glance . . .

Born Mary Alice Franklin Hatwood on May 24, 1940, in Altavista, VA; daughter of a construction worker and Josephine Austin; married Donald Futrell, October 8, 1977. *Education*: Virginia State College, B.A., 1962; George Washington University, M.A., 1968; additional graduate study at University of Maryland, 1965, Univ. of Virginia, 1978-79, and Virginia Polytechnic Institute and State Univ., 1979-80.

Career: High school teacher, Alexandria, VA, 1963-80; Education Association of Alexandria, president, 1973-75; VA Education Assn., president, 1976-78; National Education Assn., Washington, DC, secretary-treasurer, 1980-83, president, 1983-89; George Washington Univ., associate director, Center for the Study of Education and National Development, 1989-92, director of Center for Curriculum Studies and Technology, 1992-95, dean, Graduate School of Education and Human Development, 1995-.

Memberships: National Education Assn., board of directors, 1978-80, head of human relations commission, until 1980, sec.-treas., 1980-83; Education International, president, 1993; World Confederation on the Origins of Teaching Profession, president, 1990-93, executive committee vice president, 1988-90, chair of women's caucus, 1984, chair of finance commission, 1986-89, president, 1990; American Assn. of Colleges of Teacher Education; American Assn. of State Colleges and Universities; Democratic Natl. Committee, women's council; ERAmerica, natl. chairperson; U.S. Natl. Commission to UNESCO; International Labor Rights Education and Research Fund, advisory council; Natl. Democratic Institute for Intl. Affairs; National Labor Committee for Democracy and Human Rights; Project VOTE; Martin Luther King Jr. Federal Holiday Commission, bd. of advisers; Natl. History Day, trustee.

Awards: American Black Achievement Award, 1984; Distinguished Service medal, Columbia Univ., 1987; honorary degrees: Virginia State Univ., George Washington Univ., 1984; Spellman College, 1986; Central State Univ.; Eastern Michigan Univ., 1987; Adrian College; George Washington Univ., 992.

Addresses: *Office*—George Washington University, 2134 G St. NW, Washington, DC 20037-2797.

andria. Things became tense following the school's desegregation in 1965, but Futrell banded together with teachers, administrators, and parents to hold discussion meetings that defused some of the hostilities. Still, there were lingering signs of institutional racism in Virginia at the time. For instance, when communities merged their formerly segregated schools to comply with federal law, a surplus of teachers was often the result, and sometimes black teachers were demoted to non-teaching positions. Irate, Futrell worked to correct these and other subtle injustices.

The experience politicized her and she became active in a state group, the Virginia Education Association (VEA), in 1967. Although Futrell was determined to serve on the VEA board of her school district, she faced strong opposition, and the district refused to distribute her campaign literature. Accordingly, she did not win a seat, but challenged the election in court and won.

During this era Futrell went back to school, earning an advanced degree from George Washington University. She continued to teach in Alexandria schools, and served in local teachers' groups. Elected president of the Education Association of Alexandria in 1973, she ran for the presidency of the VEA three years later, and once again, was counseled to stay out of the race. Instead, she won the election and became the group's first African-American president. Around this time she married Donald Futrell, physical education teacher and coach. During her stint as VEA president, she took a leave of absence from her teaching job, but went back to the classroom in 1978. That same year, she was elected to the board of her union, the National Education Association (NEA), and became head of the union's human relations commission.

Two years later, Futrell was elected secretary-treasurer of the NEA, a full-time post for which she gave up her teaching job. The NEA was the leading teachers' union in the United States, with 1.7 million dues-paying members. Again, Futrell faced some determined opposition in her campaign: her male opponent for the secretary-treasurer post claimed that Futrell was unsuited to the job, too political, and would work only for minorities in the union. She won the campaign anyway, and three years later, when she decided to run for the presidency, she ran unopposed.

Futrell took the helm of the second-largest employees' union in the United States in 1983, at a contentious time in its history. There was much talk of educational reform during this era: the National Commission on Excellence in Education issued a study that warned of a "rising tide of mediocrity" in public education, and other research provided evidence that some schools were failing to provide an adequate education for some students—even in basic reading and math skills. Researchers and education advocates advocated tougher standards and a number of other measures to remedy the situation.

At the time, some saw teachers' unions like the NEA as the main obstacle to improving education standards in the country. Teachers' jobs were protected, some argued, and poorly performing teachers were protected, to the ire of school boards and disgruntled parents by union laws. Yet Futrell argued that the declining educational situation in the United States was hardly the fault of teachers. Several other economic and social factors made educating students for an increasingly complex world a tough job. "Teachers are easy prey," Futrell said in an interview with the *New York Times* in 1983. "We're easy people to blame. If we should be blamed for anything, though, it should be for not standing up to protest against all the burdens that society puts on us."

Futrell earned a reputation for making such frank statements, and soon became one of the most vociferous critics of the conservative Republican president of the United States, Ronald Reagan. The president had set a notoriously anti-union tone to his administration in 1981 when he fired all members of a national union of striking air traffic controllers. Reagan advocated the abolition of the Department of Education, and urged reforms that would establish competitive, business-like standards within the teaching profession—instead of union-negotiated contracts with school districts that set salaries, Reagan's idea of a "merit pay" system would give teachers pay increases based on job performance. Meanwhile, Futrell was adamant that the profession was changing, and a new era was coming. She vowed to battle any Republican cutbacks to education. "If we sit back and do nothing, they will push us around," she told *People*. "Teachers are no longer going to be the passive little old ladies who accept what's handed to them."

In the summer of 1983, Reagan spoke before the NEA's rival union, the American Federation of Teachers (AFT), at their national convention, and claimed that the NEA's new curriculum plans for students, which included conflict resolution and multiculturalism units, amounted to "brainwashing." In press interviews at the time, Futrell pointed out that her union was a large contributor to Democratic political candidates and causes. She did concede that some of America's teachers were not doing their jobs, a figure that was perhaps as high as ten percent, but noted that such statistics were common to many fields. Underperformers, she told *People*, "sift through in every profession, even at the White House."

Futrell's energetic work as NEA president caused the rank and file to re-elect her twice. She was also invited to serve on the Carnegie Forum on Education and the Economy, which issued a 1986 report on the teaching profession. It called for higher base salaries for teachers and an overhaul of the certification system. Futrell, however, did not agree with report's suggestion about instituting merit pay in the profession. "Ultimately, the attitude of experts like Futrell may be the key to the

Carnegie program's success or failure," noted *Time*'s Ezra Bowen. "For just as teachers are central to the study's implementation, they will also determine whether the program will be accepted or rejected."

In the end Futrell did manage to impact the teaching profession through her leadership: she was influential in the formation of National Board for Professional Teaching Standards (NBPTS) with the AFT, and enjoined her NEA members to support it, despite some opposition. This was one of her greatest legacies in six years as NEA president. She stepped down in 1989, but was already active in number of other endeavors, including the Martin Luther King Jr. Federal Holiday Commission. Futrell next became associate director of the Center for the Study of Education and National Development at George Washington University. In 1995 she was named dean of the Graduate School of Education and Human Development at the university. She has been integral in revising the education curriculum at the school, which has become a model for other colleges and universities.

Futrell and other forward-thinking educators argued for a more team-based approached to learning, and she also stressed that mentor programs for new teachers are crucial to the ultimate success of the teaching profession at every level. "We know that teachers who receive mentoring during their first year or two are far more likely to stay in the profession longer and to be more successful than those teachers who were not mentored," she told Goldberg in the *Phi Delta Kappan*. She also used the occasion to reflect on the special challenges that urban schools faced in the United States. Futrell spoke of "a covert pressure among minority youths not to achieve academically in school," as she stated in the interview with Goldberg. "It's perceived as acting 'white' and not being macho. Parents have to encourage their kids to excel academically and then support their efforts to do so. Churches, sororities, fraternities, businesses, and neighbors have to be involved in this problem."

Sources

Books

Contemporary Newsmakers 1986, Issue Cumulation, Gale, 1987.
Notable Black American Women, Book 1, Gale, 1992.

Periodicals

Ebony, July 1989, p. 76.
New York Times, July 3, 1983.
People, July 25, 1983, p. 54.
Phi Delta Kappan, February 2001, p. 465.
Time, May 26, 1986, p. 58.
U.S. News & World Report, June 10, 1985, p. 94.

—Carol Brennan

Bob Gibson

1935—

Baseball player, coach

Hall of Fame pitcher Bob Gibson was a member of the St. Louis Cardinals' lineup for nearly twenty years. He began his career as a pitcher in the Major Leagues when he first signed with the Cardinals in 1957. Gibson remained with the Cardinals until the mid-1970s, pitching in several World Series and winning MVP honors. After retiring from play, Gibson went on to coach for the Atlanta Braves, as well as the Cardinals.

Gibson was born on November 9, 1935 in Omaha, Nebraska. Gibson's father died three months before he was born, leaving his mother to provide for a family of seven children by doing laundry. The Gibsons moved into the Logan Fontenelle projects in Omaha in 1942. The move was a big step up from rented houses where family had been living. Bob Gibson grew up in an integrated housing project. Though the family was poor, Gibson's young life was filled with sports—baseball, football, and his favorite sport, basketball. In high school, he played baseball for his local YMCA team in the summer, but he was not able to play at Omaha Technical High School until his senior year. At Omaha Tech, whites played baseball, and blacks ran track.

As a senior on the baseball team, he made the varsity team as an outfielder and utility player. Though he hit .368 in baseball, he was really known as a basketball player. His coach even wrote to Indiana University about him, but the basketball program wrote back informing the All-State player that the team had filled their quota of blacks for the year (which was one). So Gibson turned to baseball. He rejected an offer from the famous Negro League Kansas City Monarchs because the Negro Leagues no longer interested him after Jackie Robinson broke into Major League Baseball in 1947. The St. Louis Cardinals had a minor league team in Omaha. The Cardinals offered him a contract, but Gibson's big brother, Josh, who had coached and mentored him all his life, told him he must get an education. Gibson finally accepted a scholarship to play basketball from Creighton, a private Catholic university in Nebraska.

Gibson started on the varsity basketball team at Creighton for three years. After his senior season Gibson stood as the school's all-time leading scorer, but he attracted very little attention at the professional level from the NBA. In the end he was able to parlay a great performance at a college All-Star game into a deal with the Harlem Globetrotters. In the spring of 1957 Gibson focused in on baseball, which had always been his

At a Glance . . .

Born Robert Gibson on November 9, 1935, in Omaha, NE, son of Pack and Victoria Gibson; married Wendy Nelson (second wife); children: Annette, Renee (previous marriage), Chris (with Nelson).

Career: Baseball player, coach. Signed with the St. Louis Cardinals, 1957; made first major league appearance, 1959; pitcher for the Cardinals, 1959-1975; Atlanta Braves, assistant coach, 1982-84; broadcaster for ABC, ESPN, and the Cardinals radio program, 1985-94; Cardinals, assistant coach, 1995-97.

Awards: World Series MVP, 1964, 1967; National League MVP, 1968; National League Cy Young Award, 1968; National League All-Star, 1962, 1965-70, 1972; National League Gold Glove, 1965-73; elected to Major League Baseball Hall of Fame on first ballot, 1981.

Addresses: c/o The St. Louis Cardinals, 250 Stadium Plaza, St. Louis, MO 63102.

second sport. While in college he still played in the outfield, but he did possess a 95-mile-an-hour fastball. Again, Gibson received little interest from professional teams, but he was good enough to sign with the Cardinals for a $1,000 bonus.

When Gibson showed up to practice for the first day, Omaha Cardinal manager Johnny Keane told him to throw some batting practice. Right then and there Keane decided Gibson was a pitcher. He could throw hard, but had little control so he was sent to Columbus, Georgia—a team playing in a league integrated only four years before by Hank Aaron. Gibson finished the season with a 4-3 record and then immediately reported to the Harlem Globetrotters, where Gibson became roommates with Meadowlark Lemon. After one winter with the Globetrotters, the Cardinals offered him money not to play basketball and he quit for good to become a big league pitcher.

Made It To The Majors

In 1958 Gibson made his way from a minor league training center, back to Omaha, and, by the end of the season, to the Cardinals' Triple A team in Rochester, New York, where he finished with a 5-5 record and the hardest fastball in the league. Gibson made the big league club in 1959 but split his time between St. Louis

and Omaha. It took Gibson until the middle of the 1961 season, when the Cardinals brought in Johnny Keane to manage the club, to get into the starting rotation for good.

The appointment of Keane was key to Gibson's career at that point. Instead of being constantly criticized, Keane built up the young pitcher comparing him favorably in the press with Los Angeles Dodger great Sandy Koufax. Gibson told William Ladson of *The Sporting News* about the effect Keane had on his career: "He saw something. I don't know what it was. But I was a pretty good athlete ... I was a good ballplayer until I got into pro ball and then I couldn't pitch anymore ... I just knew that Johnny Keane had confidence in me." By the middle of the next season, Gibson had made the All-Star team. But late in the year with Gibson at 15-13 and a 2.85 earned run average (ERA) he fractured his ankle and was finished for the rest of the 1962 season.

Though he started slowly, recuperating from the injury, Gibson and the Cardinals were a much-improved team in 1963. In the following campaign, the team and its ace would get better. In 1964 the Cardinals won the National League pennant with Gibson coming out of the bullpen for the last game of the year. He brought his 19 victories to the World Series against the Yankees. Three days after winning the season-ender, Gibson lost the second game of the series to the Yankees 8-3. Gibson started the fifth game at Yankee Stadium with the series tied 2-2. Gibson cruised through the powerful line up to take a 2-0 lead into the ninth. With a man on first the next Yankee batter Joe Pepitone connected with a shot that hit Gibson square in the backside and bounced toward third base. Instead of going down, Gibson pounced on the ball and somehow managed to throw the runner out. It turned out to be a game-saving play as the next batter tied the game with a home run. Gibson and the Cardinals were able to hang on to the victory in the tenth.

But Gibson was not done yet. Gibson had pitched four games in ten days and then was sent out to the hill to determine the series in Game seven. After six innings Gibson had a 6-0 lead. In the seventh Mickey Mantle hit a three-run home run, but Cardinal manager Keane left his starter in. In the ninth Keane told Gibson to just throw as hard as he could. Though the Yankees hit two home runs to make the score 7-5, Gibson got the last outs and secured the Cardinals first World Championship in 18 years. Gibson won two games and set a World Series record for strikeouts with 31. He was named Most Valuable Player (MVP) by *Sport Magazine*. Gibson told Rick Hummel of the *St. Louis Post-Dispatch* about pitching during the World Series: "People will ask, 'Were you tired?' You don't get tired till after the Series is over. The World Series is once in a lifetime. If you don't want it, go home."

The next two seasons the Cardinals stumbled but Gibson won 20 and 21 games respectively. The 1967 season was a different matter. By the all-star break Gibson had won 10 games and the Cardinals were three and a half games ahead of their closest opponents. In his next start against Pittsburgh, Pirate great Roberto Clemente lined a shot right off Gibson's shin. The mark left a baseball imprint in his tibia, but Gibson would not come out of the game. Two batters later, Gibson came down on the leg and the bone snapped between the knee and the ankle. Gibson, whose leg had been fractured after the initial contact, would be out for eight weeks.

He came back to finish the season and lead the Cardinals into the World Series against the Boston Red Sox. Gibson won the first game, the fourth game, and then it was his turn again to take the mound for the seventh game. Gibson rose to the occasion again pitching a three-hitter and adding a home run of his own to win the game 7-2. Gibson went on to win his second World Series MVP on the strength of his three-win and 27-strikeout performance. Gibson tied a World Series record set in 1905 for fewest hits allowed in three series starts with 14. Gibson was even invited to Washington D.C. for a state dinner with the Japanese president where he met President Lyndon Johnson.

Pitched Landmark Season

Gibson's 1968 season, considered by many in baseball to be the greatest single season by a pitcher in the history of the game, started slowly. After his first three starts he was winless and then won only three of his first ten appearances. After a third of the season was over, Gibson's record stood at 3-5, but his ERA was a sparkling 1.32. He even lost a one-hitter early in the season. Gibson and the Cardinals got on a roll in June. He pitched five straight shutouts and 47 consecutive scoreless innings. By the mid point in the season, Gibson's ERA was an otherworldly 1.06. By the end of July Gibson's ERA was even lower at 0.96 and he had not been taken out of the game for three months.

At the end of the 1968 season, Gibson's statistics were staggering. Gibson finished the year at 22-9, with 300 innings pitched, 13 shutouts, and an ERA of 1.12. And all for a club that averaged 2.8 runs a game on the nights he pitched. Gibson talked about his lack of run support with Edes Gordon of *Baseball Digest*: "In '68, I had 13 shutouts and lost five 1-0 games. That's 18 games in which I gave up one run of less. I lost nine games with and ERA of one. How do you do that? It drove me crazy. And people wonder why I was always grumpy—when I'd get one run, win or lose." Gibson won the league MVP and the Cardinals again won the National League pennant to face the Detroit Tigers in the 1968 World Series.

True to form, Gibson started and won the first game of the series setting a World Series record by striking out 16 batters. With the Cardinals up two games to one Gibson won his seventh straight World Series game—a record that still stands—and led the Cardinals to a three game to one advantage. But St. Louis lost the next two games, and as was the custom for the Cardinals, they would let Gibson win the seventh. Through six innings the score was tied at zero. Gibson had retired 20 of 21 batters and broken Sandy Koufax's record of 31 strikeouts in a World Series. But it was not to be Gibson's day. The Tigers scored four runs in the seventh and went on to win the World Series, spoiling Gibson's near-perfect season. After Gibson and other pitchers of 1968 dominated the game so totally, baseball decided to make several rule changes. The pitchers mound was lowered from 15 to 10 inches and the strike zone was shrunk. The umpires also cracked down on the inside pitch, one of Gibson's most feared weapons.

The 1969 season brought more of the same excellence from Gibson, though his team stumbled to fourth place in a six-team division. Gibson won his 20th game on the last day of the season against 14 losses. He pitched a career high 314 innings and despite the rule changes racked up an ERA of 2.18. The consequence of the season's failing was that the Cardinals were broken up. In 1970 the club was not the same despite Gibson's 23 wins and a second Cy Young Award. He also won his sixth straight Gold Glove award and hit .303 to become the last pitcher in Major League Baseball to hit .300 and win 20 games in a season.

In 1971 Gibson struggled with a pulled thigh muscle through the first half of the season but won 10 of his last 13 decisions to finish the year at 16-13 including a no-hitter against Pittsburgh on August 14. The 1972 season brought more milestones for Gibson including the Cardinals record for most career victories (211). At the age of 36 Gibson finished the year 19-11 with a 2.46 ERA. He also hit five home runs—only Ted Simmons and Joe Torre hit more for the Cardinals that season.

As Gibson grew older his life on and off the field was becoming more complicated. He and his wife, Charline, were on their way to a divorce and very few of his old Cardinals teammates were left from the days when they won three National League pennants. Gibson helped found the Community Bank of Nebraska with the help of financier Warren Buffett and was principal investor in an Omaha radio station.

Retired Due to Injuries

Gibson missed much of the middle of the 1973 season after tearing cartilage in his knee. He finished 1973 with a record of 12-10 and a realization that at the age of 38 wondering if his body could take much more of the pounding. Every time he pitched in 1974 he was forced to undergo the draining of his knee. His elbow sometimes swelled up so that he could not straighten his arm. Still he battled his way to an 11-13 record, but after losing the last game of the season, he announced that 1975 would be the last year of his glorious career.

Though he had high hopes for his final season, Gibson was now raising his two daughters, Annette and Renee, alone. The physical and mental stress of being a professional athlete and a full-time parent caused both facets of his life to suffer. In baseball, he was demoted to the bullpen, but at home he hired Wendy Nelson, who Gibson later married, to look after his girls while he was gone. Gibson got his first victory coming out of the bullpen on July 28. Win number 251 would be the final victory of his career because he was used very little for the rest of the season.

Gibson received a motor home from the Cardinals on Bob Gibson Day and went traveling after his retirement. He also opened a restaurant, but still looked to get back into baseball. In 1981 he became the New York Mets "attitude coach" under his former teammate Joe Torre. Before joining the Mets, Gibson became a father again, this time to a son, Chris. Also in 1981 Gibson was inducted into the Baseball Hall of Fame on the first ballot.

Torre and all the coaches were fired after the 1981 season, but Gibson thought 1982 would be better. He was lead to believe that he would be managing the Cardinals minor-league club, but senior Cardinals management vetoed the idea. In the end, Gibson went back to work for Torre, this time as an assistant coach for the Atlanta Braves. Gibson and Torre stayed in Atlanta until after the 1984 season when all the coaches were fired.

After coaching Gibson began broadcasting on the radio, first on ABC's *Monday Night Baseball* and then mainly with the Cardinals. Gibson still wanted a job in baseball, and after Joe Torre was named manager of the Cardinals, Gibson came home in 1995. Before introducing his new assistant coach to the media, Torre told Bob Klapisch of *The Sporting News* about his long time friend: "Just say he's proud, he's opinionated, sometimes he doesn't have a lot of tact. But above all, Bob Gibson loves baseball."

Sources

Books

Gibson, Bob and Lonnie Wheeler, *Stranger to the Game: The Autobiography of Bob Gibson* Viking Penguin, 1994.

Periodicals

Baseball Digest, September 2000.
The Sporting News, February 27, 1995; August 3, 1998.
St. Louis Post-Dispatch, November 2, 2001.

—Michael J. Watkins

Whoopi Goldberg

1955—

Comedienne, actress, social activist

Whoopi Goldberg's life and career have followed similar circular journeys: both began with ingenuous hope then slipped dangerously toward extinction, only to be resurrected by a rediscovery of the dormant initial promise. Throughout her acting career, she has not forgotten the lessons she learned in her early, difficult life. There is, in a sense, no division between Whoopi Goldberg the actress and Whoopi Goldberg the person, as Paul Chutkow pointed out in *Vogue*: "She seems much the same way she has often appeared on-screen: fresh, direct, exuberant, no cant, no can't." Goldberg's unpretentiousness and determination imbue her best characterizations—they are direct and empathetic. She remained committed to her art. "Simply, I love the idea of working," she admitted to Aldore Collier in *Jet*. "You hone your craft that way." And she continued her committed to rectifying disparaging social conditions affecting the unfortunate, and to which she was once subjected. Her success was earned, and she offered no platitudes for its achievement, only a realistic vision: "Take the best of what you're offered," she told Chutkow, "and that's all you can do."

Born Caryn E. Johnson in New York City in 1955, Goldberg wanted to be a performer from the very beginning. "My first coherent thought was probably, I want to be an actor," she recounted to Chutkow. "I believe that. That's just what I was born to do." She was acting in children's plays with the Hudson Guild Theater at the age of eight and throughout the rest of her childhood immersed herself in movies, sometimes watching three or four a day. "I liked the idea that you could pretend to be somebody else and nobody would cart you off to the hospital," Goldberg explained to

Cosmopolitan's Stephen Farber.

But by the time she reached high school, Goldberg had lost her desire and vision. It was the 1960s, and she was hooked on drugs. "I took drugs because they were available to everyone in those times," she told Farber. "As everyone evolved into LSD, so did I. It was the time of Woodstock, of be-ins and love-ins." Goldberg dropped out of high school and became lost in this culture, delving further into the world of drugs and ending up a junkie. Finally she sought help, cleaned herself up, and, in the process, married her drug counselor. A year later, Goldberg gave birth to her daughter, Alexandrea. Less than a year afterward, she was divorced. She was not yet twenty years old.

In 1974 Goldberg headed west to San Diego, California, pursuing her childhood dream of acting. She performed in plays with the San Diego Repertory Theater and tried improvisational comedy with a company called Spontaneous Combustion. To care for her daughter, Goldberg had to work as a bank teller, a bricklayer, and a mortuary cosmetologist. She was also, for a few years, on welfare. During this period, she went by the name "Whoopi Cushion," sometimes using the French pronunciation "Kushon." After her mother pointed out how ridiculous the name sounded, Goldberg finally adopted a name from her family's history.

Developed Insightful Comic Routine

In a significant step, Goldberg moved north to Berkeley, California, in the late 1970s and joined the Blake

At a Glance . . .

Born Caryn E. Johnson in November of 1955, in New York, NY; daughter of Emma Johnson (a nurse and teacher); married first husband, c. 1972 (divorced, c. 1974); married David Edward Claessen, September 1986 (divorced, 1988); married Lyle Trachtenberg 1994 (divorced 1995); children: (first marriage) Alexandrea Martin.

Career: Film, television, and theater actress and comedienne, 1985-; San Diego Repertory Theater and comedy group Spontaneous Combustion; worked as a bank teller, a bricklayer, and mortuary cosmetologist, 1974- late 1970s; member of the comedy troupe Blake Street Hawkeyes Theater; developed own one-woman show, late 1970s-85; host, *The Whoopi Goldberg Show*, 1992; *Hollywood Squares*, producer, talent; co- host for *Comic Relief* benefits. Television appearances include: *Star Trek: The Next Generation*, *Bagdad Cafe*, 1990. Guest television appearance: *Moonlighting*, among others; host, Academy Awards, 1994, 1996, 1999, 2002.

Awards: Golden Globe Award for best actress in a dramatic role, Academy Award nomination for best actress, both for *The Color Purple*, 1985; Image Award, NAACP, 1985, 1990; Grammy Award for best comedy recording, for *Whoopi Goldberg*, 1985; Emmy Award nomination, for guest appearance on *Moonlighting*, 1986; Academy Award for best supporting actress, for *Ghost*, 1991.

Addresses: *Office*—Gallin/Morey Associates, 8730 Sunset Blvd., Penthouse West, Los Angeles, CA 90069.

Street Hawkeyes Theater, a comedic avant-garde troupe. With this group, Goldberg was able to realize her powerful acting and comedic abilities, developing a repertoire of 17 distinct personae in a one-woman show that she labeled *The Spook Show*. She performed the show on the West Coast, then toured the country and Europe in the early 1980s before landing in New York City.

Among her sketches were four rueful—and sometimes sublime—characters: Fontaine, a profanity-spewing drug dealer with a Ph.D. in literature who travels to Europe looking for hashish, only to openly weep when he comes across Anne Frank's secret hiding place; a

shallow thirteen-year-old surfing Valley Girl who is left barren after a self-inflicted abortion with a coat hanger; a severely handicapped young woman who tells her prospective suitor who wants to go dancing, "This is not a disco body;" and a nine-year-old black girl who bathes in Clorox and covers her head with a white skirt, wistfully hoping to become white with long blonde hair so she can appear on *The Love Boat*.

Although Brendan Gill of the *New Yorker* decided Goldberg's sketches were "diffuse and overlong and continuously at the mercy of her gaining a laugh at any cost," the majority of critical and popular reaction was positive. Cathleen McGuigan writing in *Newsweek* believed that Goldberg's "ability to completely disappear into a role, rather than superficially impersonate comic types, allows her to take some surprising risks." And Enid Nemy, in a review of Goldberg's show for the *New York Times*, found the performer's abilities extended beyond mere comic entertainment and that her creations—seemlessly woven with social commentary—"walk a finely balanced line between satire and pathos, stand-up comedy and serious acting." These realistic and ranging performances also caught the attention of famed film director Mike Nichols. After seeing Goldberg's premiere performance in New York, Nichols offered to produce her show on Broadway in September of 1984.

Film Debut Earned Critical Praise

Another Hollywood figure entranced by Goldberg's sensitive performances was director Steven Spielberg, who at the time was casting for the film production of author Alice Walker's *The Color Purple*. Spielberg offered Goldberg the lead role of Celie—her first film appearance. Goldberg told Audrey Edwards of *Essence* how badly she wanted to be a part, any part, of the film: "I told [Alice Walker] that whenever there was an audition I'd come. I'd eat the dirt. I'd play the dirt, I'd be the dirt, because the part is perfect."

"As Celie, the abused child, battered bride, and wounded woman liberated by Shug's kiss and the recognition of sisterhood's power, Whoopi Goldberg is for the most part lovable and believable," Andrew Kopkind wrote in a review of the movie for the *Nation*. "She mugs a bit, pouts and postures too long in some scenes, and seems to disappear in others, but her great moments are exciting to behold." *Newsweek*'s David Ansen concurred in assessing Goldberg's film debut: "This is powerhouse acting, all the more so because the rage and the exhilaration are held in reserve." For this performance, Goldberg received a Golden Globe Award and an Academy Award nomination.

But the film itself failed to receive the praise bestowed on Goldberg. "The movie is amorphous," Pauline Kael wrote in the *New Yorker*. "It's a pastoral about the triumph of the human spirit, and it blurs on you." Much criticism was aimed at the selection of Spielberg, a white male, to direct a story that focused on the Southern rural black experience, has a decidedly matriarchal point-of-view, and offers cardboard representations of its male characters. Even Goldberg herself was criticized when she defended Spielberg and the film. In an interview excerpted in *Harper's*, director Spike Lee questioned Goldberg's allegiances: "Does she realize what she is saying? Is she saying that a white person is the only person who can define our existence?... I hope people realize, that the media realize, that she's not a spokesperson for black people." Goldberg countered by defining for Matthew Modine in *Interview* the breadth of her social character: "What I am is a humanist before anything—before I'm a Jew, before I'm black, before I'm a woman. And my beliefs are for the human race—they don't exclude anyone."

Increased Exposure Allowed Social Activism

Despite the lukewarm reception to the film as a whole, Goldberg's fortunes rose. In addition to her awards for her film portrayal, she won a Grammy Award in 1985 for her comedy album *Whoopi Goldberg* and received an Emmy nomination the following year for her guest appearance on the television show *Moonlighting*. The increased exposure, recognition, and acceptance allowed Goldberg to pursue social activities focusing on issues that affected her when she required public assistance and that she has tried to call attention to since her early stand-up routines.

Beginning in 1986, Goldberg hosted, along with Billy Crystal and Robin Williams, the annual *Comic Relief* benefit that raises money for the homeless through the Health Care for the Homeless project. "People would like the United States to be what we're told it can be, without realizing that the price has gone up—the price, you know, of human dignity," she explained to Steve Erickson in *Rolling Stone*. "Homelessness in America is just disgusting. It's just disgusting that we could have this big, beautiful country and have families living in dumpsters. It makes no sense." Her protests are not limited to this one social imbalance; Goldberg also campaigned on behalf of environmental causes, the nation's hungry, AIDS and drug abuse awareness, and women's right to free choice. She has been recognized with several humanitarian awards for her efforts.

Increased exposure, though, did not translate into increased success for Goldberg, as she went on to star in a succession of critically assailed movies: *Jumpin' Jack Flash*, *Burglar*, *Fatal Beauty*, *The Telephone*, *Clara's Heart*, and *Homer and Eddie*. It seemed that as soon as she had risen, she had fallen. "On the strength of her past work as a stand-up comic, Goldberg deserves better," Lawrence O'Toole wrote in a review of *Burglar* for *Maclean's*. "If she keeps making thumb-twiddling movies like this one, she is unlikely to

get it." And in a review of *Clara's Heart* for *People*, David Hiltbrand noted that ever since her debut film, Goldberg "has barely kept her head above water while her movies went under. After this, she'll need her own lifeboat."

Goldberg was vexed by gossip and rumors that Hollywood was ready to write her off. "In less than five years she went from Hollywood's golden girl to a rumored lesbian/Uncle Tom with a bad attitude and a career on the skids," Laura B. Randolph described in *Ebony*. "In Hollywood, that combination is almost always terminal, and insiders whispered that she should pack it in and be happy to do guest spots on the *Hollywood Squares*." Ironically, Goldberg would resurrect *Hollywood Squares* years later.

Goldberg remained steady, though, disavowing critical displeasure. "I've just stopped listening to them," she explained to Chutkow. "I've taken crazy movies that appeal to me. I don't care what other people think about it. If it was pretty decent when I did it, I did my job." And that seems to be the tenuous thread that connects her box-office disappointments: her strong performance marred by poor direction or a poor final script. The *New York Times*'s Janet Maslin, reviewing *Fatal Beauty*, wrote what could be taken as an overall assessment of Goldberg's failed showings: "It isn't Miss Goldberg's fault, because Miss Goldberg is funny when she's given half a chance."

Ghost Revived Career

Goldberg seemed simply to need the right vehicle to transport to the audience her comic approach underscored by biting social and tender humanitarian elements. Her chance came with the 1990 film *Ghost*. "Thank God Whoopi finally has a part that lets her strut her best stuff," Ansen proclaimed. Although some critics didn't fully embrace the film (the *New Yorker*'s Terrance Rafferty called it a "twentysomething hybrid of *It's a Wonderful Life* and some of the gooier, more solemn episodes of *The Twilight Zone*"), most critical and popular response was overwhelmingly positive—especially to Goldberg's portrayal of the flamboyant yet heroic psychic, Oda Mae. It was a part for which she lobbied studio executives for more than six months, and her persistence paid off. Considered a sleeper when it was released, *Ghost* was the highest-grossing movie of 1990. And Goldberg won an Oscar for her performance, becoming only the second black female in the history of the Academy Awards to win such an honor—the first was Hattie McDaniel, who won for *Gone with the Wind* in 1939.

In a decisive indication of her acting range, Goldberg immediately followed her comedic role in *Ghost* with a substantive dramatic role in *The Long Walk Home*. The film is a poignant evocation of the bus boycott in Montgomery, Alabama, in 1955—a pivotal event in the American civil rights movement. Goldberg portrays Odessa Cotter, a housekeeper who, because of the boycott, is forced to walk almost ten miles to work, regardless of blistering or bleeding feet. Throughout, the character maintains her composure and integrity. Chutkow quoted Richard Pearce, the director of the film, on Goldberg's successful characterization: "What her portrayal of Odessa revealed about Whoopi was a complex inner life and intelligence. Her mouth is her usual weapon of choice—to disarm her of that easy weapon meant that she had to rely on other things. It's a real actress who can bring off a performance like that. And she did."

Goldberg also confirmed her far-reaching, unassailable talent in the arena of television. Beginning in the 1988-89 season, she earned accolades for appearing on a recurring basis as a crew member on the successful series *Star Trek: The Next Generation*. And while her 1990 stint in the series *Bagdad Cafe* was short-lived, Goldberg in 1992 secured the coveted position of late-night talk show host. *The Whoopi Goldberg Show* devoted each program to just one guest; Goldberg interviewed actress Elizabeth Taylor on the show's debut, and subsequent programs featured such celebrities as heavyweight boxing champion Evander Holyfield.

The year 1992 also brought a series of successful film roles to Goldberg. She began the year portraying a homicide detective in director Robert Altman's highly anticipated and subsequently acclaimed Hollywood satire *The Player*. In mid-year Goldberg donned a nun's habit as a Reno lounge singer seeking refuge from the mob in a convent in the escapist comedy *Sister Act*, one of the biggest box-office draws of the summer of 1992. The film, according to *Detroit Free Press* film critic Judy Gerstel, worked "as summer whimsy mainly because of Goldberg's usual witty, lusty screen presence." And in the fall she turned again to a dramatic role, starring in *Sarafina: The Movie*, a film adaptation of the musical about Black South African teenagers' struggle against apartheid. *Sarafina* was shot entirely on location in Soweto, South Africa.

Goldberg's constant quest for a range of roles—what led Maslin to label her "one of the great unclassifiable beings on the current movie scene"—is not the mark of a Hollywood prima donna but of an actor committed to her craft. "None of my films cure cancer," Goldberg explained to Chutkow. "But they have allowed me to not just play one kind of person, which is important to me. Nobody knows how long this stuff is gonna last, and you want to have it and enjoy as much of it and be as diverse as you can."

Roast Caused Conflict

Goldberg was the honoree at a Friars Club roast in 1993. Her then-boyfriend, Ted Danson, performed a racy skit in blackface that included the N-word and jokes about the couple's sexual lives. Many in attendance were outraged and talk show host, Montel Williams, walked out during the performance. Many editorials were written concerning the affair and the media was relentless in its coverage. Members of the National Political Congress of Black Women sent a letter, which was quoted in *Jet*, to the Friars Club, stating "The use of the most vile, profane, deprecating language in describing African Americans in general and African-American women in particular is patently wrong." The couple split soon after.

In 1994 Goldberg married once again, to union organizer Lyle Trachtenberg, whom she met on the set of *Corrina Corrina*, a film in which she played a housekeeper who wins the heart of a widower and his child. The couple divorced a year later, after which Goldberg entered into a five-year relationship with actor, Frank Langella, who co-starred with her in *Eddie*. During the following years, Goldberg starred in a number of films that displayed her diverse acting abilities. In 1996 she starred in *The Associate*, a comedy where Goldberg plays a brilliant financial analyst who is passed over for a promotion. For revenge, she dresses as a man, and starts her own business. In *Ghosts of Mississippi* (1997) Goldberg played the widow of the slain Medger Evers. For a short time, Goldberg strayed from Hollywood and returned to the stage where she took over Nathan Lane's character in the play, *A Funny Thing Happened On The Way To The Forum*.

For the remainder of the 1990s, Goldberg starred in and played small parts in several made-for-television movies and films, numerous television shows, and her characteristic voice was used for several characters in some animated films. She has also taken part in many tributes to other performers and movers and shakers in Hollywood. After ten years of staying put Goldberg went on tour during the summer of 2001. Goldberg said, AI don't generally get out a lot because I'm going through the change."

Whoopi, a pioneer and somewhat of a maverick, broke more boundaries when she emceed the 66th Academy Awards, in 1994. She was the first African American to host the award ceremony, and the first solo female to host the awards. That year, The Academy Awards was the highest rated show of the season. She was invited to host the Academy Awards in 1996, 1999, and again in 2002. Goldberg remained passionate about portraying real people and telling real stories. She established her own production company, One Ho Productions. The company helped bring back the popular *Hollywood Squares* with Tom Bergeron as host and Goldberg in the center square. In 2001 she bought the film rights to the book, *Destined To Witness: Growing Up Black in Nazi Germany*, which is based on the memoirs of Hans J. Massoqoui, who was the former managing editor of *Ebony* magazine. Goldberg said, "It's a story that needs to be told. People don't realize that during the course of the 30s and 40s in Germany, there wee a lot of Black people trying to survive and not making it." According to *Jet*, this novel "marks the first time in literature that the experiences and ultimate survival of a Black youth growing up in Nazi Germany have been chronicled."

Selected works

Books

Alice (for children), Bantam, 1992.

Albums

Whoopi Goldberg, Geffen, 1985.
(With others) *The Best of Comic Relief*, Rhino, 1986.
(With others) *The Best of Comic Relief 2*, Rhino, 1988.
(With others) *The Best of Comic Relief 3*, Rhino, 1989.
(With others) *The Best of Comic Relief '90*, Rhino, 1990.

Films

The Color Purple, 1985.
Jumpin' Jack Flash, 1986.
Burglar, 1987.
Fatal Beauty, 1987.
The Telephone, 1988.
Clara's Heart, 1988.
Homer and Eddie, 1989.
Ghost, 1990.
The Long Walk Home, 1990.
Soapdish, 1991.
The Player, 1992.
Sister Act, 1992.
Sarafina: The Movie, 1992.
Sister Act 2: Back In The Habit, 1993.
Boys On The Side, 1995.
Corrina, Corrina, 1994.
Ghosts of Mississippi, 1997.

How Stella Got Her Groove Back, 1998.
The Rugrats Movie, (voice only), 1998.
Girl, Interrupted, 1999.
Kingdom Come, 2001.
Call Me Claus, (TNT Original), 2001.

Sources

Christian Science Monitor, March 27, 1986.
Cosmopolitan, December 1988; March 1991; April 1992.
Detroit Free Press, May 29, 1992.
Ebony, March 1991.
Entertainment Weekly, April 2, 1999, p. 36.
Essence, March 1985.
Harper's, January 1987.
Interview, June 1992; October, 1999, p. 126.
Jet, April 24, 1989; August 13, 1990; April 22, 1991; January 13, 1992; June 1, 1992; November 1, 1993, p. 56; October 27, 1997, p. 64; April 23, 2001, p. 64.
Maclean's, April 6, 1987.
Nation, February 1, 1986; December 10, 1990.
New Republic, January 27, 1986.
New Statesman, August 23, 1991.
Newsweek, March 5, 1984; December 30, 1985; October 20, 1986; July 16, 1990.
New York, December 12, 1988; April 2, 1990.
New Yorker, November 5, 1984; December 30, 1985; July 30, 1990.
New York Times, October 21, 1984; October 30, 1987; February 14, 1988; February 9, 1990.
Parade, November 1, 1992.
People, October 17, 1988; April 2, 1990.
Rolling Stone, May 8, 1986; August 9, 1990.
Time, December 17, 1990; June 1, 1992.
Variety, March 13, 2000, p. 51; December 10, 2000, p. 26.
Vogue, January 1991.

—Rob Nagel and Christine Miner Minderovic

Meredith Gourdine

1929-1998

Olympian, physicist, engineer,

Many people of varying notoriety excel in specific fields. This is what makes them successful or famous. For Meredith Gourdine, excelling in athletics simply wasn't enough. After earning a silver medal in the 1952 Olympics in Helsinki, Finland, Gourdine parlayed a wealth of knowledge, teamed with a vast academic background into a noteworthy career. His post-Olympic path would be that of a highly recognized physicist, engineer, holder of nearly thirty U.S. patents (some accounts have the number as high as 70) and the founder of a engineering system that would be an enormous benefit to removing smoke and fog.

Born September 26, 1929 in Newark, New Jersey, Gourdine was raised in Brooklyn, where his father worked as a painter and janitor. Attending Brooklyn Tech High School, he didn't start running until his senior year. While in high school, Gourdine would work eight hours after school, helping his father with painting jobs. In an article found at www.princeton.edu, Gourdine recalled his father's advice during those times. "My father said, 'If you don't want to be a laborer all your life, stay in school.' It took." Being an excellent swimmer, Gourdine earned a swimming scholarship to the University of Michigan. He decided to attend Cornell, where he paid his way through the first two years.

While at Cornell in the early 1950s, the six-foot, 175-pound Gourdine excelled in track and field. He won championship titles in the Intercollegiate Association of Amateur Athletes of America, and another five titles in the Heptagonal Games. In 1952 he led Cornell

to a second-place finish in the National Collegiate Athletic Association Championships. Gourdine later qualified for the summer Olympics that year. Gourdine finished second in the broad jump event, settling for a silver medal with a leap of 24 feet, 8 1/4 inches. He lost by an inch and a half. In the same article at www.princeton.edu, Gourdine said "I would have rather lost by a foot. I still have nightmares about it.'"

After the Olympics Gourdine worked for four years in the private sector. According to a profile found at inventers.about.com, Gourdine served as a technical staffer at Ramo-Woolridge Corporation for a year before becoming the senior research scientist at Caltech Jet Propulsion Laboratory in 1958. Two years later he was named lab director at Plasmodyne Corporation and would become chief scientist of the Curtiss-Wright Corporation from 1962 to 1964. Also in 1964 Gourdine was named to the President's Panel on Energy and ultimately established Gourdine Systems on a $200,000 loan from family and friends. In 1973 he started Energy Innovations in Houston.

Gourdine's attention to detail and extremely high intelligence would be the foundation for his most notable scientific discoveries in electrogasdynamics. According to a Gourdine profile found at www.mit.edu, his particular field of study is "basically the generation of energy from the motion of gas molecules which have been ionized (electrically charged) under high pressure." The article also described Gourdine as "one of the first, and remains one of the most respected, scientists in electrogasdynamics." For Gourdine, suc-

At a Glance . . .

Born Meredith Charles Gourdine September 26, 1929 in Newark, NJ; died November 20, 1998 in Houston. Survived by wife, Carolina Bailing; one son, Meredith, daughters (from a previous marriage) Teri, Traci, and Toni; five grandchildren.

Education: Bachelor's of Science, Cornell University, 1953; Ph.D. in Engineering Physics, California Institute of Technology, 1960.

Career: U.S. Naval officer; Ramo-Woolridge Corporation, technical staffer; Caltech Jet Propulsion Laboratory, senior research scientist; Plasmodyne Corporation, lab director; Curtiss-Wright Corporation, chief scientist; founded Gourdine Systems in Livingston, NJ; founded Energy Innovations in Houston, 1973; holder of more than 30 U.S. patents.

Awards: Olympic silver medal, Broad Jump, Helsinki Olympics, 1952; Guggenheim fellowship, 1960; Ramo-Woolridge fellowship.

cess came from developing a practical use for a complex scientific procedure.

Gourdine earned patents from 1971 to 1973 for his invention called "Incineraid." Gourdine established a method to help remove smoke from buildings and also a way to remove fog from airport runways. Those systems created clear air by introducing a negative charge to airborne particles. Those negative charges made the particles electromagnetically charge to the ground, where they would drop and be replaced by fresh air. Gourdine would later earn additional patents related to electrogasdynamics, including applications to circuit breakers, acoustic imaging, air monitors and coating systems. He also created the Focus Flow Heat Sink, which is a method used to cool computer chips.

His impressive work in science and technology earned him respect and praise from his peers. Physicist H. E. Blackwell, in a tribute appearing at www.wellblack-.com, spoke highly of Gourdine. "Having had a vague memory of an *Ebony* article on Dr. Gourdine in the early 70's, I had been surprised to first run into him at the Johnson Space Center in 1992. I had been more surprised to find that he had lost his sight years before. More surprising was that he had not let blindness deter his creative work. He was filled with energy and ideas for new technology. Some years later when he asked me to assist him with some tasks, I found remarkable the manner in which he was able to carry complex equations in his head and manipulate them with ease."

Despite his intelligence and fortitude, Gourdine would eventually surrender to illness. He developed diabetes, a disease that would ultimately cause him to not only lose his sight, but one of his legs. According to an obituary appearing at www.sportsillustrated.cnn.com, Gourdine's ex-wife, June Hubbard, said that at the time of his death, he was undergoing twice-weekly dialysis treatments. He passed away at age 69 at St. Joseph's Hospital in Houston. The cause of death was listed as complications from multiple strokes. Gourdine had earned more than 30 patents, an Olympic silver medal and the respect and admiration of his peers and family. Like his colleagues, Hubbard was quoted as having high esteem for her former husband. "That man, he never gave up no matter what. When he was losing his eyesight, when he lost feeling in his hands. He just kept on and on despite his disabilities," she told sportsillustrated.cnn.com.

Sources

http://inventors.about.com
www.math.buffalo.edu
www.princeton.edu
http://sportsillustrated.cnn.com
http://web.mit.edu
www.wellblack.com

—John Horn

E. Lynn Harris

1957—

Author

E. Lynn Harris had a secret he kept from his co-workers for a long time. The first person he spoke to about his secret was well-known author Maya Angelou. In 1983 she was speaking at a corporate conference in the company where Harris worked. It was there that he confessed his secret to her. He wanted to become a writer. "She told me I should write something every day," he said in *People* magazine, "even if it was just one word." This dedication to his dream has made Harris an extremely popular author today.

E. Lynn Harris was born in Flint, Michigan in the late 1950s. His mother was a single parent who raised him and his three sisters on her salary from factory jobs. "My mother was a single parent who always worked two jobs," Harris told the *Chicago Tribune*. "We have never been a sit-down-at-the-table-and-discuss-our lives-type. But there has always been a lot of love there." Harris recalled watching white families on television and wondering why his family did not act the way they did. "I realize now that we, black families, respond to things differently," he added in the *Tribune*.

When Harris was four years old his mother moved to Little Rock, Arkansas, where Harris spent the remaining time of his growing up years. His mother had a small four room house. *The Houston Chronicle* said that as a teenager Harris "used to lie about his modest, single-parent background and pretend to be the scion of a well-off family." "I started working odd jobs at age 12 to help support the family," said Harris in *The Atlanta Constitution*. Even though life wasn't easy he managed to do right. "My mother is my greatest

inspiration because she worked so hard to bring us up right. She leads by example." According to *The New York Times*, Harris was 14 when he first met his father, who was killed a year later.

Harris attended high school several miles away from his home and commuted the distance daily. The school was a predominately white school. Harris said he attended the school because students received a better education there than the schools closer to his home. When he graduated, Harris went on to attend the University of Arkansas in Fayetteville. It was there that he decided he was going to become a writer. He majored in journalism and received his degree in 1977. While at Arkansas Harris was the first black male cheerleader, the first black yearbook editor, and president of his fraternity. He told *The Houston Chronicle* that he was in that workaholic mode, being the most popular, but not having any friends.

To this day Harris remains an Arkansas Razorback fan. He seems more devoted than their other big fan Bill Clinton. "I get upset and depressed for a day when Arkansas loses. I don't even read the sports pages. It's just my passion," he told *USA Today*. He went on to tell the story of how he rushed through a book signing and interviews one night a couple of years ago during the NCAA basketball tournament, "it was the one time that I prayed no one would show up," he said.

"I was miserable because I was living a lie," he told *The New York Times*. "Mr. Harris said he fretted over his looks and lied about his sexuality for years," the paper continued. "He drank too much. He was lonely." Mr. Harris relates one story where he called his mother crying because he had broken off a relationship with a lover. He said in *The Commercial Appeal*, that his mother told him "You're my baby and I love you no matter what." "And I said, 'I know mom, but sometimes you need somebody more than your mother to love you.'" She didn't know at the time that Harris was gay. When asked about his sexuality Mr. Harris has given different answers. To some reporters he has said he is gay and has known this for many years. At other times he has said that he relates to one of the characters from his first two novels, Raymond Tyler, Jr., "I see myself as a gay man, but when I see an attractive woman," he said in *The Dallas Morning News*, "or think about settling down and making a home for myself, I still feel that ambivalence. I think it's an issue that troubles a lot of men."

After college Harris was hired immediately by IBM. He spent approximately the next thirteen years selling mainframe computers for IBM as well as AT&T and Hewlett-Packard. He lived in Dallas, Houston, and New York City before moving to Atlanta. Harris has said he was earning $90,000 a year at his sales job before he left. *The Houston Chronicle* called him, "successful but not happy." The article also added, "... he turned to writing as a form of therapy to help alleviate feelings of depression." "Part of the depression was that being black and gay had caused me so much pain," he said in *The Houston Chronicle*, "If someone understood the pain that living this life could cause, maybe they would

see that nobody would go out willy-nilly and choose it, and they would show more empathy." As with many gay men it took some time before Mr. Harris could feel comfortable with his sexuality.

After leaving his high powered sales job, Harris began writing. When he completed his first book he sent it to several publishers. Not a single publisher would agree to publish the manuscript. Some even went so far to say that black people didn't want to read about the things he was writing. Even a national publisher of gay books rejected the manuscript. After some soul searching and getting over the pain of all the rejection letters, Harris decided he would publish his own book. According to *Publishers Weekly* he contacted AIDS agencies and they were able to provide the money he needed in exchange for a portion of the proceeds in return for helping him promote the book. He was also able to find a printer that would work with him to arrange payment for their work. "I got the book printed right before the Christmas of 1991, and that's when the horror started," he said to the magazine. "I had over 5,000 copies in rented office space. At the first book party we sold only 42, and I felt sick."

He began carrying around boxes of the book in the trunk of his car. He left copies at beauty salons, women's groups, black-owned bookstores and even went door-to-door in an effort to sell the book. Bookstores began calling him when customers began requesting the book they had seen in beauty salons. It wasn't long before *Essence* magazine named his book one of their ten best of the year. He worked hard enough that eventually he had sold 10,000 copies of the book that he published. For many first books, published by major publishers, this is considered to be a successful book. All Harris' work finally netted him a contract with a publisher. Doubleday signed him to a writing deal, after reading an article about him in *The Atlanta Constitution*. They re-issued the first book *Invisible Life* in paperback, and published in hardcover his second book *Just As I Am*.

Harris became well-known. He is greeted by hundreds of fans when he arrives for book signings at stores around the country. His third book spent several weeks on *The New York Times* bestseller list. "Slowly I'm seeing more men, slowly I'm seeing more whites," Harris said recently in *The Houston Chronicle*. "But the majority are Black women. They are very fervent in their support." Being a former salesman, he knows that his fan base has grown because the amount of time his latest book has spent on the bestseller lists. On why his books are popular Harris told the *Chicago Tribune*, "The characters and situations are so real that people learn something about themselves and about other people." He also felt that the books touch everyone in the black community, both gay and straight. "Most of the black community believe that certain people like upstanding or popular black people can't be (gay or bisexual)," he told the Chicago paper. The *Tribune* also added that "the popularity of his novels have forced the African American community to examine this once hidden side of the black culture."

Harris began working on his memoirs, tentatively titled, *For Colored Boys Who Have Considered Suicide When Being Gay Was Too Tough*, a word play on the title of Ntozake Shange's play *For Colored Girls Who Have Considered Suicide/When The Rainbow Is Enuf*. He was also working on the sale of the screen rights of his books, so that they can be made into movies, as well as two other novels. In 2002 Harris received the Writers for Writers Award from Barnes & Noble for his E. Lynn Harris Better Days Literary Foundation, an organization that helps mentor up-and-coming writers.

By 1994 Harris could claim that he was the first African American male to be at the top of *Blackboard*, the African-American best-seller list. By 2000 his first six novels had sold over one million copies and he was the first African American male to equal the achievements of his female counterparts. Harris' characters often show up from book to book, which helped to keep his readers hooked. Or, perhaps his readers are hooked because his plots, according to Clarissa Cruz, writer for *Entertainment Weekly*, could be described as "*Soul Food* meets *Melrose Place*." Harris's latest character, Yancey Harrington Braxton, a broadway diva, is jilted at the altar in *Not a Day Goes By*, and records an "autobiographical" song in Harris's subsequent novel, *Any Way the Wind Blows*. Having first hand knowledge of marketing, Harris asked Booby Daye to write music and lyrics for "Yancey's Song" and asked Yvette Carson, a back-up singer for Whitney Houston, to record the song. Harris' publisher, Doubleday, produced 15,000 promotional CD singles that feature the same cover art and title, *Any Way the Wind Blows*.

At book signings, Harris is surprised when people tell him how much they love him, give him hugs, and bring him food. He liked the fact that people tell him how much his stories have touched their lives. In an interview with Ebony magazine, Harris was asked where he finds his inspiration. Harris replied, "My faith in God and in myself, from people I consider role models—my mother and my aunt, someone like John H. Johnson and Linda Johnson Rice. He's from Arkansas, and I always look to him as a hero. If a man from Arkansas could create *Ebony*, I could become a success, too."

Selected writings

Invisible Life, 1992.
Just As I Am, 1994.
And This Too Shall Pass, 1996.
If This World Were Mine, 1997.
Abide With Me, 1998.
Not A Day Goes By, 2000.
Any Way The Wind Blows, 2001.

Sources

Periodicals

The Advocate, June 24, 1997, p. 110; August 29, 2000, p. 67.
The Atlanta Constitution, June 9, 1992, p. D1.
Chicago Tribune, December 5, 1994, p. C1.
The Commercial Appeal (Memphis), April 4, 1996, p. 1C.
The Dallas Morning News, April 3, 1996, p. 1C.
Ebony, October 2000, p. 23.
Entertainment Weekly, September 2000, p. 38.
Essence, April 1996, p. 88.
The Houston Chronicle, April 14, 1996, p. 20.
The New York Times, March 17, 1996, p. A43.
People, April 15, 1995, p. 115.
Publishers Weekly, December 6, 1993, pp. 29, 32; April, 19, 2000, p. 44;June 26, 2000, p. 50; June 25, 2001, p. 49; July 30, 2001, p. 53.
USA Today, August 17, 1994, p. 7D.

On-line

Publishers Weekly, http://publishersweekly.reviews news.com, February 25, 2002.

—Stephen Stratton and Christine Miner Minderovic

Isaac Scott Hathaway

1874-1967

Sculptor, educator

Best known for his busts of prominent African Americans, most notably Paul Lawrence Dunbar, Booker T. Washington, and Frederick Douglass; Isaac Scott Hathaway also designed the Booker T. Washington and George Washington Carver half dollar pieces. Hathaway's career developed during the Harlem Renaissance, a time in which African-American poets, artists, writers, and intellectuals made their presence felt in American culture. Yet in many ways, Hathaway's ideas and principles anticipated the Harlem Renaissance.

Hathaway, born in 1874 in Lexington, Kentucky, was one of three children. His mother died when he was just three years of age. His two sisters, Fannie and Eva, were sent off to be raised by their grandmother, while he remained with his father, the Reverend Hathaway of the Christian Church in Lexington. His father provided Isaac with a stimulating childhood and a good education.

Hathaway decided to become an artist at a very early age for very compelling reasons. At the age of nine, while accompanying his father on a tour of a museum that exhibited the busts of famous Americans, young Isaac was determined to find the bust of his favorite hero and role model, Frederick Douglass. Disappointed not to have found what he was looking for, he asked his father why Douglass was not among the busts that were on display. Reverend Hathaway explained to his son that, at that time, there were no trained black sculptors who could provide the public with statues and busts of prominent blacks. In addition, his father explained that while there were many important and famous blacks who deserved to be honored, their likenesses would not be displayed in public places. Determined, Isaac Hathaway declared, according to www.liu.edu, "I am going to model busts of Negroes and put them where people can see them."

A determined and inventive young artist, Hathaway fashioned his first art studio out of a chicken coop. He pursued his art education with a mission, receiving training at several schools. He attended Chandler College in his hometown of Lexington for a while and then moved to Pittsburgh to study ceramics at Pittsburgh Normal College. Wanting to learn more about fine arts, Hathaway enrolled in the Art Department of the New England Conservatory of Music in Boston and later the Cincinnati Art Academy in Cincinnati. He also received additional ceramics education at the College of Ceramics at the State University of New York at Alfred, New York.

After college, Hathaway became an elementary school teacher, thereby applying his diverse educational background to support his artistic endeavors. Conversely, he used his knowledge of art to enhance his effectiveness as an educator. For example, he prepared plaster of Paris models for his science classes, also creating the human skeleton to teach his students about the human body.

After Hathaway gained local fame as a sculptor, his friends and peers who appreciated his talents and his work, suggested that he establish his own company so that he could distribute his sculptural work on a national level. His company was first called the Afro Art Company, and then at a later time changed its name to the Isaac Hathaway Art Company. Essentially, Hathaway fulfilled his boyhood dream of becoming an artist who would create sculptures and busts of prominent African Americans such as his hero, Frederick Douglass, as well as Booker T. Washington, Paul Lawrence Dunbar, George Washington Carver, Richard Allen, Mary McLeod Bethune, Dr. Charles Drew, and C.C. Spaulding. His work was sold to various public places, including libraries, schools, churches, places of business, and government buildings. Hathaway also produced masks, plaques, and bronze sculptures.

A versatile figurative artist, Hathaway was able to work with large figures as well as miniatures, and was the first artist to make death masks of prominent African Americans. Isaac Scott Hathaway was also the first African American to design a coin for the United States. In 1946 Hathaway was commissioned by President Harry S. Truman to design a half dollar coin, according to www.liu.edu, "to commemorate the life and perpetuate the ideas and teachings of Booker T. Washington." A few years later, in 1951, Hathaway was chosen to design the commemorative George Washington Carver half dollar piece.

Hathaway was an esteemed educator as well as a talented artist and innovator. Much of his work was done in ceramic, a medium in which he excelled. He taught at several colleges, including the Tuskegee Institute, Alabama A&M College, and Alabama State College, where he founded and headed Ceramic departments. As he lived and worked in Alabama, it is not surprising that his favorite medium contained Alabama clay. After years of working with his mixture of clay, he developed a method that gave the final product a translucent quality. At one time during his career, Hathaway was a sculptural designer for the New National Museum of the Smithsonian Institute.

Hathaway's art has been largely ignored perhaps because he was a classical, figurative artist whose career developed during a time when experimentation was the norm. Historians could state that his career flourished because it coincided with the Harlem Renaissance, but essentially, Hathaway's ideals enhanced the teachings and ideals of that era. Hathaway claimed, "that the art of a people not only conveys their mental, spiritual, and civic growth to posterity, but convinces their contemporaries that they can best portray in crystallization their feelings, aspirations, and desires."

Sources

Books

Cederholm, Theresa Dickason. *Afro-American Artists*. Trustees of the Boston Public Library, 1973.
Walker, Rosalyn. *A Resource Guide to the Visual Arts of Afro-Americans*, 1971.

Periodicals

Negro History Bulletin, January, 1954.

Online

http://www.liu.edu/cwis/cwp/library/aavaahp.htm.

—Christine Miner Minderovic

Jessie Mae Hemphill

1937—

Blues musician, singer

A regular performer at blues festivals as late as the early 1990s, Jessie Mae Hemphill, outfitted in a sequined hat and shiny purple halter top, stood out onstage for her age as well as her appearance. With a wink in her eye and a gold tooth flashing, Hemphill played guitar, bells attached to her legs, her foot tapping a tambourine. The music of her one-woman band was haunting—familiar, yet new. It drew from the traditions of North Mississippi Delta region—music born of slavery, reared in poverty, and perfected on the farmland. Hemphill played it with her own style, updating classic lyrics with her own words—"the thoughts I have about times and about living and life," she wrote in the liner notes to her album *She-Wolf*. Her distinctive mix of new and old Delta traditions with day-to-day observations, won Hemphill international acclaim as a blues woman. She, however, was just carrying on the family tradition.

Hemphill was born Jessie Mae Graham in Senatobia, Mississippi. Though some sources cite her birth date as 1932 or 1934, the majority agrees that she was born in 1937 on October 18th. Whatever the date, one thing is sure—Hemphill was born with music in her blood. Her father, James Graham, was a blues pianist and her mother, Virgie Lee Graham, was skilled in many instruments, though she did not identify herself

as a musician. Hemphill has said that, although her mother was not interested in playing music, her Aunt Rosa was, and she believed that they both inherited their passion for music from Hemphill's maternal grandfather, Sid Hemphill. The elder Hemphill was a well-known leader of fife-and-drum groups and had a successful career that spanned fifty years. Fife-and-drum, a traditional music native to the North Mississippi Delta region, has long interested ethnomusicologists because of its links to African musical styles. Sid Hemphill recorded with famed musicologist Alan Lomax in the 1940s. Sid Hemphill, in turn, had his musical roots sown by his father, Doc Hemphill, a Choctaw Indian and famed fiddler. This rich generational musical heritage has driven Jessie Mae Hemphill's own musical career. "All of the Hemphills was music players. And so I'm the last one. I'm just trying to play to keep the Hemphill music going. And trying not to let my granddaddy down," she told *Guitar Player* in 1991.

Began Picking the Guitar at Eight

With such a musical pedigree it was almost inevitable that Hemphill would become a musician at an early

At a Glance . . .

Born Jessie Mae Hemphill on October 18, 1937 (some sources cite 1932 or 1934), in New York, NY; daughter of Virgie Lee Graham and James Graham, a blues pianist; married J.D. Brooks (divorced).

Career: Singer, songwriter, guitarist, percussionist. Began performing as a child; in infrequent appearances with blues bands and drum-and-fife groups, 1950s-60s; began a solo career as Jessie Mae Hemphill, 1970s; recorded first album, *She-Wolf,*1980; second album, *Feelin' Good,* 1990; toured extensively throughout the United States and Europe, until 1995.

Awards: W.C. Handy Traditional Female Artist of the Year, 1987,1988, 1994; W.C. Handy Acoustic Album of the Year, for *Feelin' Good*, 1991.

Addresses: *Home*—P.O. Box 975, Senatobia, MS 38668.

age. She was eight years old when she began to learn guitar. "When I was little," she told *Guitar Player*, "my granddaddy started me off to playing guitar, and I started off playing blues. I liked the spirituals, but I played the blues because I thought that would get me somewhere in the money line faster than the spirituals would." The first complete song she learned was her Aunt Rosa Lee's "Bullyin' Well" which later appeared on her album *She-Wolf*.

Following her grandfather's lead as a multi-instrumentalist, Hemphill did not confine herself to just the guitar. She soon began learning drums and eventually picked up the tambourine, fife, flute, trombone, saxophone, harmonica, and piano. As a teen she began to perform and even won contests for her tambourine skills. Further cementing her link with her heritage, Hemphill learned to play instruments with clear African roots, including the quills—homemade cane pipes similar to panpipes—and the diddley bow, a one- stringed instrument that is plucked or played with a glass bottle. However, it was for the guitar, drum, and tambourine that Hemphill became best known. Hemphill learned from listening to her relatives, noting for *Guitar Player* that her Aunt Rosa showed her how to play songs. Hemphill also said that she had to "learn how to make the sound in my head."

During the1950s and 1960s, though she was already a skilled performer, Hemphill worked a series of menial jobs including stints in grocery stores and dry cleaners. She moved to Memphis during this time and, while still

a teenager, married J. D. Brooks. Music found its way back into Hemphill's life when she landed a job at a Memphis blues club. This led to her running her own club for a brief while. It wasn't until the 1970s that Hemphill would turn to her inherited role as a musician full-time.

When her marriage ended, Hemphill left Memphis and returned to Mississippi and her musical roots. She dropped her married name and adopted her more famous family name. About this time Hemphill caught the attention of Dr. David Evans, a noted ethnomusicologist, blues scholar, and talented musician in his own right. In the liner notes of Hemphill's album, *She-Wolf*, Evans wrote, "I was struck with what a fresh approach she had to an old style of music." He continued, "She had drawn on the deepest traditions of the blues and African-American folk music to create truly contemporary country blues, not nostalgic recreations of an earlier musical era."

In 1979 Evans received a grant from the National Endowment of the Arts to record and produce Mississippi blues music. Under his tutelage the High Water Recording Company was created as a division of the University of Memphis. One of its first artists was Hemphill. That first recording featured the Hemphill original compositions, "Jessie's Boogie" and "Standing in My Doorway Crying." The latter became a hit and was the top selling record on the High Water label. Following this success, Evans introduced Hemphill to the French label Vogue Records who promptly signed her to record her first album, *She-Wolf*.

Developed Award-Winning Sound

Shortly following the release of *She-Wolf* Vogue Records changed artistic direction and as a result *She-Wolf* languished with little promotion and no stateside audience. The album wouldn't be released in the United States until the late 1990s. The inertia of *She-Wolf* couldn't stop Hemphill and she kept right on playing, writing music, and developing her distinct, hypnotic sound. London's *The Independent* described Hemphill as a "powerful and mesmerizing performer who is like a female version of John Lee Hooker and Howlin' Wolf combined." The blues establishment also took notice and Hemphill won the esteemed W.C. Handy Award for Traditional Female Artist of the Year in both 1987 and 1988.

In 1990 her second album, *Feelin' Good*, was released on Evans's High Water label. With this album Hemphill drew the attention of blues aficionados from around the globe. One reviewer wrote on the Harmony Ridge Music website, "She's haunting, sexy, and full of the raw energy only someone with the blues in their blood can be." The album also scored Hemphill another Handy award in 1991 for Acoustic Album of the Year. Hemphill penned most of the songs on *Feelin' Good*.

Drawing from traditional blues topics of love lost and found, poverty and hard work, sex and salvation, Hemphill continued a tradition of singing for and of the people. She told *Guitar Player*, "[The songs] don't be all from me … It be what I think other-folks is feeling—the trouble that other womens is having. All us women have the same kind of trouble with our guys. Some of my blues is kinda sad blues, 'cause sometimes I be feeling down and out, and I know some other womens do too. So I play them so it will hit somebody."

Juggled Popular Blues with Delta Traditions

Hemphill's fame reached its peak in the early 1990s. She was in demand at blues festivals and concerts all over the United States and Europe. As the general public lapped up her music, it also stirred the interest of academic folklorists. Hemphill performed for folklore societies in Memphis and Washington D.C. "Jessie Mae's strongest musical influences come from her family and the local folk music tradition near her home in Como, Mississippi," wrote Evans. Those traditions include the fife-and-drum of which Hemphill told www.mississippitalking.com, "[It was] my granddaddy's music, it came from Africa. My granddaddy knew it, and his daddy knew it too." Even with her hectic schedule, Hemphill managed to find time to perform with fife-and-drum groups back home in Mississippi.

As her fame was spreading, so was her reputation as a real "She-Wolf" of the blues. On stage Hemphill nurtured a sexuality normally reserved for male singers. She wore sequins and low cut tops, and flirted with the audience. Photographer Bill Steber, who has photographed many traditional blues musicians, wrote on his website: "Female blues guitarists of Hemphill's generation are rare because of the social strictures and danger associated with the lifestyle. Jessie Mae, however, has always known how to take care of herself in a hostile world. 'My mother carried her gun all the time,' says Hemphill. 'She was a pistol-packing mama so I'm a pistol-packing mama'." Her willingness to step outside traditional female roles was also expressed in her songwriting and performing. Of *She-Wolf*, a reviewer for www.retroactive.com wrote, "Hemphill uses the opportunity to display the full range of her powers. When she sings 'Do the disco baby. Do it, baby, do it' on "Jump Baby Jump," you know what she's talking about now, and [it is] every bit as salacious as any of Mr. Hooker's nastier moments."

In 1994 Hemphill won her fourth Handy Award, again for Traditional Female Artist of the Year, and her career seemed destined to continue its phenomenal growth. However, a debilitating stroke left her partially paralyzed, making it impossible for her to play guitar again. Though her career effectively came to a halt, her fame continued to grow. In 1997 *Feelin' Good* was re-vamped and re-issued on CD by the HighTone Records

label. A year later, *She-Wolf* was finally released in the United States, also on HighTone Records. The releases once-again stirred the interests of blues lovers and scholars, making Hemphill something of a cult icon in the blues community.

In November of 2001 she sang and played tambourine as part of the "The North Mississippi Hill Country," a concert in Brooklyn Heights, New York that brought her together with other homegrown Mississippi talent, including legends Otha Turner and T-Model Ford, as well as more famous newcomers Lucinda Williams, the North Mississippi All-Stars, and the Jon Spencer Blues Explosion. The concert was filmed by acclaimed German filmmaker Wim Wenders for *The Blues*, a PBS series set to premiere in 2003.

Carried on Delta Tradition

Despite her continuing fame and ever-growing audience, Hemphill's life was still a struggle. This daughter of the North Mississippi Delta blues, home-grown fourth generation blues musician, innovator and tradition saver, lived alone for many years in a ramshackle trailer in Como, Mississippi with her pet poodles. However, organizations such as the Sunflower River Blues Association of Clarksdale, Mississippi, whose aim is to assist blues pioneers who have fallen on hard times, has helped Hemphill find better housing.

Hemphill has also not been forgotten by cultural historians. Students in Mississippi have written about her life as part of "The Mississippi Writers and Musicians Project," which shares the rich cultural tradition of Mississippi with high school students. And she speaks to students as part of the Blues Project of George Mason University. One student wrote on the Blues Project website of a 2000 visit, "When we met Jessie Mae Hemphill … she seemed to have a great perspective on how the music brought the community together for celebration and to share their lives with each other … As we sat and listened to her I felt as if we were hearing her own history as a blues woman, but it also told me what life has been like as a whole in the Delta for the past century."

Selected discography

She-Wolf, Vogue/Blues Today, 1980 (French Release); HighTone/HMG, 1998 (reissue).
Feelin' Good, High Water, 1990; HighTone/HMG, 1997 (reissue).
Giants of Country Blues, Vol. 3, Wolf, 1991 (compilation with other artists).
Deep South Blues, HighTone/HMG, 1999 (compilation with other artists).
Mali To Memphis: An African-American Odyssey, Putumayo World Music, 1999 (compilation with other artists).

Sources

Periodicals

The Atlanta Journal-Constitution, August 16, 1998, p. C3.
Guitar Player, October 1991, p27; May 1998, p. 47.
The Independent (London, England), April 4, 1998, p. 39.
The New York Times, Nov 12, 2001, p. E1.

On-line

www.bluesaccess.com/No_30/horwitz.html
www. catfishkeith.com
Bill Steber Photography, http://gallery64.com/steber_b/descrip/(14)Steber_JessieMaeH.htm
Harmony Ridge Music, http://www.hrmusic.com/discos/fafram17.html
http://www.mojoworkin.com/bluesrag/features/highwaterii.html
http://www.mississippitalking.msstate.edu/issue-04/blues/artist3.html
The Blues Project, http://www.ncc.gmu.edu/CFS/bluesproject.htm
www.retroactive.com/mar98/jessiemae.html

—Candace LaBalle

Darrin DeWitt Henson

1970(?)—

Choreographer, actor

Darrin DeWitt Henson, one of the actors on the popular Showtime series *Soul Food*, has earned legions of fans among viewers. Although fans of the hit series may not realize it, they were already familiar with Henson's dance moves before they knew him as a television star. In addition to acting, Henson has also choreographed a number of dance routines for some of music's hottest performers.

Henson was raised in the Bronx, New York, along with his four brothers. His father was a professional horse trainer and his mother was a homemaker. He remembers having a love for dance from the age of five. He began perfecting his dance skills in his back yard, with stints in between the television and a mirror. Henson's first paying job as a dancer came when he was ten. "We were at a birthday party and listening to James Brown and I remember getting in the middle of the dance floor," he explained in an interview with *Dance Magazine*. "I started popping and this old man gave me five dollars and that was it. I knew what I wanted to do," he continued.

Henson grew up in the place many people call the home of break-dancing. Never formally trained for dance, his first sources for moves were the break-dancers in his community. He also added material from the dance steps he saw in popular music videos. "I'd come home from school and go into my backyard … I'd have the boom box blasting, and my friends and I would get into it and see what we could come up with," Henson told *People Weekly*.

Henson began dancing semi-professionally in high school with a New York group. Soon after his 1988 high school graduation, he left that group to join a break-dancing troupe for the Ringling Brothers and Barnum &Bailey Circus. With a new decade rolling in, Henson found new ways to flex his dancing style and began working in videos, which helped create a style of his own. He was featured in the Salt-N-Pepa "Whatta Man" video and began working with the likes of video vanguards such as Michael Jackson, who unknowingly provided Henson with some of his first moves. "I studied dance by watching Michael Jackson videos," he told *Dance* magazine. "I would put a mirror in front of the television and practice. Everything happened in my bedroom."

But Henson became restless with dancing behind others. "As a dancer I got frustrated working with a lot of choreographers," he said in *Dance*. "I didn't like their steps. I didn't think they were good enough. I got frustrated into being a choreographer." He began his career as choreographer working with diverse stars ranging from Deborah Cox and Dru Hill to Prince. By the late 1990s he had founded Dance and Entertainment Workshop, his own dance company, where he took the mentoring that he was receiving from fellow dancers and artists a step further. This was also the time that his clients like Christina Aguilera, Britney Spears, N'Sync, and Jennifer Lopez began knocking at his door.

Henson provided Aguilera with her moves for the "Genie in a Bottle" music video. He also lent his dancing skills to Spears in "You Drive Me Crazy," and eventually landed not only N'Sync's most memorable video "Bye, Bye, Bye," but he was hired to choreograph their 1998, 1999, and 2000 world tours. To combat spreading himself too thin, he personally trained instructors from his dance company to be able to take on the role of teaching the steps and participating in the videos and shows he produced. "I'm basically mentoring a lot of people," he told *Dance*. "I want to see the product get better ... and there's jobs that I have no time to do, because I'm so busy."

Henson felt less challenged by his role as choreographer, so he began putting time into his acting career. He had landed small roles in shows like ABC's *NYPD Blue* but still wanted something more. He finally won a role on Showtime's TV series *Soul Food* in 2000. The series had been adapted from the immensely popular film *Soul Food* and has proven to be just as successful. It has also given Henson a stronger presence in the spotlight, allowing people to put a face to his name. When he won the 2000 MTV Video Award for Best Choreographer of the Year with the "Bye, Bye, Bye" choreography for N'Sync, many viewers were surprised to see the actor on stage with the band. Henson's dual role shows that "[b]rothers are not only in front of the camera, but also behind the camera and we are helping to develop the artists that we see today," he explained in an interview with *Jet*.

Henson the actor has been so successful in his stint in front of the camera that his series was renewed for a second season and he was gearing up for his feature film debut in *Jack of All Trades*. Spreading his acting

wings hasn't limited his love for dance. Henson was scheduled to choreograph the Spice Girls in concert and launched Darrin's Dance Grooves, a seminar series that he takes to different cities to teach children to dance. He also put together an exercise video for those average viewers wanting to try their luck with his dancing techniques. In the video, viewers could learn the steps that made both Henson and N'Sync famous, while getting in shape.

Henson's advice to the youngsters in his classes is to practice, practice, practice. "Get in front of that mirror and do it 'til you got it," he advised in *Dance*. "Pick your favorite video and practice the dance steps." For Henson, choreographer to fellow stars, the method is proven, tried and true.

Selected works

(as choreographer)

"Genie in a Bottle," music video, Christina Aguilera.
"You Drive Me Crazy," video, Brittany Spears.
"Bye, Bye, Bye," video, N'Sync.
"Love Don't Cost A Thing," video, Jennifer Lopez.
"Play," video, Jennifer Lopez.

(as actor)

Beverly Hills 90210.
NYPD Blue.
New York Undercover.
Double Platinum, (made-for-TV movie), 1999.
Soul Food, 2000-.
Jack of All Trades, (film).

Sources

Periodicals

Dance, April 2000, p. 95.
Jet, October 30, 2000, p. 57.
People Weekly, July 9, 2001, p. 77.
Time, September 11, 2000, p. 112 .

On-Line

Darrin's Dance Grooves, www.darrinsdancegrooves. com
Internet Movie Database, http://imdb.com

—Leslie Rochelle

Andre and Suki Horton

Skiers

The world has watched as Tiger Woods carved a path for African Americans in golf. In tennis, it was the Williams sisters, Serena and Venus, who've broken the color barrier with their vicious serves and incredible stamina. Decades before any of these trailblazing athletes were born it was baseball legend Jackie Robinson who integrated America's favorite pastime. These athletes have truly been pioneers, opening their respective sports to new generations of young black athletes. However, there are a handful of sports in the United States that as of yet remain mostly Caucasian pursuits. Skiing is one of them. As one avid African- American skier explained to *Ski Magazine*, "Every time my family and I went skiing, we were always the only black family on the slopes. There's nothing bad about that, but I guess you like to see that you are not the only one in your group participating in this great sport."

Many factors are pointed to as an explanation of this, including money—skiing is a very expensive sport to participate in. Also, African Americans have not historically participated in this sport, so it is not something that is passed down to their children. According to a National Brotherhood of Skiing (NBS), an African-American skiing organization, quoted in *Ski Magazine*, a third factor is geographic, "There are not many African Americans living in resort towns....They are not living in close proximity to skiing on a daily basis from the time they are very young." A sister-brother duo from Anchorage, Alaska is poised to change this, not only showing that African Americans can ski, but that they can also become ski champions. By 2002 Andre and Suki Horton were the top-ranked African American ski racers in the country, and with their sights set on the 2006 Olympics, they may just become the top-ranked ski racers.

Began Skiing Before Schooling

Andre Horton was born in Anchorage, Alaska on October 4, 1979. Little sister Andreana "Suki" Horton followed on May 3, 1982. Elsena, their mother, who was white, had moved to Alaska years earlier and had met and married their father Garry, an African- American stationed at a nearby military base. When Andre was born, Elsena, a native of Idaho and avid skier, wasted no time introducing Andre to the great snowy outdoors. He strapped on his first pair of skis when he was just five. Suki soon wanted to take after her big brother and first hit the snow when she was only three. She told *Rocky Mountain News* in 2001, "I've always wanted to be like Andre. I've always wanted to follow my brother." The siblings became bound through their love of skiing and now are virtually inseparable as best friends and training partners. "One never speaks without the other coming up in the conversation," noted www.blackvoices.com.

Andre began his skiing life as a Nordic skier, which involves cross-country skiing. "I started out in Nordic skiing, then Nordic jumping and cross-country skiing," he told *Rocky Mountain News*, but by age seven he had switched to Alpine skiing, characterized by speeding downhill. Suki also gravitated to this adrenaline-fueled sport. Growing up they spent almost every free moment skiing. They began entering local ski races as pre-teens, racking up wins and impressing the skiing community.

When Andre was 14 he started training with Gordon Stewart of Stewart Sports in Alaska, who would later come to train and manage both Andre and Suki. Horton told *Ski Magazine*, "I met Gordon when I was a pretty chubby 14 year-old. He's been training with

At a Glance . . .

Born Andre Horton was born on October 4, 1979, in Anchorage, AK; born and Andreana "Suki" Horton born May 3, 1982, in Anchorage, AK. *Education*: Both attend sporadic classes at University of Alaska.

Career: The Hortons began skiing when they were very young, Andre at five and Suki at three; as pre-teens they began to compete in Alpine races; together they make up the National Brotherhood of Skiers (NBS) Elite Team; both Hortons have appeared in a training video produced by Stewart Sports, Anchorage, AK. *Suki*: member, Western Region Elite Ski team.

Awards: *Andre*: Alaska State Champion, 1998; first African-American skier selected to the U.S. Ski Team Development Program, 2000; 9th place overall finish in the U.S. Alpine National Championships, 2001; first African-American to win an FIS race in Europe, 2001; 4th place, NorAm Competition, 2001; 1st place, Mt. Bachelor's Northwest Cup Finals, 2001. *Suki*: Alaska State Champion, 1998; U.S. Ski Team's Junior Development Group, 1997; selected to compete in the U.S. Alpine National Championships three years in a row; 2nd place, Western Region Downhill FIS series, 2001.

Addresses: *Home*—Anchorage, AK. *Management*—Stewart Sports, 209 West Dimond, Studio 5, Anchorage Alaska 99515, (907) 566-4055, Gordon@stewartsports.com.

me ever since; now he's like a brother." Andre didn't stay chubby for long. He grew to six foot one and packed on muscle like a bodybuilder. "I didn't want to play football because I didn't want to get wrecked and not be able to ski race," Andre told the *Rocky Mountain News*. "A lot of my friends would say, 'You're huge, man. Why don't you play football, put pads on and hit people. You could go to college and be famous. or something'." He further explained, "A lot of people put athletics and fame together. I'm not really like that. I like ski racing. I have a passion for it."

Found Support in NBS

By their early teens, the Hortons had become Alaska state champions and were winning races throughout the Western United States. However, according to

www.blackvoices.com, "They determined the races they would participate in based on what the family could afford." Then, when Andre was 15 he discovered the National Brotherhood of Skiers (NBS). "I saw two other black-American racers at an FIS (International Ski Federation) race in Oregon. That was totally amazing to me—I'd never seen another black ski racer. They were on scholarships from NBS and told me about the program." Schone Malliet, NBS Competition Director, explaining the organization to www.blackathlete.com said, "African-Americans, motivated by their passion for skiing, were inspired to create opportunities for young people to pursue the sport, and pursue it competitively." Malliet continued, "Realizing the financial commitment, the NBS has made it its mission to provide funding, training and support for young African-American men and women in pursuit of an Olympic medal." It costs about $30,000 to pursue a competitive skiing career. Costs arise from equipment, training, club fees, and travel expenses.

Both Andre and Suki promptly became members and their commitment and athleticism was rewarded with NBS skiing scholarships. Of the three youth ski teams the NBS sponsors, the Elite Team is the top. As of 2002 Andre and Suki were this team's only members. The NBS's financial aid, along with their family's unwavering support, and Stewart's careful training and management, meant that Olympic gold could become more than an incredible dream for the Hortons. The dynamic duo were finally in a place to actually pursue this goal.

By the time they graduated high school—Andre in 1998 and Suki in 2000—they had not only become ski racing powerhouses, but had taken on a number of other hobbies. Andre learned jazz trumpet and photography and began working part time for the Anchorage Daily News as a photographer for their Perfect Life segments. Suki took up violin, becoming quite accomplished. She also became an avid rollerblader. Both of the Hortons pursued athletics, enjoying weightlifting, interval training, and mountain biking. They even appeared in a training video for Stewart Sports together. However, nothing was dearer to their hearts than skiing and ski racing, and, according to Stewart, they both shared the same goal—finishing in the top ten in the 2003/2004 World Cup and scoring a medal at the 2006 Winter Olympic Games.

Began Pursuing Olympic Dreams

The road to the Olympics is paved not only with hard work and dedication on the part of the athlete, but also on a series of competitions, both national and international. Membership in the FIS is also important as is ranking in FIS sponsored competitions. Both Suki and Andre have competed in FIS events and Andre made skiing history at a 2001 competition in Sella Nevea, Italy when he came in first place in an FIS downhill

Suki and Andre Horton

competition. "Today was a spiritual victory for me," Andre wrote on the NBS website. "For the 100 or so Italians watching the race, they witnessed the first ever black-American to win a FIS race in Europe!" Making the win more impressive was the fact that the majority of competitors were Italians who were familiar with the course.

Another important step in the Olympic quest is nomination to the United States Ski Team's development program. Members of the development train with the top U.S. skiers and are considered Olympic hopefuls. In 2000 Andre cleared that hurdle, being elected to the 2001-2002 team. This allowed him the opportunity to train with the U.S. Ski Team at their world class facilities in Park City, Utah. With this appointment, Andre also became the first African American on the U.S. Alpine Ski Team. He scored some of his most impressive achievements training with the U.S. World Cup team in Chile in 2001. In four time trials, Andre beat his teammates. In one of those trials, he finished a full second over the rest of the team. "I was ecstatic!" Andre said on www.stewartsports.com. He continued, "at the team meeting I have never been so red. Dale the Men's [World Cup] head coach was talking about the day and then said, 'if anyone could have caught Horton, well … good job Horton.'"

Suki also has been elected to the U.S. Ski Team in the Junior Division. After being hailed for her championship finishes in the Slalom and Giant Slalom races at the 1995 Junior Olympics, Suki made the U.S. Ski Team's Junior Development Team in 1997. In addition, both Hortons have had the chance to ski against U.S. champions at the U.S. Alpine National Championships. Suki was nominated to compete in this prestigious race three times in a row. She even finished second behind gold medallist Picabo Street at a race in Vermont. A knee injury in 1999 forced her to take time to recuperate.

Praised by Other Skiers

Both Andre and Suki drew accolades from skiing professionals. Lester Keller, a U.S. Competition Director told www.blackvoices.com, "Andre is probably one of the strongest athletes we've got in the national system." Of Suki, Keller said, "Suki is a tough kid and a strong competitor. She likes to compete and likes to be the best." The NBS, which has long pursued the goal of having a black skier at the Winter Olympics was also confident of the Hortons' abilities. "In 2002, I would like to see at least one or two of our youths on the U.S. Ski Team and competing in the Olympics," Bessie Gay, president of the NBS was quoted in *Ski Magazine*. "By 2006, I would like to see our youth reaching the podium."

In addition to their awesome skiing talent, Suki and Andre have impressed the skiing—and sports community at large—with their easy going personalities. Numerous. articles have described them as "good-natured," "fun-loving," and "laid-back." "[Andre] is a great guy to be around and an inspiration to the other team members," Keller told www.blackvoices.com. This easy charm, coupled with their wholesome good looks and sparkling smiles, has caused many to bet that the Hortons will become awesomely famous. as media darlings and African-American athletic pioneers. For their part, the Hortons would rather focus on skiing.

Both Hortons acknowledged feeling pressure due to the hope African-American skiers and the media have pinned on them. Of the references to him being the Tiger Woods of skiing, Andre told the *Rocky Mountain News*, "I've thought about the Tiger Woods stuff, but those are huge shoes to fill because he's talented at what he does." He continued, "If it works out that way, fine. But I'm trying to keep a level head about it." Following a devastating knee injury that effectively eliminated Andre's chances of making it to the 2002 Olympics, he countered the pressure he was feeling by telling www.blackvoices.com. "I know there are so many people who want to see me get into the Olympics. When it comes down to it, it's Andre Horton who has to make the sacrifices and has to train to get to the Olympics and on the U.S. Ski Team and no one else."

Suki has also felt the burdens of being considered a pioneer. "There is more pressure because there are people who have helped me along the way, and I want to pay it off," she told *Ski Magazine*, referring to the obligation she felt to help NBS reach its goal of having a black skier on the winners podium at the Olympics. Still, like the NBS, the Hortons were committed to the sport of skiing. Though the burden of being a trailblazer was a lot for a young athlete already juggling the hectic schedule demanded of a world-class skier, the Hortons were up for the challenge. Suki summed it up best, again invoking Woods, when she told *Ski Magazine*, "When I saw Tiger Woods, and the way that everyone started playing golf after he won, I though maybe I can make an impact by making the U.S. Ski Team." She continued, "I realized that what I do out there could affect a lot of people."

Sources

Periodicals

Rocky Mountain News, (Denver, CO), April 1, 2001, p. 3C.
Ski Magazine, January 2000.

On-line

www.blackathlete.com/skiing.htm
www.blackvoices.com/sports/andre_suki
www.easternpaskicouncil.org
www.nbs.org
www.skinet.com
www.stewartsports.com

—Candace LaBalle

Iman

1955—

Model, actress, businesswoman

"She's the High Priestess—we all call her that (Iman means priest in Arabic)," declared designer Fernando Sanchez about exotic model Iman in *Vogue*. "Of course she's dramatic, but behind the slightly grand attitude she is very professional ... And whatever happens ... she'll handle it: make them laugh, keep them in awe—whatever is needed to cover a disaster. But beyond the fact that she's famous, Iman is the perfect model, she gives *expression* to the clothes." Her long neck and elegant gait made her a favorite of top designers as a runway model in international showrooms. Commenting on the native Somalian beauty, who has been called "Iman the Magnificent" and "Queen of the Runway," Bill Blass told *Vogue* that "the truth is, she's a great actress. She uses her body like an instrument."

Born in 1955 in Mogadishu, the capitol of the East African country Somalia, Iman Mohamed Abdulmajid is the daughter of a Somalian diplomat father and a gynecologist mother. Her mother gave her the masculine name "Iman," the model divulged to Linda Konner in *Glamour*, in hopes that she would compete equitably with others since she was "a woman with a man's name." Although Somalia was impoverished, Iman grew up with her two brothers and two sisters in a white house on one of the most beautiful beaches on the Indian Ocean. Throughout her childhood, Iman's family took camping trips to the desert, which comprised most of Somalia. Asked about her mysterious demeanor as a showroom model, Iman told Konner, "Now, *every* time I'm on a runway, I deliberately think of Somalia, and I try to take the people watching me to where I am in my head. I want them to *see* what I *see*—the desert, and the stars that go on forever, illuminating the darkness."

Although Somalia was predominantly Muslim and women were regarded as second-class citizens, Iman learned a different set of attitudes from her parents. Allowed to marry four wives under religious law, her father chose to marry only one woman. Iman related to Konner that her mother, a pioneer thinker, advised her frequently, "Iman, you don't have to lie down with a dog. You have a choice; you don't have to do anything you don't want to do. One good woman is far better than ten men." The family relocated to Kenya after being driven out of Somalia in 1969 when Iman was about fourteen years old. She finished high school and enrolled at the University of Nairobi to study political science. Able to speak five languages, Iman was hardly the legendary cattle herder the press portrayed her as after her modeling debut, when high fashion photog-

At a Glance . . .

Born Iman (pronounced "ee-mahn") Mohamed Abdulmajid in 1955, in Mogadishu, Somalia; daughter of a Somalian diplomat and a gynecologist; married Spencer Haywood (a professional basketball player; divorced, 1987); married David Bowie (a musician), April 24, 1992; children: (first marriage) Zulekha; (second marriage) Alexandria Zahra Jones. *Education*: Attended University of Nairobi; graduated from New York University.

Career: High fashion model and actress; discovered by photographer Peter Beard in Africa, mid-1970s; film appearances: *The Human Factor*, 1979, *Out of Africa*, 1985, *No Way Out*, 1987, *Surrender*, 1989, *Star Trek VI*, 1991, *House Party 2*, 1991, *Heart of Darkness*, 1194, *Exit to Eden*, 1994, *The Deli*, 1997, *Omikron: The Nomad Soul*, 1999; television appearances: *Miami Vice, The Cosby Show, Dream On, In the Heat of the Night*, 1989; and in music videos, including Michael Jackson's "Remember the Time," 1992; creator of documentary *Somalia Diary*, BBC, 1992; contributor to *Vogue* magazine; established cosmetics line to be mass marketed, 1992; launched couture cosmetics line, I-Iman, 2000; autobiography, *I Am Iman*, 2001.

Selected awards: Mayor Tom Bradley declared February 29, 1980, "Iman Day" in New York City.

Addresses: *Agent*—c/o Elite Modeling Agency, 111 East 22nd St., New York, NY 10010.

rapher Peter Beard discovered her on his way to the country to pick up supplies.

"I really first saw her one day," Beard recalled in *Vogue*, "as I was driving down Standard Street in Nairobi with Kamante, who was, as you know, [writer] Isak Dinesen's faithful retainer. Iman was dead anxious to get out of Africa." In her autobiography, *I Am Iman*, Iman explained that she did not even know what modeling was when she was approached by Beard. Just months before Beard sent Iman's photos to Wilhelmina, a prestigious modeling agent, Iman had married, in rebellion, her teenage sweetheart. Iman knew the marriage was a mistake, so that when Peter called with the offer to go to America to become a model, she leapt at the chance—more to escape the marriage than to become a model. In October of 1975, Iman, the

young college student, traveled to New York, where upon her arrival, she thought that her new home was worse than a third world country. New York was in the midst of a garbage strike, the city was filthy and the climate was cold. Iman told Ingrid Sischy writing for *Interview* magazine, "It was worse than any village I saw in Africa."

A publicity blitz that bypassed the customary interview route of aspiring models brought Iman immediate employment with Wilhelmina and with luminary fashion designers, including Bill Blass. Audiences were more likely to crowd showrooms to catch a glimpse of the model-star than to view the clothes in a collection. Instantly attaining international fame, Iman divulged to Konner later in her career, "I'm a ... black model, succeeding in a country that craves blonde, blue-eyed teenagers. I've taken work away from blonde women. I've even taken work away from men. I'm secure within myself—independent, a survivor."

Working with fashion photographers more in partnership than seclusion, Iman applied her own make-up and often styled her own shots while modeling. She also commanded unheard of fees, such as $100,000 for one designer collection. French designer Thierry Mugler described Iman at the top of her profession in *Vogue*, "She feels the atmosphere of the crowd (and holds their attention like nobody else). She knows how to use those hips. I know how to dress them. We go to the extreme together."

Iman's career almost ended in 1983 when she was nearly killed in a taxi cab accident. Her shoulder was dislocated, and she also broke three ribs as well as her collarbone and cheekbones. After she fully recovered, Iman received a merchandising contract to market a line of authentic African fabrics called *kikois*. With an acting career underway by the 1980s, Iman revealed in *Essence*, "I'm a workaholic. I feel that when I wake up in the mornings, if I'm not working, attending acting class, going to the gym ... the world is passing me by. Whatever this rat race is about, I'm a part of it. I'm one of the rats!"

In 1987 Iman divorced basketball star Spencer Haywood. The couple had been married for eight years and had a daughter, Zulekha. In 1989 Iman quit modeling. She simply woke up one day and said to herself, AThis is it. This year I'm closing up shop." A few years later, Iman began dating British rock star David Bowie and married him in a civil ceremony in Lausanne, Switzerland, on April 24, 1992. In November of that year, the model lost a long custody battle with Haywood over their daughter. Craving more children, Iman disclosed in *People*, "I'm an old woman. But I'll try to squeeze one in." After Bowie gave her a 10.5-carat canary diamond to celebrate their union, she had a bowie knife tattooed on her right ankle. After several years of trying to conceive a child, Iman decided to rely on an African custom to stimulate fertility. The custom is to hold another woman's baby. So, Iman borrowed fellow model Christy Brinkley's baby and several months after, she conceived. In August of 2000 Iman and David welcomed the birth of their daughter, Alexandria Zahra Jones.

Iman planned to broaden her acting career beyond the scope of cameo appearances in such motion pictures as *Star Trek VI*. She experimented with videos, including Michael Jackson's "Remember the Time," in which she gave the pop superstar a kiss. She also completed a documentary called *Somalia Diary* for the British Broadcasting Corporation (BBC) about famine in her native country, which she visited for the first time in twenty years in October of 1992. That year a *People* correspondent commented on Iman's enduring beauty: "The face, the frame, the name: all so perfectly exotic (or perhaps, since they all belong to Iman), so perfectly Ixotic." One of the first black models to appear on major magazines covers and lure prestigious cosmetic companies to offer contracts, Iman divulged in *People*, "I'm happy with my life. Everything is going the way I wanted it to."

In 1992 Iman, who always had to mix two or more foundation colors to find the right shade of make up, decided to create a reasonably priced line of cosmetics for women of color. Two years later the line was mass marketed and licensed to "Color Me Beautiful", selling only at J.C. Penney department stores. In 2000 she established a couture cosmetics line for all women, I-Iman, that was sold at Sephora cosmetics stores. Her business ventures have been successful, establishing "ethnic" cosmetics during a decade when many other prominent cosmetics companies followed suit and created their own line of cosmetics for women of color.

In 2001 Iman published her autobiography, *I Am Iman*, not only to convey to the public who she is and where she came from, but to address universal issues such as self-esteem, identity struggles, and the pressures of pop culture. *Essence* described *I Am Iman* as "a strikingly impressive photo-autobiography."

Sources

Black Enterprise, November 1994.
Essence, January 1988; November 2001.
Glamour, September 1989.
Interview, October 1994.
Newsweek, November 2, 1987.
Oakland Press (Oakland County, MI), October 19, 1992.
People, May 4, 1992; May 18, 1992; May 8, 2000.
Vogue, October 1989; December 1992.
WWD, March 3, 2000.

—Marjorie Burgess and Christine Miner Minderovic

Rafer Johnson

1934—

Athlete

When American athlete Rafer Johnson won the gold medal for the decathlon in the 1960 Olympics, he also earned the title of "world's greatest athlete," usually appended to the first-place finisher in this grueling track and field event. Johnson never competed again after his victory, but instead devoted his energies to a career in public service. In 2000 he was a spectator at the Sydney Olympic Games to watch his daughter compete —an honor he deemed more important to him than his gold- medal victory, he told *Sports Illustrated* writer Brian Cazeneuve. "My greatest joy is seeing how my children turned out," declared Johnson.

The future Olympian was born in 1934 into a Texas family of cotton-field laborers, and spent his first few years in a house without electricity or running water. He was the oldest of five children in the family, which moved to Kingsburg, California, a small farming town in the San Joaquin Valley. Though the community was home to residents mainly of Swedish extraction, Johnson recalled that he enjoyed the advantages of living in a small town, and believed it inspired him later in life. "I knew *every* kid in school and they knew me," Johnson told *Los Angeles Times* writer Eric Sondheimer. "You looked after your neighbor, after your

friend. People helped me, people advised me, people corrected me. I always wanted to be this person willing to give something back."

Trained for Olympics

At Kingsburg High School in the early 1950s, Johnson was encouraged by his track coach, Murl Dodson. One day, the student athlete complained to his mentor that he felt he was not fulfilling his potential, so Dodson took Johnson to watch another athlete prepare for a race. The track star was Bob Mathias, also from the San Joaquin Valley, who had won the 1948 Olympic decathlon and was at the time training for the 1952 Games.

It was a turning point for Johnson. "I decided I wanted to be the best in the world, too," Betty Barnacle, a Knight-Ridder/Tribune News Service reporter quoted him as saying. "It wasn't ego. I just wanted to accomplish it and it was a giant step. It was one of the key things that happened to me. Once I told someone what I wanted to be, it freed me as an athlete."

Johnson went on to attend the University of California at Los Angeles, where he was captain of both the track and field teams, and president of the student body as well. He was also the first African American at the school to pledge a national fraternity. In 1956 his athletic talents qualified him for the decathlon event of the Summer Olympic Games, which were held in Melbourne, Australia that year. The decathlon was one of the Olympics' most grueling tests: athletes took part in ten events over a two-day period that included a series of jumps and hurdles as well as the discus throw, shot put, javelin, and pole vault; they also ran a 400-meter race and the final 1500-meter. Johnson took second place and a silver medal.

Classic Olympic Moment

Johnson was such a standout athlete during his college career that *Sports Illustrated* named him "Sportsman of the Year" in 1958. Around this time Johnson began training alongside another standout UCLA track star, C. K. Yang, for the 1960 Summer Olympics in Rome, Italy. At those Games, Johnson served as captain of the

U.S. team, and carried the American flag in the opening ceremonies. His decathlon performance was a memorable one: in the final event, the 1500-meter race, Johnson crossed the finish line visibly exhausted, just steps ahead of Yang. Both men set world decathlon records in event, and Johnson decided to use the opportunity to exit gracefully—he never competed again.

Instead Johnson went to work for People to People International, an American goodwill agency, and acted in films. He was often cast as an African warrior in combat in *Tarzan* pictures of the 1960s, but also appeared in the 1979 mini-series *Roots: The Next Generation*. For a time, he worked as a sports broadcaster, and also devoted his energies to recruiting Peace Corps volunteers. Romantically he was linked to Gloria Steinem, a glamorous and well-known women's rights activist at the time. Johnson also volunteered for Democratic presidential hopeful Robert Kennedy in 1968. When Kennedy won the California primary in June, he and his entourage were passing through the Ambassador Hotel. Shots were fired, and Kennedy fell. Johnson pushed Kennedy's pregnant wife, Ethel, out of harm's way, then lunged toward the gun—along with another unofficial bodyguard, gridiron star Rosey Grier—and disarmed the assailant, Sirhan Sirhan.

Johnson was devastated by the moment, but credited Kennedy's sister, Eunice Kennedy Shriver, for helping him regain some perspective. Shriver and her husband—parents of television journalist Maria Shriver—had recently founded the Special Olympics, a competition for developmentally and physically disabled children and adults. Johnson became a founding board member of the California Special Olympics, and dedicated himself to helping the organization grow to a size of 25,000 participants in 68 programs across the state. Over the years, Johnson has also served on the California State Recreation Commission, a Fair Housing group, and a federal committee on mental retardation.

"Their Own Dreams"

Johnson married Betsy Thorsen in 1971, with whom he had two children. He kept his 1956 silver and 1960 gold medals in a bank vault, and on rare occasions took them out—for show and tell at children's school, or at the school where his wife taught. He felt that to have them—or his other trophies and awards—on display at home might discourage his children from excelling themselves. "I wanted my kids to have their own dreams," Johnson told *Sports Illustrated*'s Cazeneuve. "I'd already done so much." The daughter and son knew little of their father's fame until he drove them to the opening ceremonies of the 1984 Summer Games in Los Angeles. Only then did Johnson reveal to the youngsters, then nine and 11, that he had been asked to light the torch, a great symbolic honor.

In the opening ceremonies, Johnson sprinted up the steep stairs, torch in hand, and lit the flame that marked the formal kick-off of the Games. The 49-year-old received rousing cheers. Recalling the moment, Johnson said that he felt less like himself than he did an "Olympian" instead, as he told *Sports Illustrated* writer Robert Sullivan. When he came out of the stadium tunnel of the Los Angeles Coliseum, he observed "something special going on. As I ran I could see tears in the eyes of some of the athletes. I felt a part of all those great Olympians on the field. I was tied to all those in the stands. I think the torch run may be the great legacy of these Olympic Games. I think it tied us together and made it all warm—a feeling of binding us all together," he told Sullivan.

Still, the athlete recalled in another interview that it was a shaky moment. Johnson said that he "nearly fell off," according to *Independent Sunday* journalist Ronald Atkin. "I would have done if they hadn't put a fibreglass pole up there for me to hold on to. We had practised a few times but I had never seen the stadium all dressed up and full of people. It was an incredible sight."

Second Generation of Olympians

In 1995 Johnson revisited the stadium in Rome where he won his gold medal when he took part in a documentary film on Olympic history. He and the silver medallist that day, Yang, have remained friends over the years, and Johnson is also close to his brother, Jimmy, who played for the San Francisco 49ers. Johnson's children recalled that the 1984 torch-lighting honor ignited "Olympic fever" in both of them: both Jennifer and Josh attended their father's alma mater, UCLA, where Josh excelled in javelin and almost qualified for the 2000 Olympic team. Jenny, wife of former UCLA gridiron star Kevin Jordan, became a standout professional beach volleyball, and competed in the 2000 Sydney Games. A proud father accompanied her to the Games. "I've never played volleyball, so I can't tell her what to do, although she wouldn't listen to me anyway," Johnson said in an interview with Knight-Ridder/Tribune News Service reporter Chris Tomasson. Johnson-Jordan noted that her father's humble attitude had always been a positive influence in her life. "My dad never talked about what he had accomplished, and that took a lot of pressure off me," she told Tomasson.

Johnson lives in Sherman Oaks, California, but returns to Kingsburg occasionally for events at Rafer Johnson

Junior High School. He is the author of a 1998 memoir, *The Best That I Can Be*, in which he credited those who encouraged him or did not allow prejudice to stand in the way of helping him in his athletic career. He also, however, recalled certain hardships. His father was an alcoholic who sometimes came to his track events drunk. "I came to dread the weekends," Johnson wrote in his autobiography. "It was as if there were two of him: The kind, hard-working family man who showed affection for his wife and children, and the hell-raising drunk who would stay out 'til all hours and come home with a chip on his shoulder, slamming doors and roaring at the top of his lungs, ready to pull my mother out of bed and beat her at the slightest provocation."

The Best That I Can Be earned positive reviews. A *Publishers Weekly* review noted that while Johnson's recounting of incidents of racism was "inevitable" in such a book, "his tone is candid, rarely displaying rancor when recalling even recent racism or when discussing the disapproval of his interracial marriage." *Booklist*'s Wes Lukowsky noted that many contemporary biographies have an element of the scandalous that is publicized to boost sales, but Johnson's story "will stand out as unique because it is the autobiography of an uncommonly decent, ethical, and likable man."

Selected writings

(With Philip Goldberg) *The Best That I Can Be* (autobiography), Doubleday, 1998.

Sources

Booklist, July 1998, p. 1826.
Fresno Bee, June 9, 1996, p. D1; February 11, 1999, p. E1.
Independent Sunday, (London, England), September 17, 2000, p. 6.
Knight-Ridder/Tribune News Service, November 6, 1997; September 13, 2000; September 22, 2000.
Library Journal, July 19998, p. 99.
Los Angeles Times, November 5, 1997, p. 3; May 9, 2000, p. D1.
People, July 10, 2000, p. 149.
Publishers Weekly, June 29, 1998, p. 44.
Sports Illustrated, August 20, 1984, p. 96; September 11, 2000, p. 20.

—Carol Brennan

Leontine Kelly

1920—

Religious leader

A highly respected religious leader, Leontine Kelly was the first African-American woman to be elected bishop of a prominent Christian denomination. The Methodist church approved the ordination of women as ministers in 1956, and in 1984 Kelly, at the age of 64, was elected bishop, becoming only the second woman and first African-American Methodist bishop. Her duties included supervising the California and Nevada conferences of the United Methodist church, which consisted of approximately 100,000 members.

Born to the Reverend David DeWitt Turpeau, Sr. and Ila (Marshall) Turpeau in Washington, D.C. on March 5, 1920, Leontine was the seventh of eight children. The Turpeau family left Washington, D.C., lived in Pittsburgh for two years, and then settled in Cincinnati by the time Leontine was ten years old. Leontine's father was an ordained Methodist Episcopal minister who served as the district superintendent, a post that is one rank below bishop. Her mother, Ila, a community leader and a co-founder of the Urban League in Cincinnati, was the first African American to have served on the Cincinnati Camp Fire Girls Committee. In 1970 the *Cincinnati Enquirer* named Ila one of the outstanding women of the year. Both parents were supporters of the NAACP and worked hard to develop a dialogue between segregated communities.

It was in Cincinnati that Kelly first learned that the role of the church extended beyond providing a place for people to gather and worship. She also learned that the parsonage in which the family lived had been a station on the Underground Railroad, and still contained the

tunnel that led to the church. Her father was an role model to Kelly. A dedicated man who felt that it was the duty of all Christians to be socially and politically active, Reverend Turpeau always supported political, cultural, and economic activities in the communities where he worked as a pastor. Although the religious community in which Kelly grew up was segregated, her father insisted that it was the duty of the African-American churchgoers to be, according to africanpubs.com, "racial missionaries" to white churches, and to act as positive role models to facilitate a change in attitude toward the African-American community.

Kelly attended the Harriet Beecher Stowe School, where Jennie D. Porter was principal. Porter was the first African-American principal in Cincinnati and the first African-American to earn a Ph.D. at the University of Cincinnati. Her message to the schoolchildren was that gender and race are not and should not be barriers to success. As a young woman, Kelly also admired Mary McLeod Bethune, and as an adult woman she modeled herself after Bethune by using her position of authority to educate.

After attending Woodward High School, Kelly went to West Virginia State College. Having completed her junior year, she quit school, married Gloster Bryant Current, and started a family. Current was a religious man who, before marriage, played in and directed his own orchestra. Following his marriage to Kelly, he held various posts for the NAACP, and worked as an assistant pastor in two United Methodist churches. In the mid-1950s, Kelly and her husband divorced.

At a Glance . . .

Born Leontine Turpeau on March 5, 1920, in Washington, D.C.; married Gloster Bryant Current (divorced); married James David Kelly, 1958; children: Angella Patricia Current, Gloster Bryant Current, Jr., John David Current, Pamela Kelly (adopted). *Religion*: Methodist Episcopal.

Career: Schoolteacher; Virginia Conference Council on Ministries, staff member; Asbury Hill United Methodist Church, Richmond, VA, pastor, 1976-83; United Methodist Church, Nashville, TN, national staff, 1983-84; California-Nevada Conference, San Francisco, CA, bishop, 1984-89.

Awards: Grass Root Leadership Award (SCLC), 1981; honorary doctorate, Garrett Evangelical Theological Seminary, 1984.

Addresses: *Office*—330 Ellis, San Francisco, California, United States 94102.

Deeply affected by the divorce, Kelly turned to meditation and Bible study, which considerably strengthened her faith.

In 1956 Leontine married James David Kelly, a Methodist minister. Two years later, the family moved to Richmond, Virginia, where Kelly completed her B.A. at Virginia Union University. She became a social studies teacher and a lay speaker in the Methodist church. In 1966 the Kelly family moved to Edwardsville, Virginia, where the Galilee United Methodist Church had hired James. Kelly herself was very active in the church and became a popular speaker. When James Kelly died, in 1969, the congregation of Galilee Church asked Leontine, to her surprise, to take her husband's place. Until that time, Kelly had never considered joining the ministry even though she had been surrounded by pastors all her life.

Kelly accepted the challenge and began theological studies, receiving her masters of divinity degree from the Union Theological Seminary, in Richmond, in 1976. During her studies Kelly remained at the Galilee church until 1975 when she became the director of social ministries for the Virginia Conference Council of Ministries. In 1977 she was appointed pastor of Asbury Hill United Methodist Church, where she stayed until 1983. During her time at Asbury Hill, the congregation doubled. She became a member of the national staff of the United Methodist Church and served as the Board of Discipleship's evangelism executive.

Only highly esteemed ministers are considered for the position of bishop, and Kelly's years in the ministry, as well as her years serving as a national staff member made her an excellent candidate. She was first identified in 1982 as a likely successor to the first female bishop, Marjorie Swank Matthews, who was, according to church rules, expected to retire in 1984. In 1984 Kelly was nominated for, and elected bishop. She also made history by being one of two or three bishops to have been, according to africanpubs.com, "elected bishop by one jurisdiction while serving as a member in a different jurisdiction."

Kelly retired as bishop in 1988, after four years of service. In 2000 Kelly was inducted into the National Women's Hall of Fame. Her adopted daughter, Pamela Kelly, nominated Kelly for the honor. Also in 2000 in honor of Kelly's eightieth birthday, the family established a scholarship fund at United Methodist-related Africa University in her name. In a speech at the 15th World Conference, Bishop Desmond Tutu, according to africanpubs.com, said the following about Kelly: "I would like to give you one very good theological reason why women ought not to be ordained, least of all made bishops. It is Bishop Kelly. She was superb ... She really made men understand why women say that when God created man she was experimenting!"

Sources

http://www.africanpubs.com/Apps/bios/1139Kelly Leontine.asp
http://www.black-collegian.com/afroican/trailblzr.shtml
http://umns.umc.org/00/oct/493.htm

—Christine Miner Minderovic

Florynce Kennedy

1916-2000

Lawyer, political activist, lecturer

Flo Kennedy has had a remarkably long and visible career as a lawyer, militant activist, and feminist. Since the 1950s, when as an attorney she fought for royalty rights due the estates of musical legends Billie Holiday and Charlie Parker, Kennedy has unflinchingly attacked racism, inequity, and hypocrisy wherever she has found it. An original member of the National Organization for Women (NOW) and the founder of the Feminist Party, Kennedy has been a vocal spokesperson for women, blacks, homosexuals, and other minorities, and a staunch defender of civil rights. Variously called outspoken, outrageous, profane, and a woman of "immeasurable spirit," Kennedy was once described in *People* as "the biggest, loudest, and indisputably, the rudest mouth on the battleground where feminist activists and radical politics join in mostly common cause." Fellow feminist and friend, Gloria Steinem, has said that for those in the black movement, the women's movement, the peace movement, and the consumer movement, "Flo was a political touchstone—a catalyst." Steinem, founder of *Ms.* magazine, also claimed that "Five minutes with Flo will change your life."

Born Florynce Rae Kennedy on February 11, 1916 in Kansas City, Missouri, she was the second of Wiley and Zella Kennedy's five daughters. Wiley was first a Pullman porter with the railroad and later owned a taxi business. Zella worked outside the home only during the Depression. Neither parent was very strict, and Kennedy wrote in her autobiography, *Color Me Flo: My Hard Life and Good Times,* that her parents' protective attitudes combined to make her and her sisters feel very special. "All of us had such a sense of security because we were almost never criticized," she

recalled. She has suggested that her upbringing contributed significantly to her anti-Establishment outlook. "I suspect that that's why I don't have the right attitude toward authority today, because we were taught very early in the game that we didn't have to respect the teachers, and if they threatened to hit us we could just act as if they weren't anybody we had to pay any attention to," she wrote. She learned from her father that sometimes it is necessary to go to extreme measures to defend oneself. Kennedy remembers that her father showed up at school with a gun because the principal had threatened to whip her, and that her father once stood up to the Klu Klux Klan with a shotgun in hand.

Kennedy's childhood, while not always prosperous, was a happy time. Zella instilled both tenacity and optimism in her daughter. "Zella never accepted poverty, and yet she didn't resent it either, and we laughed a lot when we were really desperately poor," Kennedy wrote of her mother in *Color Me Flo.* "She always made an effort to maintain some kind of esthetic surroundings.... She was determined to have rose bushes, although our yard had too much shade.... But every year Zella decided she was going to have grass and roses.... We never had a single rose from any of those bushes, yet she persisted in going out and buying them. It was Zella who epitomized hope for us—she never gave up."

Aimed for Law School

Kennedy graduated from Lincoln High School in Kansas City at the top of her class, but she did not

At a Glance . . .

Born Florynce Rae Kennedy on February 11, 1916, in Kansas City, MO; died December 21, 2001, in New York; daughter of Wiley (a Pullman porter and taxi owner) and Zella Kennedy; married Charles Dudley Dye (a writer), 1957 (deceased). *Education:* Columbia University, B.A., 1948, J.D., 1951.

Career: Lawyer, political activist, lecturer, author. Lawyer in private practice in New York, NY, 1954-66; founder and director of Media Workshop and Consumer Information Service, 1966; founder and director of Feminist Party, 1970; national director, Voters, Artists, Anti-Nuclear Activist and Consumers for Political Action and Communication Coalition (VAC-PAC); national director, Ladies Aid and Trade Crusade.

Member: National Organization for Women 1966-70; New York Bar Association.

immediately go on to college. Although she felt that one day she probably would attend college, opportunities for higher education for blacks were limited "really kind of unheard-of," she stated. Instead, Kennedy opened a hat shop in Kansas City with her sisters, an enterprise that was fun, if not exceptionally prosperous. While Kennedy admitted she may have been "a little more outspoken, a little crazier than the rest" in high school, she was more interested in boys than politics. Within a few years of graduation, however, she was involved in her first political action. She helped organize a boycott when the local Coca- Cola bottler refused to hire black truck drivers.

Following her mother's death from cancer, Kennedy and her sister Grayce moved to New York in 1942. Ignoring those who advised her to become a teacher or a nurse at City College, Kennedy enrolled at Columbia University in 1944 as a pre-law student. She supported herself working at various part-time jobs. She explained her decision in 1976: "I thought anybody with the brains and energy to become a teacher ought to want to become something better." She elaborated, "I find that the higher you aim the better you shoot, and even if it seems you're way beyond yourself ... it always turns out that you can do a lot more than you thought you could." When in her senior year she again aimed high, attempting a concurrent enrollment at Columbia Law School, she was refused admission. Told she had been rejected not because she was black but because she was a woman, Kennedy was no less incensed. She promptly wrote the dean a letter suggesting the move was racially motivated and hinting that a lawsuit might

follow. In 1948 she was admitted to the law school, one of eight women and the only black member of her class. She received her B.A. in 1948 and was awarded her law degree in 1951.

After law school Kennedy clerked with the law firm of Hartman, Sheridan, and Tekulsky, and she was admitted to the bar in 1952. By 1954 she had opened an office on Madison Avenue. It was rough going at times, and she had to take a job at Bloomingdale's one Christmas in order to pay the rent. The late 1950s brought Don Wilkes, a law partner, and Charles "Charlie" Dye, a Welsh writer ten years her junior whom she married in 1957. Neither relationship was to last long. After several disappointing legal defeats, Wilkes ran off with most of the firm's assets, leaving Kennedy over $50,000 in debt. Although Dye was very supportive during this crisis, the marriage was rocky due to his alcoholism, and he died soon after.

Activism Began With Media Workshop

Before Wilkes left, the firm had taken on a case for blues singer Billie Holiday. When Holiday died, Kennedy continued to represent the estate, and later she represented the estate of jazz great Charlie Parker as well. In both situations Kennedy successfully fought the record companies to recover money from royalties and sales due the estates. Kennedy's experience with this estate work signaled the beginning of her disillusionment with law. "Handling the Holiday and Parker estates taught me more than I was really ready for about government and business delinquency and the hostility and helplessness of the courts," she wrote in her memoir. She continued: "Not only was I not earning a decent living, there began to be a serious question in my mind whether practicing law could ever be an effective means of changing society or even of simple resistance to oppression."

As a result of these experiences, as well as her conviction that a government conspiracy shrouded the assassination of President Kennedy, the enterprising attorney began to reassess her ability to effect social change through the judicial system. In 1966 Kennedy set up the Media Workshop in order to fight racism in media and advertising. When Benton and Bowles, a large ad agency, refused to provide the Workshop with requested hiring and programming information, the group picketed the Fifth Avenue office. "After that they invited us upstairs," Kennedy recalled, "and ever since I've been able to say, 'When you want to get to the suites, start in the streets.'"

Thus began Kennedy's career as an activist. She was highly visible in this role during the 1960s, picketing the Colgate-Palmolive building with members of NOW, and also protesting at WNEW-TV. The group's media protest led them to CBS, where they were arrested for refusing to leave the building. Eventually CBS withdrew the complaint.

In 1966 Kennedy represented activist H. Rap Brown and was present at the four Black Power Conferences, and at the Black political caucuses as well. She also attended the first meeting of the fledgling National Association for Women, but she was soon disappointed by NOW's reluctance to go head-to-head with the issues of the day. "I saw the importance of a feminist movement, and stayed in there because I wanted to do anything I could to keep it alive, but when I saw how retarded NOW was, I thought, 'My God, who needs this?'" In November of 1971 Kennedy founded the Feminist Party. Its first action was to support Shirley Chisholm's presidential candidacy. Nothing was to big for Flow to tackle. Kennedy, who coined the oft repeated phrase, "If men could get pregnant, abortion would be a sacrament" sued the Roman Catholic church in 1968 for interfering with efforts to liberalize abortion laws. The following year, she organized a group of people to challenge the constitutionality of New York's abortion law, which was subsequently liberalized in 1970.

Launched a Speaking Career

The speaking career that would take Kennedy through the next two decades began in 1967 at an anti-war convention in Montreal. She became incensed when Black Panther Bobby Seale was not allowed to speak. She wrote in her memoir: "I went berserk. I took the platform and started yelling and hollering." An invitation to speak in Washington followed, and her lecturing career was born. Kennedy's activist and speaking careers continued throughout the 1970s and 1980s, and included the Coat Hanger Farewell Protest on the abortion issue, anti-Nixon demonstrations, picketing Avon International for support for the three-hour *Celebrate Women* TV program, the MAMA March—the March Against Media Arrogance—and the organization of a demonstration, a "pee-in," at Harvard University protesting the lack of women's restrooms. In 1971 Kennedy co-authored *Abortion Rap* with Diane Schulder, and in 1981 she wrote *Sex Discrimination in Employment: An Analysis and Guide for Practitioner and Student,* with William F. Pepper. She was national director of Voters, Artists, Anti-Nuclear Activists and Consumers for Political Action and Communications Coalition (VAC-PAC) and also national director of the Ladies Aid and Trade Crusade. According to a *Jet* magazine article published in 1986, these organizations' "commandments" include "Thou Shall Not Use Our Dollars to Finance Racism and Sexism on Network Television." Kennedy, who called herself

"radicalism's rudest mouth," challenged military spending, suggesting that the government had contracted a new social disease, "Pentagonorrhea."

In 1986 Kennedy was "roasted" by friends and colleagues at a 70th birthday party in New York City. Among those honoring her at the event were activist Dick Gregory and civil rights attorney William Kunstler. That Flo Kennedy's career has lengthened to four decades is no surprise when one considers her approach to activism. She described her philosophy about her struggles and victories in her autobiography as being "like a successful bath; you don't expect not to take another bath.... Countermovements among racists and sexists and nazifiers are just as relentless as dirt on a coffee table.... Every housewife knows that if you don't sooner or later dust ... the whole place will be dirty again."

Known for her flamboyant attire, which included her "signature" cowboy hat and pink sunglasses, Kennedy remained active, even from her bed. During the last few years of her life, she was bedridden due to a number of health conditions, but was still going after large organizations. At age 81, she was involved in a sexual harassment case against a large civil rights organization, the National Urban League. She died in New York, at the age of 84.

Selected writings

(With Diane Schulder) *Abortion Rap,* McGraw Hill, 1971.
Color Me Flo: My Hard Life and Good Times, Prentice-Hall, 1976.
(With William F. Pepper) *Sex Discrimination in Employment: An Analysis and Guide for Practitioner and Student,* Michie Co. (Charlottesville, VA), 1981.

Sources

Books

Kennedy, Flo, *Color Me Flo: My Hard Life and Good Times,* Prentice-Hall, 1976.
Notable Black American Women, Gale, 1992.

Periodicals

Essence, May 1995, p. 140.
Jet, March 31, 1986, p. 6; January 15, 2001, p. 18.
Los Angeles Times, December 28, 2000, p. B8.
off our backs, February 2001, p. 16.
People, April 14, 1974, p. 54.

—Ellen Dennis French and Christine Miner Minderovic

Dany Laferriere

1953—

Writer

The unconventional and controversial novelist Dany Laferriere has chronicled for North American audiences the nightmarish atmosphere of the Duvalier dictatorship that terrorized the Caribbean island nation of Haiti in the 1970s and 1980s. Laferriere experienced the terrible events of his homeland firsthand, fleeing Haiti for his life in 1978. Yet Laferriere has also trained a keen eye on his adopted North American home. Living first in Montreal, Canada, and then in Miami, he has produced novels and other less classifiable writings that satirize North American sexual attitudes and examine relationships between the races.

Laferriere was born in the Haitian capital of Port-au-Prince on April 13, 1953. His father, Windsor, was a Haitian politician who ran afoul of the government and was eventually exiled. Many of Laferriere's writings are autobiographical, and his 1991 novel *L'odeur du café* (The Aroma of Coffee) is thought to represent his own childhood; its central figure is a ten-year-old boy whose grandmother is steeped in Haiti's traditional belief system. Laferriere became a journalist in the 1970s.

That was a difficult position to hold during the dictatorship of Haitian leader Jean-Claude ("Baby Doc") Duvalier, one of a family dynasty of leaders whose power was ruthlessly guarded by a secret paramilitary police force known as the *tontons macoutes*. Laferriere co-founded a weekly magazine called *Le petit samedi soir*, but when his friend and associate Raymond Gasner was found murdered in 1978, he left Haiti and settled in French-speaking Montreal, Canada.

Delivered Nude Weather Forecast

Despite that point of connection, life in Montreal was harsh and alien for Laferriere. During his first year there, he recalled in a book of poetic memoirs entitled *A Drifting Year*, he occasionally was forced to dine on "steak on the wing"—on pigeons he trapped in a city park. For several years Laferriere worked in a tannery—an industrial plant that processes animal hides—while beginning to write. His wit began to attract attention among educated Montrealers, and his situation improved rapidly. During a stint as a television weatherman he startled viewers by delivering the forecast in the nude. In 1985 Laferriere's first novel was published; entitled *Comment faire l'amour avec un Nègre sans se fatiguer* (How to Make Love to a Negro Without Getting Tired), it described, like many of his other works, aspects of his own experiences.

The novel's central character is a young writer, named Man, who shares a Montreal apartment with an African roommate, Bouba, who spends much of his time listening to jazz and reading the Koran. Laferriere's novel examines white North American stereotypes of blacks and focuses the reader's eye on the experiences of those at the bottom of the social hierarchy, framing these issues largely within a series of sexual relationships the two men have with white women in Montreal.

Novel Translated into English

The book's subject matter stirred some controversy, but it was positively reviewed and was soon translated into

English and published in the United States as *How to Make Love to a Negro*. Despite the troubles Laferriere had lived through and the serious nature of the issues addressed in his writing, much of his work is marked by a certain desperate humor (well captured by his regular translator David Homel), and *How to Make Love to a Negro* was no exception. Structured like many of Laferriere's other books as a series of short, sharp observations, the book announced a major new talent.

Laferriere's novel was made into a film that was shown without incident in French Canada, but its English title, intended as satirical, stirred protests when the film was released in the United States in 1990. The *New York Times* refused to run ads for the film, which fell out of sight after a few showings. That year, Laferriere gave up on Montreal's long winters and moved to Miami, a city with a large Haitian population. He still speaks French much better than English and continued to play a role in Montreal's literary life. "My heart is in Port-au-Prince. My spirit is here in Montreal. My body is in Miami," he explained to the Montreal *Gazette*. "When I want political drama, I'll go to Haiti. For intellectual discussion, I need Montreal. For real crime, there's Miami."

Returned to Haiti

Laferriere's second novel, *Eroshima* (1991) continued to explore the theme of interracial relationships, de-

picting a romance that develops between a black man and a Japanese woman. Many of Laferriere's novels and other writings, however, have returned to his own experiences. Laferriere returned several times in the 1990s to a somewhat freer Haiti, and several of his books consist of innovatively structured reflections on his home country. *Down Among the Dead Men* (1997) is divided into sections designated as "Real Country" and "Dream Country"—the "real" sections depict Laferriere's reunions with his mother and friends, while the dream sequences treat the Haitian rituals of voodoo and the widespread belief in zombies.

Behind all the wit and satire in Laferriere's writing lies a concern with the effects of poverty on the psyches of the world's downtrodden. "If we were really human beings," a Haitian tells him after he asks about zombies, "do you think we could survive this famine, and those heaps of garbage and trash you see at every street corner?...Here, there are no good people or bad people—there are just dead people." Laferriere's 1996 novel *Pays Sans Chapeau* (A Country Without a Hat)—the title refers to the Haitian belief that no one should be buried in a hat, which might block the path of the deceased to the afterlife—is set in Haiti, and his first book of the new millennium, *Le cri des oiseaux fous* (The Cry of the Crazy Birds), is a depiction of the last 24 hours the author spent in Port-au-Prince before leaving for Montreal in 1976.

Not withstanding his focus on Haiti, Laferriere, who lives in Miami with his wife and three daughters, aged 20, 15, and 10 in 2001 ("our five-year plan," he once explained to the Montreal *Gazette*), has continued to unleash sharp observations of North American culture. *Why Must a Black Writer Write About Sex* (1994) was an uncategorizable mix of fiction, commentary, and satire in which Laferriere, among other things, imagines a conversation with author James Baldwin. Baldwin explains that he is one of only a few black people in heaven—the others "decided to choose hell ... they felt more comfortable with the familiar." Despite the failure of his initial foray into movies, Laferriere has been reported to be at work on several other film scripts, one of them an adaptation of his novel *Dining with the Dictator*.

Selected writings

Comment faire l'amour avec un Nègre sans se fatiguer (How to Make Love to a Negro), 1985, trans. 1987.
Eroshima, 1991.
L'odeur du café (The Aroma of Coffee), 1991, trans. 1993.
Le gout des jeunes filles (trans. as Dining with the Dictator), 1992.
Cette grenade dans la main du jeune, est-elle un arme ou un fruit? (trans as. Why Must a Black Writer Write About Sex?), 1993.
Chronique de la derive douce (trans. as A Drifting Year), 1994, trans. 1996.

Pays sans chapeau (trans. as Down Among the Dead Men), 1996, trans. 1997.
Le charme des après-mide sans fin (The Charm of the Endless Afternoon), 1997.
Le cri des oiseaux fous (The Cry of the Crazy Birds), 2001.

Sources

Periodicals

The Gazette (Montreal, Quebec, Canada), June 8, 1996, p. H1; December 13, 1997, p. H3.
Maclean's, December 26, 1994, p. 35.
Ottawa Citizen, November 9, 1997, p. E4.
Publishers Weekly, September 6, 1993, p. 87; October 31, 1994, pp. 57 58.
Toronto Star, November 8, 1997, p. M18; January 9, 1999, Entertainment section.
Washington Post, July 6, 1990, p. N43.
World Literature Today, Spring 2001, p. 307.

On-line

Contemporary Authors Online, The Gale Group, 2001. Reproduced in *Biography Resource Center,* Gale, 2001, http://www.galenet.com/servlet/Bio RC

—James M. Manheim

Willie Lanier

1945—

Football player, businessman

Throughout his illustrious professional football career, Willie Lanier displayed the ferocity and tenacity that made him the preeminent linebacker of his time. Playing for the Kansas City Chiefs during a time when the middle linebacker position was considered a thinking position—and, therefore, exclusive to white players—Lanier broke through the color barrier. According to chiefswarpath.com, Chiefs owner Lamar Hunt was quoted as saying about Lanier, "His destiny was to be the prototype middle linebacker of his era."

Willie Lanier was born in Clover, Virginia, on August 21, 1945. He attended Maggie Walker High School in Richmond, Virginia. Upon graduation, Lanier had planned to attend Virginia State University, study business administration, and find a job somewhere in central Virginia. Professional football was not a part of this original plan. However, Lanier, seeing a more racially tolerant environment in the North, decided that he would rather attend Morgan State University, in Baltimore, Maryland. Since he also wanted to play on the college's football team, Lanier telephoned Morgan State coach Earl "Pappa Bear" Banks. "He told me that there was no scholarship available, and I told him I wasn't looking for a scholarship," Lanier told the

Times-Dispatch. "I told him I just wanted to go to school to get an education."

Banks invited Lanier to take the Morgan State entrance exam. Lanier obliged, and promptly scored in the top ten percent of the entire incoming freshman class. Without a scholarship, Lanier financed his first semester with a student loan and a work-study arrangement. On the football field, he made a name for himself, his play from 1963 to 1966 ranking him among the greatest players to have ever played at Morgan State. He eventually earned an athletic scholarship, and through this success on the field, his dedication to his studies remained intact. He completed his education in four years, earning a degree in business administration. "You were supposed to graduate in four years," Lanier told the *Times-Dispatch.* "That was the expectation. Everybody did it at that time, and there was no question why you were in school."

Lanier earned his degree in 1967, and was selected by the Kansas City Chiefs in the second round draft. Nicknamed "Honey Bear" by his teammates, Lanier was tough as nails on the football field. He was also nicknamed, "Contact." "I always had a history of being someone who played the game physically and would be

At a Glance . . .

Born William Lanier on August 21, 1945, in Clover, VA. *Education*: Morgan State University, business administration degree; University of Missouri-Kansas City, graduate school, attended.

Career: Kansas City Chiefs, 1967-77; Wheat First Union, senior vp and capital markets liaison, currently.

Memberships: Virginia State University, board of visitors; United Way of Greater Richmond; YMCA; The Garfield Child's Fund; WCVE Public TV, Central Virginia; Industrial Development Authority of Chesterfield County; Huddle House, Inc, board of directors.

Awards: NFL Man of the Year, 1972; Linebacker of the Year, NFL Player's Association, 1970-75; Chiefs' Super Bowl IV, Defensive Star; All AFL/AFC, seven times; played in two AFL All Star Games; six Pro Bowls; elected to Kansas City Chiefs, Hall of Fame, 1985; Pro Football Hall of Fame, 1986; Virginia Sports Hall of Fame, 1986; NFL 75th Anniversary Team, 1995; Virginian of the Year, 1986.

Addresses: *Office*—Wheat First Union, Senior Vice President and Capital Markets Liaison, 901 E Byrd St, 5th Flr, Richmond, Virginia, United States 23219 (804) 649-2311.

very much involved in hard tackles," Lanier told the *NFL Insider*. "You start with a high degree of intelligence about what it takes to perform and how to protect yourself and make sure that you play every game of every season at a very high level...."

During his professional career, Lanier had 27 interceptions and 15 fumble recoveries. He also played in the Super Bowl IV, in which the Chiefs defeated the Minnesota Vikings, 23-7. While Lanier's numbers looked impressive, nothing showed his true colors as a player than a goal line stand in the AFL Divisional Playoff Game against the Super Bowl champion New York Jets. Thanks to Lanier's leadership, the Jets were able to earn only a field goal and were defeated by the Chiefs. Against the Vikings, the Chiefs weren't pre-

dicted to win, but Lanier, teamed with such veteran stars as defensive tackle Buck Buchanan and linebackers Bobby Bell and Jim Lynch, created one of the AFC's top defenses. "The Kansas City defense only gave up 20 points in three (playoff victories over) the New York Jets, Oakland, and then Minnesota," Lanier told the *NFL Insider*.

Lanier retired from football following the 1977 season. He had amassed some great honors, including being named to the first six AFC-NFC Pro Bowl games. In 1971 Lanier was named the Defensive Most Valuable Player. He was inducted in the Chiefs's Ring of Honor in 1984—the ring is displayed around the upper deck facing at Arrowhead Stadium. In 1986 Lanier was inducted in the Pro Football Hall Of Fame. Finally, in 1999 Lanier was named one of the middle linebackers on "Dr. Z's All-Century Team." Lanier was also named one of *The Sporting News*'s 100 Greatest Players. "Playing in the Super Bowl and being inducted into the Hall of Fame were caps on my athletic career," Lanier told the *Times-Dispatch*. "But I never saw them as caps on my life."

Unlike many athletes of his time, Lanier's transition away from football was smooth. One of the first post-football things that Lanier did was enroll in the graduate school at the University of Missouri-Kansas City. "That's what other students with business degrees were doing," Lanier told the *Times- Dispatch*. "I didn't see any reason why I should be any different." Employed as senior vice president and capital markets liaison with Wheat First Union in Richmond, Virginia, Lanier has spent the past 21 years in the investment business. He has also, along with NFL Hall of Famer Jim Brown, explored the possibility of formulating the first black-owned NASCAR team.

Sources

Books

Who's Who Among African Americans, 14th ed. Gale Group, 2001.

Periodicals

NFL Insider, January 28, 2001.
The Charlotte Observer, February 13, 1999.
Sports Illustrated, August 30, 1999.
Times-Dispatch (Richmond, VA), 1998.

On-line

www.chiefswarpath.com
The Sporting News, www.sportingnews.com

Denise Lewis

1972—

Olympian

As a young girl growing up in Britain, Denise Lewis had fantasies of fame and glamour in the worlds of song, dance or acting. She became a household name, but not via the arts. The youngster blossomed into a gifted and beautiful woman, one who would earn Olympic gold in perhaps its toughest event, thanks to a constant effort of training, sacrifice and intense focus.

Born August 27, 1972 in West Bromwich, England, Lewis would sing and dance for her mother in their living room, dreaming of stardom. Raised exclusively by her Jamaican-born mother, Lewis' father left the family before she was born. By the time she was 15, track and field training was the biggest part of her life. In an article written by Ted Kessler for London's *The Observer*, a vivid portrait of a determined young athlete is painted. "Now Denise is 15. It's neither raining nor snowing in Birmingham this evening, which is good. But it is sleeting, which is bad. Worse, Denise is outside and alone in the dark, pounding round an empty running track.... She could be with her school friends down the precinct, chasing boys and learning to smoke.... But she's here, running determinedly in circles, cold, wet, lonely."

Always competitive as a youth, Lewis harnessed it in a way that helped foster her talent. In primary school, she'd organize lunchtime races against the fastest boy. During her high school years, Lewis was so determined and focused, she participated in any sport offered to her. "I was good at them all," she told the *Observer*. "And I was a big fan of Jackie Joyner-Kersee, and battles that Daley (Thompson) had in the decathalon

with Jurgen Hingsen, so the heptathlon seemed the natural thing for me to do." She pleaded with her mother to be formally trained in track. Her mother hired Darrell Bunn. Her perseverance and dedication meant a 90-minute journey on two buses and one train straight after school and she rarely got home before nine, but she loved all the discipline she attempted.

The heptathlon is one of the most grueling endurance events in women's track and field, if not all sports in general. Over a two-day span entrants participate in seven events with escalating points awarded based on placement. The higher the place in each event, the more points awarded. The winner is the one with the most accumulated points after the last event. The day's first events consisted of the 100-meter hurdles, the high jump, shot put and 200-meter dash. The second day featured the long jump, the javelin throw and the 800-meter run. An intensely physical regimen requiring a hard-to-come-by mix of bursting speed, tremendous upper-body strength, endurance and an extremely high tolerance of pain. For this, Lewis was becoming a prodigy.

Lewis placed fifth at the European Junior Olympics in 1991. The next year, she finished 19th in the long jump at the European Championships, but stunned everyone when she beat the event's recordholder in the long jump one month later at the Commonwealth Games. She said that would be the point of realization for her. "When I won gold there I had a word with myself," she explained to the *Observer*, 'Denise, you are actually better than you think you are. Get with it

At a Glance . . .

Born August 27, 1972 in West Bromwich, England; one child.

Career: Heptathlete. Olympics, bronze medalist, 1996, gold medalist, heptathlon, 2000; World Championships, seventh place, 1995, second place, 1997; European Junior Championships, fifth place, 1991.

Awards: Awarded OBE, 2001.

girl!' She stopped going to nightclubs and kicked her focus and desire into high gear. "I'm ambitious, I'm determined, I set high standards for myself."

Her competitive nature would vault her up the track and field ranks. In 1995 she finished seventh at the World Championships. In 1996 she was third at the Atlanta Olympics. Later at Gotzis, Austria, she broke the UK record with 6,645 points and finished as the second-ranked heptathlete in the world. She saw more accolades and continued improvement in 1997, breaking the UK and Commonwealth records, placing second in the World Championships. A nagging ankle injury created a slow start in 1998, but she did win the European Championships. And when she finally walked away with Olympic gold at the 2000 games in Sydney, Australia, Lewis had the unmistakable claim as one of the top female athletes in the world.

In an interview with Alison Kervin at www.btinternet.com, Lewis' post-Olympic image was detailed as forever changed. And despite being known mainly for her track and field accomplishments, readers are reminded of Denise Lewis, the person, rather than the athlete.

"Since she hobbled over the line to complete the 800 metres in Sydney and win heptathlon gold, her life has changed beyond measure." "People knew who I was before, but that's different from being famous," Lewis told Kervin.

Her success also brought about a new world of opportunities. She was invited to model clothes and endorse various types of women's wear for English designers. The British Broadcasting Company (BBC) began discussions with her in 2001 to become a new sports correspondent. Perhaps most importantly, Lewis began focusing on life after sports in 2001, specifically, those involving the pitter patter of little feet. On November 2, 2001, the BBC reported that Lewis was pregnant and may miss the 2002 Commonwealth Games in Manchester. The 2000 Olympic gold medallist and her partner, Belgian sprinter Patrick Stevens, are expecting their first child in April of 2002.

As for her future Lewis told *The Observer* that she has a vision of how things might pan out. "She's in her early 50s. She's still looking good and feeling fit. She's a mother of three kids, living somewhere warm by the sea." If Lewis, who applied an immense amount of time and energy into making her previous dreams come true and attain the impressive goal of an Olympic gold medal and the recognition of being one of the top female athletes in the world, puts forth the same effort, her dream of a relaxing existence will become reality.

Sources

www.btinternet.com
www.birchfieldharriers.com
www.news.bbc.co.uk
www.observer.co.uk
www.sportsaid.org
www.sportsillustrated.cnn.com

—John Horn

Ray Lewis

1975—

Professional football player

Ray Lewis emerged from tiny Lakeland, Florida to become one of the National Football League's (NFL) most feared defensive players of the modern era. Lewis's passion for football grew out of his love of wrestling, a sport that he excelled in at Lakeland Kathleen High School. Lewis's father had won state wrestling titles at Kathleen, and that motivated Lewis to set new records there. On the football field Lewis has exuded the same kind of passion and desire. His prowess in football at Kathleen attracted the attention of all of the state's major colleges. Once Lewis decided on the University of Miami, he worked to become one of the best players in the school's history.

After three years of college, Lewis entered the NFL and was taken by the Baltimore Ravens. The previous season, the Ravens had moved from Cleveland to Baltimore and had not yet developed a team identity. But Lewis quickly established an identity for himself through his tenacious defensive playing. He combined speed and power with the ability to change the game with one hit or one big play. During the 2000 season, Lewis led the Ravens to a victory over the New York Giants in Super Bowl XXXV at Raymond James Stadium in Tampa, Florida.

As a youngster Lewis's determination to succeed as an athlete was formidable. At Kathleen High Lewis won the Class 4A 189-pound state title, while earning at the same time Florida High School Athletic Association All-State honors. But most of Lewis's notoriety came through football, which would prove his vehicle to stardom. On Kathleen's football team, Lewis was named the most valuable player during both his junior and senior years. During his career, Lewis played running back and linebacker, and returned kicks. He also had ten quarterback sacks in two years as well as several kick return touchdowns.

Such athletic prowess helped him to earn a full football scholarship to the University of Miami, where Lewis played for then-coach Dennis Erickson. Off the field, however, Lewis suffered a major loss: his roommate, Marlin Barnes, was murdered. Lewis wears a t-shirt under his uniform that symbolized the bond that he had with Barnes. He told the *Baltimore Sun*, "[w]hen he passed away, he became my motivation. I do this for him." Despite the setback, Lewis was named a second-team All-American after his junior season with the Hurricanes. He also was the runner-up for the coveted Dick Butkus Award, which is given to college football's

At a Glance . . .

Born Ray Anthony Lewis on May 15, 1975, in Bartow, FL; son of Ray Lewis, Sr. and Sunseria Keith; children: Ray Anthony III, Rayshad. *Education*: University of Miami.

Career: Professional football player. Baltimore Ravens, linebacker, 1996-.

Awards: Named NFL Defensive MVP, Super Bowl MVP; selected to Pro Bowl, five times; first-team All-Pro.

Addresses: c/o Baltimore Ravens, 11001 Owings Mills Blvd, Owing Mills, MD 21117.

best linebacker each year. All of the success prompted Lewis to enter his name into the NFL Draft, where the Ravens chose him 26th overall.

Lewis made his impact felt throughout the NFL, particularly in the American Football Conference's Central Division, where the Ravens played eight of their scheduled 16 games. As a 21-year-old rookie, Lewis was the Ravens' leading tackler, registered two and a half quarterback sacks, and one interception. For his efforts, Lewis was named to *USA Today*'s All-Rookie Team. Lewis followed up his rookie year with another outstanding campaign that included 210 tackles, which earned him team honors once again. A 13-tackle performance against the rival Cincinnati Bengals on December 21, 1997, helped him to preserve the NFL's title for tackles and put him in his first Pro Bowl ever. Before the 1998 season, Lewis signed a four-year $26 million contract, which placed his salary among the NFL's highest for linebackers. Ravens' defensive coordinator, Marvin Lewis, commented to *Sports Illustrated* about the linebacker, "[h]e's got everything you want, from great mental capacity to leadership skills to incredible intensity and athletic ability."

While Lewis's accomplishments as a football player were constant, they were overshadowed by the events of January 31, 2000. During the after-party following Super Bowl XXIV in Atlanta, Georgia, Lewis's friends Joseph Sweeting and Reginald Oakley allegedly got into a fight with Richard Lollar and Jacinth Baker near the Cobalt nightclub in upscale Buckhead, Georgia. Lollar and Baker were stabbed to death in the fracas. Lewis, Sweeting, and Oakley were charged with six counts of murder. He was jailed in Atlanta before

posting bond. He was allowed to return to his home in Maryland.

According to CNN Sports Illustrated.com, in June of 2000, a judge approved a deal that allowed Lewis to avoid murder charges and jail time by pleading guilty to a misdemeanor and testifying against Sweeting and Oakley. Lewis pleaded guilty to obstruction of justice and was sentenced to 12 months probation, which prohibited him from using any illegal substances during that time. For his involvement, Lewis was fined $250,000 by NFL Commissioner Paul Tagliabue for violating the league's morality clause.

Before Ravens' training camp in July of 2000, Lewis apologized to his teammates and asked them for their forgiveness. He determined to put the incident behind him and led the Ravens to the AFC Playoffs. In the process, the Ravens defense set a single 16-game season record for the fewest points allowed.

Lewis made one spectacular play after another, helping the Ravens to secure playoff wins over the Denver Broncos, Oakland Raiders, and Tennessee Titans. During the playoff run, Lewis was quoted by *Slam! Sports* as saying, "I'm like a pit bull with a steak. I'm bloodthirsty, but only about football." Despite constant pleas from Lewis to talk about just football, questions from members of the media kept going back to the incident from January of 2000. But in the end, Lewis felt that he had once again overcome adversity, especially after the Ravens' victory in Super Bowl XXXV. "(God) says, 'When you go through tragedy, I'll make it your biggest treasure,'" he told *Cincinnati Enquirer* contributor Paul Daughtery. "And I feel like the season I'm having is my treasure."

Sources

Books

Newsmakers, Issue 3, Gale Group, 2001.

Periodicals

APB Celebrity News, February 4, 2000.
Baltimore Sun, July 19, 1998.
Cincinnati Enquirer, January 14, 2001.
Holland Sentinel, January 24, 2001.
Slam! Sports, January 8, 2001.
Sports Illustrated, January 8, 2001.
USA Today, June 13, 2000.

On-Line

www.APBnews.com
www.CourtTV.com
www.thehollandsentinel.net
www.NFL.com

Sonny Liston

c. 1928—

Boxer

Sonny Liston was one of professional boxing's more mysterious figures. His is a biography clouded with speculation, from the uncertainly of his birthdate and suggestions that he maintained connections to the mafia, to questions about his death. Adding further color to his life story is the fact that Liston acquired the skills he used to become heavyweight champion while serving a prison sentence.

The exact date and place of Charles L. "Sonny" Liston's birth is as opaque and mysterious as the man himself. Even the controversial former heavyweight champion seems not to have known the place or year of his birth. He has said he was born somewhere between 1932 and 1935, but most often claimed the date to be May 8, 1932. His mother, however, remembered that he was born on January 8, 1932—or January 18. Liston was one of eleven children, according to his mother, but he could never recall exactly how many siblings he had and some reports list up to 25 brothers and sisters. Whatever the year and whatever the date, Liston was born on a cotton plantation in Sand Slough Arkansas to Tobe and Helen Liston, who were tenant farmers on the plantation.

Despite all the family around, Liston grew up in isolation trying to avoid his father. His favorite activities were swimming at a nearby lake and riding the family mule. Liston got into trouble from a young age and received some savage whippings from his father. The beatings were so bad that the marks on his back were noted after his autopsy in 1970. Liston was quoted in *Sports Illustrated* as saying in regard to his upbringing: "I had nothing when I was a kid but a lot of brothers and sisters, a helpless mother and a father who didn't care about any of us. We grew up with few clothes, no shoes, little to eat. My father worked me hard and whupped me hard."

As a result of the constant conflict, Charles was sent to live with his brother, Ward, when he was about 16. Shortly thereafter, Liston's father died and his mother came to live with Ward for one season's farming. She moved on to St. Louis and her son followed her in 1946. He supposed that St. Louis was like the other small towns he had lived in and just showed up one night wandering around the city. He had no idea where his mother lived, but by chance he ran into some people who knew her.

Liston tried working and perhaps tried school, but the young man found both equally unpleasant. After three

At a Glance . . .

Born Charles L. Liston c. 1928, in Sand Slough, AR; died on December 30, 1970; son of Tobe and Helen Liston (tenant farmers); married Geraldine Clark; children: Danielle.

Career: Professional boxer. Learned boxing at Missouri State Penitentiary, 1950-52; won Golden Gloves World Title, 1953; professional boxer, 1953-70; won heavyweight championship, defeating Floyd Patterson, 1962; lost title to Cassius Clay, 1964.

years, Liston began to rob small stores and service stations. On January 16, 1950, one month into the crime spree, he was apprehended. He pled guilty to robbery and larceny and was sentenced to the Missouri State Penitentiary in Jefferson City.

Learned to Box While in Prison

Though some prison officials remembered Liston as a man who was always fighting, his official record was clear. He gravitated toward the Catholic priest who was also the director of athletics in the prison. The priest introduced the aimless young man to boxing. Liston took on all comers at Jefferson City. After he beat a heavyweight from St. Louis, some local newspaper men spread the word about Liston and soon began a campaign to release him. The campaign succeeded and he was released on October 30, 1952 to become a professional boxer. Besides boxing, Liston learned to write his name in prison, though, he was still unable to read.

Liston was entered into a Golden Gloves boxing tournament in St. Louis. He won this local tournament and went on to win the Midwestern regional title by defeating the 1952 Olympic Heavyweight champion. After winning the National Championship he became Golden Gloves champion of the World, defeating the West German champion in one round on June 22, 1953. In four months Liston had become the best amateur heavyweight fighter in the world and signed a professional contract.

Through his first year as a professional, Liston breezed through the competition until his first loss to Marty Marshall, a man ten pounds lighter. On September 7th, Marshall broke Liston's jaw and defeated him in a close eight-round decision. Liston later said that the reason he did not knock the smaller man out was that he was told to carry Marshall for a few rounds to give the fans a show. He said he was surprised by the punch that broke his jaw and ended up losing. The broken jaw set

Liston back six months, but strengthened his appeal with gamblers because his odds were now better.

In April of 1955 Liston again faced Marshall and beat him badly, knocking Marshall down four times to score a sixth-round technical knockout. But for all his prowess in the ring, outside the ring Liston's life was as complicated as ever. From 1953 until 1958 Liston was arrested 14 times in St. Louis. The most serious incident involved Liston assaulting a police officer for which he received 30 days in jail. Liston was jailed for offenses connected to his heavy drinking and was even questioned about his connection to the mob. It was rumored that Liston was a leg-breaker for the local mob-controlled unions.

Legal Problems Hindered Boxing Career

On September 3, 1957 his life seemed to stabilize when Liston married Geraldine Clark, but after a particularly nasty altercation with a policeman, Liston had no peace in St. Louis. Between the time of his arrest and sentencing he was arrested five more times. He was arrested four days after his wedding and held on two consecutive days for two separate robbery charges. With all the problems Liston had with the law, he fought only once in two years.

In 1958 Liston came to Chicago to fight. By this time his original managers, men who discovered him and sprung him from prison, had been pushed aside or bought out. But when he traveled to Chicago, he impressed a whole new set of "managers" who wanted a piece of Liston. Before a fight in March of 1958 Liston signed a five-year contract with Joseph "Pep" Barone. Liston fought once more in St. Louis and then moved to Philadelphia where his career would be directed in secret by Frankie Carbo and Blinky Palermo, two ruthless mobsters who controlled much of the boxing world throughout the 1950s and 1960s.

Liston's star immediately began to rise. He continued to win and his bouts were appearing on radio and then television. Though Carbo during this time was on the run from the law and then in prison, Liston fought in Miami Beach and Las Vegas. His record stood at 34-1, with 24 knockouts by the end of 1961, and he was being guaranteed up to $10,000 per fight. But his success was always under suspicion because of the people with whom he associated. Liston was even questioned about his managers, or undercover managers, in front of a senate subcommittee in Washington D.C. regarding corruption in the boxing world.

Despite his questioning and the police harassment, he fought and beat all the top contenders in the heavyweight division. By the end of 1961, people were accusing reigning heavyweight champion Floyd Patterson of dodging Liston. Cus D'Amato, who managed Patterson, said that Patterson would never fight Liston because Liston was a criminal and didn't deserve a chance to be heavyweight champion. As if to prove D'Amato's point, the state of California barred him from fighting there, claiming he had to change managers before getting a license to fight there. To get a chance to fight for the heavyweight title, Liston decided in 1961 to buy back his contract for $75,000 over two years. Despite his gesture, D'Amato and Patterson still considered Liston morally unacceptable.

Pennsylvania License Suspended

To bolster his reputation, Liston signed with a local Philadelphia manager who had recommended by Alfred Klein, a member of the Pennsylvania State Athletic commission and former member of the Congressional subcommittee which had grilled Liston about organized crime in boxing. He signed a two and a half year contract with George Katz, which he hoped would carry him to a heavyweight title fight. But after Gibson was arrested twice in May and June of 1961, his license to fight in Pennsylvania was suspended indefinitely.

Gibson and his wife moved to Denver to live next to the rectory of a Catholic church and Father Edward Murphy, who tried to reorient Liston to society. Whether the move was a ploy or a sincere attempt to reform his life, he was reinstated after a three- month suspension and scheduled to fight on December 4, 1961. Liston received $75,000 for a pay-per-view event in which he served as the under-card for a Floyd Patterson championship fight. He beat fourth-ranked West German Albert Westphal, knocking him out in 1:58 of the first round. Westphal lay unconscious on the canvas for two minutes—longer than the fight itself lasted. The only fighter left was Patterson and, for Patterson, the only challenger left was Liston. Finally on March 16, 1962 a contract was signed which would bring the two men face to face.

No one except Patterson himself wanted the champion to face Liston. Both white and black people held Liston in disdain and did not want him to become boxing's most glamorous champion. The state of New York pulled the plug on the fight, which was moved to Chicago in September of 1962. Liston reveled in his role of Black Knight. He told the press he would kill Patterson and he would like to run Patterson down with his car. At the same time, the only person in the world who had a good word to say about Liston was Patterson himself.

When the moment came, Liston took only two minutes and six seconds to knock Patterson out. Liston thought that with the heavyweight belt in his possession, his public persona would change also. But it did not. Liston expected a hero's welcome when he returned to Philadelphia as the heavyweight champion, but when he arrived at the airport, he was met by no one. Sportswriter Jack McKinney described Liston's reaction to his chilly reception as the newly-crowned heavyweight champion in *Sports Illustrated*: "His eyes swept the whole scene. He was extremely intelligent, and he understood immediately what it meant. His Adam's apple moved slightly. You could feel the deflation, see the look of hurt in his eyes. It was almost like a silent shudder went through him."

It was less than a month before Liston was arrested again for driving his Cadillac at 15 mph. The police said Liston had been drinking and at first he would not cooperate. Liston moved to Chicago and on December 4th and moved into a 21-room mansion on the city's south side. Liston was set to fight Patterson again in the spring or 1963, but he injured his knee and the fight was moved to the summer from Miami Beach to Las Vegas.

On July 22nd, Liston defeated Patterson again in 2 minutes and 23 seconds. After the fight, chaos erupted when 21-year-old Cassius Clay (a young Muhammad Ali) jumped into the ring to begin his "I am the Greatest" speech. The crowd booed Liston in his victory. Instead of returning to Philadelphia or Chicago, Liston went back to Father Murphy in Denver and received a hero's welcome at the airport. He made a tour through the British Isles, but everywhere he went he was hounded by Clay calling him a big ugly bear and claiming he was too chicken to fight. Once, in a Las Vegas casino, Clay and his entourage found Liston playing dice. Clay began to badger the champion when Liston pulled out a handgun and fired twice at his head. Everyone hit the floor and Clay ran for the exit. Ali's manager Angelo Dundee told Randy Harvey of the *Los Angeles Times* about the incident: "We found out later that Liston heard we were coming and loaded his gun with blanks to scare Muhammad. It worked. Muhammad told me, 'I act crazy. He is crazy.'"

Lost Championship Title

Liston would defend his title against Clay in February of 1964 in Miami. The fight was a strange one. Clay and Liston were even after six rounds, but then Liston, a 7-1 pre-fight favorite, refused to come out of his corner for the seventh, claiming his left arm was numb. Liston's camp claimed that he had injured his shoulder during training camp, but no one said anything before the fight. Then it came to light that Liston's management team purchased rights to Clay's next fight for $50,000. Liston's purse was withheld, but a doctor announced that Liston's shoulder was indeed hurt. A member of Liston's camp, Jack Nilon, told Simon Barnes of *The Times* of London that "he heard something snap. After that it got progressively worse."

When Liston got back to Denver, he was arrested for driving 75 mph in a 35 mph zone, while drunk and carrying a loaded revolver. Liston was also being sued by a former publicist and the IRS had filed liens against him and his wife and his management company. He was arrested twice more in 1964, including a Christmas day lock-up for drunk driving and then resisting arrest.

On May 25, 1965. Liston fought Clay again. Even after losing to Clay the first time, Liston was an 8-to-5 favorite. The bout became famous as the "Phantom Punch" fight in which Clay tossed a lazy jab Liston's way and Liston fell over as if hit by a sledge hammer. With the loss and the allegations that Liston had thrown the fight, Liston's career as a big-time heavyweight fighter was over. He continued to fight, often in Europe until his final victory in 1970 over Chuck Wepner, who would later fight Clay for the heavyweight championship.

Liston claimed to be 38 at the time of his last fight, but his real age was more like 50. At the end of 1970 Liston's wife, Geraldine, traveled to St. Louis to spend Christmas with her mother. She returned to Las Vegas on January 5, 1971 and found her husband lying dead on the floor of her bedroom. The coroner's report implied but never implicitly said that a heart attack was the cause of death. However, traces of heroin were found in his blood. Some believed he had a heart attack. Some believed he killed himself because he was running out of money. Some believed that he accidentally overdosed on heroin. Because he was afraid of needles, some believed that he was murdered. Whatever the cause, Liston's death is as shrouded in mystery as was his life.

Sources

Books

Tosches, Nick. *The Devil and Sonny Liston*. Little Brown and Company, 2000.

Periodicals

The Los Angeles Times, February 25, 1997.
Sports Illustrated, February 4, 1991.
The Times (London, England), December 11, 1999.

—Michael J. Watkins

Patrice Lumumba

1925-1961

Former Prime minister of Congo

If the United States has the Rev. Dr. Martin Luther King Jr. and Malcolm X to remember as heroes of the battles in the civil rights movement and "symbols of liberation for people of African descent around the world," wrote Alan Riding in the *New York Times*, Congo (for many years known as Zaire) and Africa itself have Patrice Lumumba. Lumumba, a passionate nationalist, became Congo's first elected prime minister after leading the movement to wrestle control of the country's independence from Belgium in June of 1960. Two months later, vilified as a Communist by the West in the throes of the Cold War, Lumumba was overthrown and only months after that was murdered with the suspected collusion of the United States and Belgium. Though the United States was cleared of any involvement in Lumumba's death at the time, suspicions remained and independent investigations continued forty years later. According to sociologist Ludo de Witte in his book *The Assassination of Lumumba*, Belgian operatives directed and carried out the murder, and even helped dispose of the body. Lumumba's demise, wrote Bill Berkeley in the *New York Times*, was a "turning point in history that helps explain how that African nation wound up on the road to its present ruin."

Showed a Passion for Learning

Patrice Hémery Lumumba was born on July 2, 1925, in the village of Onalua in the province of Kasai, Congo, in the Batetela tribe. One of four sons of poor farmers, he began attending missionary schools at age eleven. Most missionary schools' prime directive was to prepare blacks for manual labor, and only one hour per day was given to book study, the rest to farming and other physical work. Lumumba's missionary teachers responded to the boy's ravenous hunger for knowledge and talent for learning by lending him books to read before dark, as his family was too poor to afford a candle for him to read by. Growing up, gathered with other villagers, Lumumba was told the horrific tales of atrocities at the hands of Belgian soldiers under King Leopold II. The soldiers' practice was to sever the hands of slave natives who did not gather enough rubber or ivory. Lumumba completed his primary studies in four years and went on to Tshumbe Sainte Marie Secondary School for his secondary education. For reasons unknown—some suggest his father could no longer afford school fees—Lumumba left school at age 18, after three years and with no diploma.

Lumumba went in search of work, first 150 miles away from home to Kindu, a mining town, then to Kalima, where he worked as a nursing assistant. In 1944 Lumumba set out for Kasai's second-largest city, Stanleyville (now Kisangani). Lumumba was dazzled by the cosmopolitan and European areas of the big city—its wide boulevards, lush parks, swimming pools, skyscrapers, and luxurious villas. But the city's restaurants, theaters, and hotels were off limits to Africans who were relegated to the back seats of buses and boats, and were not permitted to live within city limits.

Lumumba lived in the nearby township of Mangobo which, fortunately for Lumumba, boasted a library.

At a Glance . . .

Born Patrice Hémery Lumumba on July 2, 1925 in the village of Onalua in the province of Kasai, Congo, in the Batetela tribe; died on January 17, 1961; son of François Tolenga; married: Pauline Opangu, c. 1951; children: Patrice.

Career: Postal worker, c. 1947; writer for *Voice of the Congo,* c. 1951; arrested for misappropriating postal funds, 1956; organized Congolese Movement (MNC), 1958; elected prime minister of Congo with President Kasavubu and subsequently overthrown, 1960; arrested, escaped, captured, and delivered to Katanga secessionists, December 1960-January 1961; executed and his body destroyed, January 1961.

Lumumba spent his time reading and with Congolese youth of his age who had also come from rural villages and had been educated in westernized mission schools. They called themselves "évolués." Together, the group debated issues, listened to news on the radio, and exchanged books. Lumumba took a course to improve his French and learned several Congolese languages, including Swahili, spoken in eastern Congo and throughout East Africa, and Lingala, a trade language spoken along the Congo River.

Became Part of the "Évolué" Community

In 1947 Lumumba—because he was fluent in Congolese languages—got a job as a postal worker in the capital city of Leopoldville (now Kinshasa), nearly 1,000 miles down the Congo River, but was transferred back to Stanleyville in 1950. Back in Stanleyville, Lumumba surrounded himself with Congolese intellectuals and liberal politics. He volunteered at the local library and helped organize the first postal-workers' union. He was a founder of *Comité de l'Union Belgo-Congolaise*—a group of African intellectuals and liberal Europeans with an aim to improve race relations. Lumumba's days began at two in the morning, when he would read for a few hours before taking a bath at five and breakfasting on coffee with no sugar. In 1951 Lumumba, no fan of arranged marriages, married 15-year-old Pauline Opangu, an arrangement set up by his father. Pauline could not read, write, or speak French, but Lumumba became "completely captivated" by her "elfin charm," according to *Historic World Leaders.* The two had one son, Patrice.

In the early 1950s, Lumumba began expressing himself in editorials and poems he wrote for *La Voix du Congolese* (Voice of the Congo) and *La Croix du Congo,* two "évolué" publications. Through these writings, he became known as one of "only a dozen Congolese in a country of thirteen million who dared to express himself," according to *Historic World Leaders.* In 1952 after mounting pressure from the évolués, the colonial government announced that qualified natives would be granted a registration card which would entitle them the same privileges as Europeans, theoretically. Lumumba applied and passed the required tests, but was denied on the grounds of "immaturity." He appealed in 1954 and was among the first to receive the card. The next year, Lumumba was among a group of Congolese granted an audience with reformist Belgian King Baudouin, who was touring Congo. Lumumba was the only one in the group to answer the king's questions, and the king drew Lumumba aside to discuss the future of Congo as Baudouin's white dignitaries looked on, ignored.

The royal attention earned Lumumba regard among his fellow Congolese and the contempt of Belgian officials. He was chosen to represent the Congolese in Belgium to discuss political reform. When he returned home to Stanleyville, Lumumba was arrested for stealing about 2,500 francs from his employer, the post office. He had openly "borrowed" the money, he said, and had left a signed receipt declaring his intention to repay. Lumumba maintained his innocence throughout, but was found guilty and sentenced to two years in jail, and served 11 months. The local évolué community raised enough money to reimburse the entire sum and provide for Lumumba's family during his jail term, but colonial officials likely felt they had silenced a young reformer, if only temporarily.

Independence Sparked in Africa, Inspired Lumumba

Bent on independence for Congo, but discouraged by what had happened in Stanleyville, Lumumba went to work as a salesman for the Belgian Polar Beer company in the capital city of Leopoldville (now Kinshasa) in 1957. During that time, significant political changes were taking place across Africa, with Ghana being the first black African colony to gain independence as a nation. The Mau Mau revolt had been averted in neighboring Kenya and the prospect of independence was looking like it could become reality for several French and British colonies. Belgium finally granted limited African involvement in civic activities and held elections in Leopoldville in 1957.

Lumumba emerged as a founder of the National Congolese Movement (MNC). The group was formed in anticipation of the 1958 visit of a Belgian delegation sent to Congo to examine the political situation there and suggest plans for the country's future. The MNC petitioned the Belgian government for more native involvement in the planning of their future, and talk began to circulate of Congo's independence from Belgium, previously unheard of. From this, over a dozen political groups arose in addition to the MNC, demanding independence for Congo. The most significant of these, ABAKO, had been elected to power in Leopoldville, with Joseph Kasavubu as mayor. Another party later appeared, called Confederation des Associations du Ratanga (CONAKAT), and led by Moise Tshombe.

Lumumba and Kasavubu planned to attend the Pan-African People's Conference that year to strategize all Africa to independence. Kasavubu was unable to make the trip, but Lumumba gave an impassioned speech before the 600 delegates, citing injustices of the past and the Universal Declaration of Rights of Man and the United Nation's Charter, and arguing for an immediate end to colonialism. He declared colonialism near its end, and made it clear that Europe's future with African nations depended on support in Africa's independence, not continued imperialism. Lumumba ended his speech powerfully with: "Down with imperialism. Down with colonialism. Down with racism and tribalism. Long live the Congolese nation. Long live independent Africa." Meanwhile, freely elected ABAKO and Kasavubu were removed from Leopoldville by Belgian authorities. Lumumba campaigned for Kasavubu's release and drummed up support for the MNC throughout the colony.

Divided Elections, Unstable Nation

In April of 1959 the MNC led a meeting of Congolese political parties to organize and strengthen and to plan a provisional government, with a deadline set for January 1, 1961. Lumumba was arrested in Stanleyville for inciting disorder in October of 1959, when a riot broke out and twenty Congolese were killed after he gave a speech at an MNC conference there. He was sentenced to six months in jail, but local Belgian officials were forced to release him so he could participate in a roundtable conference between the Congolese and Belgians in Brussels. At the meeting, provincial and national elections were set for May of 1960, with Congo winning independence in June.

The elections themselves attested to how divided Congo truly was. The 137 seats in the National Assembly were split between the PSA with 13 seats, ABAKO with 12, CONAKAT with 8, and MNC with 33, and the rest went to over a dozen smaller parties. Lumumba tried in vain to unify with Tshombe's CONAKAT, as did Kasavubu. Finally, on June 23rd, Lumumba and Kasavubu allied to form a unified government of Congo, with Kasavubu as president and Lumumba as prime minister.

What set Lumumba apart from his main rivals—veteran politician and Joseph Kasavubu and Moise Tshombe, a power in the Katanga province—were his convictions and vision for a unified and independent Congo. Lumumba, at age 35, became the country's first prime minister under President Kasavubu on Independence Day, June 30, 1960. In an impromptu Independence Day speech attended by King Baudouin, Lumumba declared that the eighty years of tyrannical colonial rule and Congolese exploitation would be put in the past, and looked forward to cooperating with Belgium as an equal and independent nation.

Tried to Quell a Chaotic Congo

Within days of the victory, the country was in chaos. Congolese army mutinies led to Belgian military intervention. Lumumba reacted by cutting diplomatic ties with Belgium. On July 11, the mineral-rich province of Katanga seceded from Congo, led by Tshombe, who barred Lumumba and Kasavubu from entering the province. Under the advice of U.S. President Dwight Eisenhower, Lumumba invited United Nations peacekeeping troops to land in the country. When the UN refused to restore Katanga, Soviet leader Nikita Khrushchev sent planes, weapons, and advisors to aid Lumumba, which drew the attention and confirmed "the worst fears" of the American government under Eisenhower, according to journalist Bill Berkeley of the *New York Times*. As Lumumba tried to prevent inner turmoil from tearing his country apart at the seams, his enemies seemed to multiply. In September of 1960 army commander Joseph Mobutu arrested and ousted both Kasavubu and Lumumba and took power of Congo.

For accepting Soviet aid during the height of the Cold War, Belgians and Americans accused Lumumba of being communist, to which he replied, "We are not communist, Catholics or socialist. We are African Nationalist. We retain the right to be friends with whoever we like in accordance with the principal of political neutrality." Still, even out of office, Lumumba remained under the scrutiny of Western spies for his ties to the Soviet Union. In August of 1960, CIA Director Allen Dulles cabled the CIA chief in Congo: "In high quarters here, it is the clear-cut conclusion that if [Lumumba] continues to hold high office, the inevitable result will at best be chaos and at worst pave the way to Communist takeover.... His removal must be an urgent and prime objective." A few days later, a CIA scientist, Sidney Gottlieb, arrived Congo carrying a vial of poison intended to kill Lumumba. Gottlieb never got his chance, and the poison was dumped in the Congo River.

Lumumba managed to escape Mobutu and tried to join his followers, but was recaptured. In December of 1960, Lumumba was arrested by Congolese authorities and Belgian officials engineered his transfer to his enemies in Katanga, the breakaway province still under Belgian control. "Anyone who knew the place knew that was a death sentence," according to journalist

Kevin Whitelaw of *U.S. News & World Report*. "I prefer to die with my head unbowed, my faith unshakable, and with profound trust in the destiny of my country," Lumumba wrote to his wife from prison. He had already been badly beaten and was bleeding when he arrived in Katanga on January 17, 1961, escorted by Belgian soldiers.

Question of American Involvement Never Answered

After Lumumba and two of his aides were murdered, the bodies were cut up with a hacksaw by Belgian Police Commissioner Gerard Soete and his brother and dissolved in sulfuric acid, to destroy the evidence, according to Whitelaw's article in *U.S. News & World Report*. In a 1999 television interview, Soete displayed a bullet and two teeth he claimed to have saved from Lumumba's body. Lumumba's assassination cleared the way for the insidious regime of dictator Mobutu who, for three decades, ran Congo into poverty. The region never recovered and remains unstable and is a warground for at least five neighboring countries.

A 1975 U.S. Senate investigation led by the late Frank Church (D-Idaho) found there was "a reasonable inference" that Eisenhower authorized Lumumba's assassination, but the committee stopped short of a conclusive finding. According to journalist George Lardner Jr. in the *Washington Post*, an August of 1960 meeting of Eisenhower with the National Security Council lends to suspicions regarding U.S. involvement. Though the meeting notes themselves are inconclusive—attesting to the wisdom of Eisenhower's no-direct-quotations for meeting reports. The meeting's notetaker, Robert H. Johnson, told the *Post* that he distinctly recalled Eisenhower turning to CIA Director Dulles and perfectly audible to everyone at the meeting, saying "something to the effect that Lumumba should be eliminated." Eisenhower said "something—I can no longer recall the words—that came across to me as an order for the assassination of Lumumba."

In his research for *The Assassination of Lumumba*, Ludo de Witte found a Belgian official who help organize Lumumba's transfer to Katanga who said that he kept CIA station chief Lawrence Devlin fully informed of the plan. "The Americans were informed of the transfer because they actively discussed this thing for weeks," de Witte told *U.S. News & World Report*. Devlin, now retired, denied the claim.

Lumumba's legend has inspired scores of books, articles, art, and film. One major motion biographical picture on the subject, *Lumumba*, directed by Raoul Peck, stirred up new interest in the slain leader upon its release in 2001. Though the political thriller was produced in cooperation with Lumumba's family, and paints an admirable and respecting portrait, it is notable for its adherence to the tragic facts. "*Lumumba* is potent stuff," wrote critic *Los Angeles Times* film critic Kenneth Turan. "Complex, powerful, intensely dramatic." Critic Elvis Mitchell wrote in the *New York Times* that the film contains "a breathtaking amount of information, rolling through history swiftly and boldly yet conveying an epic investment in characterization as Lumumba's power and comrades inexorably fade, victims of the conflict in the Congo." Peck also made a well-received documentary film on Lumumba, titled *Lumumba: Death of a Prophet*, released in 1991. Lumumba was an idealist, director Peck told the *New York Times,* "because he had the option of being an opportunist like so many around him and he chose not to be."

Sources

Books

Meredith, Martin, *The First Dance of Freedom*, Harper, 1954.
Reshetnyak, Nikolai, *Patrice Lumumba*, Novosti Press, 1990.
Sarte, Jean Paul, *Lumumba Speaks*, Little, Brown, 1972.

Periodicals

Economist, August 11, 2001.
Los Angeles Times, July 20, 2001, p. F6.
New York Times, June 6, 1999, p. 29; June 24, 2001, p. 2.13; August 2, 2001, p. A20.
U.S. News and World Report, July 24, 2000, p. 63.
Washington Pos t, August 8, 2000, p. A23.

On-Line

Historic World Leaders, Gale Research, 1994. Reproduced in *Biography Resource Center,* The Gale Group. 2001, http://www.galenet.com/servlet/Bio RC

—Brenna Sanchez

Tandja Mamadou

1938—

President of Niger

One of the first "democratically-elected presidents of Niger, Tandja Mamadou, is the hope of the future to many," said the *Camel Express*, an English newsletter of the Friends of Niger. Though only history will attest to whether or not Mamadou will fulfill the hope that he has been identified with, he has already dedicated much of his life and energy to the government of Niger, creating a legacy of commitment that many countries, developed and developing, would envy. Like many post-colonial African nations, Niger has known little peace since securing its independence from France in 1960. Ranked as one of the poorest countries on Earth and possessing one of the largest foreign debts, the country has suffered greatly and continues to battle with poverty, a dilapidated infrastructure, ongoing warfare between ethnic groups, and bloody political coups.

Mamadou was born in Maine-Soroa, in the Lake Chad region of southeast Niger in 1938. He was educated at a military school and pursued a career in the Nigerian Armed Forces, where he eventually rose to the rank of Colonel. His high rank in the military afforded him close contact with the government and in 1974 Mamadou played a key role in a military coup that ousted then President Hamani Diori. Another military leader, Lieutenant Colonel Seyni Kountché, assumed the presidency and a military government was established that would last the next 15 years. During this time Mamadou held many high-level governmental posts, including that of Prefect of the Region of Tahoua (similar to governor of a state) from 1981 to 1988. Following Kountché's death in 1987, some sources close to the presidency indicated that Kountché wanted

Mamadou to succeed him as president. However, another officer, General Ali Seybou, became the next military president of Niger.

Mamadou continued to hold posts in the government under Seybou as well, including the role of Ambassador to Nigeria, one of Niger's most important neighbors. Niger relies heavily on imports of basic commodities from Nigeria including electricity. Mamadou held this post from 1988 to 1990, at which time he was appointed Minister of the Interior. He remained in this role until 1991 when Seybou dismantled the military government and instituted a civilian democracy. Soon after, Mamadou retired from the military, though not from political life.

In 1993 Mamadou ran for president of Niger in the country's first democratic elections in over two decades. Although Mamadou captured the most votes, these did not translate into a clear majority, and he lost the election in a re-run to his closest opponent, Mahamane Ousmane, amidst rumors that he was not a native born citizen of Niger. Following this loss, Mamadou assumed the leadership of his political party, the National Movement for the Development of Society (MNSD).

Ousmane's presidency was marked with periods of ethnic violence as well as continued economic instability and poverty. In 1996 the country was once again engulfed in a military coup, this time led by Colonel Ibrahim Bare Mainassara, who re-established military rule. Recognizing, however, that a military leadership

At a Glance . . .

Born Tandja Mamadou in 1938 in Maine-Soroa, near the Lake Chad region of Niger. *Education*: Completed training at a military school.

Career: Soldier and politician. Participated in the military junta that ousted President Diori, 1974; Prefect of the Region of Tahoua, 1981-88; Ambassador of Niger, 1988-90; Minister of the Interior, 1990-91; retired from military; made two unsuccessful presidential bids; active in political demonstrations against government and was arrested, 1997; elected to a five-year term as president of Niger, 1999.

would potentially threaten foreign aid, Mainassara decided to legitimize the new government with an election. Mamadou, as well as recently-ousted President Ousmane, ran against Mainassara for the post, but before the election could take place, Mainassara outlawed political rallies, replacing the electoral congress with his own cronies and becoming Niger's elected president.

During Mainassara's rule, Mamadou and other political leaders, including his former rival, Ousmane, staged a number of boycotts against the government, brazenly acting in defiance of the President. Together they formed the Front for the Restoration and Defense of the Democracy, and in 1997, in an extravagant political move, Mamadou and two other opposition leaders turned themselves into Mainassara's government to be willingly arrested as political dissidents.

Dissatisfaction with Mainassara's government grew as Niger's dire economic situation worsened. Poverty continued to rise and many civil servants, including soldiers, were not being paid. Along with the political dissidence fueled by Mamadou and others, the situation ignited and on April 9, 1996, Mainassara's own presidential guard assassinated him. Once again, a military state was declared and Major Daouda Malam Wanke, of Mainassara's guard, assumed control. Unlike previous military leaders, however, Wanke claimed not to want the presidency. He vowed instead to oversee the transition of the government to a civilian-led democracy. International watchdogs and human rights groups, aghast at the bloody assassination, were skeptical and foreign aid was suspended. But Wanke worked quickly, turning to Nigeria for assistance in planning the transition to democratic rule. Six months later, Mamadou and six other political leaders were running for office.

In November of 1999 Tandja Mamadou was elected president with sixty percent of the vote. International observers agreed that the election was conducted freely and fairly, although it is estimated that only thirty percent of the population voted. In one of his first post-election press conferences, Mamadou stated, as quoted by www.brecorder.com: "My first priority will be political stability and then institutional and social stability." He continued, "Then I will tackle the reconstruction of the country's economy and finances around which all of today's problems revolve."

Mamadou has concentrated on meeting those goals, and according to the Panafrican News Agency website, "For Niger, the year 2000 was essentially a year of concrete moves to enhance political and social stability." Among Mamadou's first actions in office was the re-establishment of ties with other African democracies, including Nigeria. Not only would this help preserve the trade ties between the two nations, but Nigeria's considerable clout could help prevent any future attempts at a military intervention in Niger's new government. Mamadou has also worked hard to rebuild relations with the international community, and within a month of his assuming office, he traveled to France to meet with government and foreign aid officials. Following his visit French aid was restored to Niger. In September of 2000 the European Union committed to 63 billion francs in development projects in Niger. Then, in December of the same year the International Monetary Fund granted Niger 53 billion francs for structural improvements.

In addition to the financial crisis, Mamadou and his cabinet have also worked on the social crises that beset their nation. In September of 2000 the president led a "Flame of Peace" ceremony to celebrate the end of the Tuareg fighting that plagued northern Niger for nearly a decade. In that ceremony over 2500 weapons turned in by rebels were burned. In January of 2001 he began a project that would build a series of mini-dams and water reservoirs. The goal of the project was to build three dams a year in each district of the country. According to a report on the Panafrican News Agency website, "the project [is aimed] at alleviating poverty by improving agricultural production through the construction of water supply facilities, the development of arid lands, and the promotion of the fisheries sector." The report went on to say that "the initiative is in partial fulfillment of the commitments [Mamadou] made to the people of Niger during his campaign for president to alleviate suffering, hunger, malnutrition, thirst, diseases, and ignorance." In that vein, Mamadou has also launched a polio immunization program, literacy programs, and subsidies for grain and other commodities. He also instituted a ban on hunting to help protect Niger's dwindling wildlife population that includes giraffes, lions, and rhinos.

Despite his successes, Mamadou's tenure has not been without controversy and opposition. Just days following his swearing-in ceremony, there was a public outcry when Mamadou, in accordance with the constitution, revealed his assets. They included six villas, three houses, two vehicles, nearly a thousand head of cattle, and numerous high-ticket items such as televisions, refrigerators, and freezers. In a country where more than sixty percent of the population lives in desperate poverty and even water is a luxury, Mamadou's admission of wealth was not welcome. Shortly afterwards, his government came under fire from human rights groups when it gave amnesty to participants in the 1996 and 1999 military coups. Famine, outbreaks of factional fighting, AIDS, tourist kidnappings, crime, and student unrest continued to plague the country, and opposition leaders regularly spoke against Mamadou, staging walkouts of government sessions, and hosting rallies in protest of the government's actions. With many challenges ahead of him, Mamadou would have to rely on his political and military experience if he would lead his country into the future.

Sources

Periodicals

The Camel Express, February 2000.

On-line

www.bbc.co.uk
Business Recorder, www.brecorder.com
www.friendsofniger.org
www.nigerembassyusa.org
Panafrican News Agency, www.allAfrica.com

—Candace LaBalle

Memphis Minnie

1897-1973

Blues singer, guitarist, composer

The blues scene in the 1920s and 1930s was diverse in style—spanning classic, urban, and country blues—but almost completely homogenous in terms of gender. Men dominated the stages of juke joints and nightclubs, with very few women breaking the ranks of blues musicians. However, there were a few exceptions who made their mark. One such woman was Memphis Minnie, the most significant female country blues singer to emerge during that era.

She is credited as being one of the first blues artists—male or female—to use the electric guitar, preceding Muddy Waters' use of the instrument by a year. Memphis Minnie's style of guitar playing reflected how she lived her life—hard-driving, passionate, and contrary to what was expected of women at the time. Although she made numerous recordings over the course of a career which spanned three decades, none of them captured the raw energy of the live performances that earned her a place next to other female blues greats like Ma Rainey and Bessie Smith. Fortunately, the power of her musical style lives on through the many well-known blues performers influenced by this dynamic musician, including Brewer Phillips, Big Momma Thornton, and Koko Taylor, as well as Rock & Roll artists such as

Chuck Berry, Elvis Presley, and the Rolling Stones.

Began Playing at a Young Age

Minnie, who also went by the names Texas Tessie, Minnie McCoy, and Gospel Minnie, was born Lizzie Douglas on June 3, 1897, in Algiers, Louisiana, a city located near the mouth of the Mississippi River, across from the old slave docks in New Orleans. Minnie was the first of thirteen children born to Abe and Gertrude Douglas, who were Baptist sharecroppers. In 1904 Minnie moved with her family to Walls, Mississippi, located just south of Memphis. Soon after the move, Minnie's parents gave her a guitar for her birthday. She quickly learned how to play her guitar and began entertaining at parties in her neighborhood, picking up the nickname "Kid Douglas." When she got a little older, "Kid" often snuck into Memphis, where she sang and played in parks and on the street corners around town for tips, meeting other musicians and getting her first taste of the early Memphis blues scene.

In the mid-1910s, Minnie joined the Ringling Brothers Circus and traveled throughout the South, entertaining crowds with her music. Eventually, Minnie quit the

Born Lizzie Douglas, June 3, 1897, in Algiers, Louisiana; died August 6, 1973, in Memphis; married Casey Bill Weldon (divorced); Kansas Joe McCoy (divorced); Little Son Joe. *Religion*: Baptist.

Career: Blues artist, member of Memphis Jug Band; recorded with Sunnyland Slim, Blind John Davis, Hambone Lewis, Charlie McCoy, Myrtle Jenkins. Recorded on several labels including Decca, Vocalian, Columbia, Bluebird, Okeh, Regal, Checker, and JOB.

Awards: Inducted into Blues Foundation Hall of Fame, 1980; *Blues Unlimited* Reader's Poll, 1973.

circus and moved to the Bedford Plantation in Mississippi. There she spent several years "woodshedding" with a guitar and mandolin player, Willie Brown, who had at one time played with both Charley Patton and Robert Johnson. According to www.worcesterphoenix.com, guitarist Willie Moore, who played with Minnie and Willie Brown said, "Wasn't nothing he could teach her. Everything Willie Brown could play, she could play, and then she could play things he couldn't play."

Minnie eventually returned to Memphis, and was already tough and street-wise by the time she established herself as part of the Beale Street blues scene, an environment that had the reputation of being rough and somewhat seedy, in which only a woman of extraordinary strength and resourcefulness could survive. As quoted in the book *Woman with Guitar: Memphis Minnie Blues*, one observer said, "Any men fool with her she'd go right after them right away. She didn't take no foolishness off them. Guitar, pocketknife, pistol, anything she get her hand on she'd use it." Economic necessity dictated Minnie's close proximity to street life as she subsidized her income with prostitution, charging the relatively large sum of $12 for her services. Minnie also gained a reputation for partying and gambling.

Created the Hard-Driving Electric Sound

For several years, Minnie was a member of the Memphis Jug Band and recorded with several artists. In 1929 Minnie was discovered by a talent scout from Columbia Records and recorded her first song, "Bumble Bee," under the name of Memphis Minnie, along with her second husband, the guitarist Kansas Joe McCoy (her first husband was guitarist Casey Bill

Weldon). The recording brought the pair enough recognition to move on to Chicago, the hub of the blues scene, where Minnie would live for the next twenty-five years. Besides being a woman in a male-dominated music scene, Minnie literally "stood out" from other musicians by playing lead guitar while standing, at a time when everyone else played their guitars sitting down. She also tried new styles of music, new picking styles, and new instruments. Minnie was the first to record with what came to be known as the "classic" 1950s blues combo: electric guitar, piano, bass, and drums. It has also been noted that Minnie was among the first to play the electric guitar in 1943, at least one year before Muddy Waters did. Writer Langston Hughes described her performance in an article about her in the January 9, 1943, *Chicago Defender*, noting, "She grabs the microphone and yells, 'Hey now!' Then she hits a few deep chords at random, leans forward ever so slightly on her guitar, bows her head and begins to beat out…a rhythm so contagious that often it makes the crowd holler out loud.…All these things cry through the strings on Memphis Minnie's electric guitar, amplified to machine proportions—a musical version of electric welders plus a rolling mill."

Minnie proved that she could hold her own with her male peers during energetic guitar contests where the winner was decided by the intensity of applause from the audience. Competing sometimes for just a bottle of whiskey, Minnie took on blues artists such as Big Bill Broonzy, Tampa Red, Sunnyland Slim, and Muddy Waters. She often won, although she sometimes picked an opportune moment during these contests to lift her skirt in order to increase the applause.

Unfortunately, Minnie was never recorded playing her characteristic hard-driving electric sound. Minnie, like many other African-American blues artists, was essentially controlled by the impresario Lester Melrose, who handled all the details of the recording business for most of the "race record" labels during that era. Melrose instructed his musicians to record a toned-down version of the blues, a formulaic approach that became known as the Melrose Sound, the Bluebird Beat, the Melrose Mess, or the Melrose Machine. Even Minnie's recordings for other labels such as Decca failed to capture her spirited approach to the blues. However, Minnie's willingness to teach and nurture other young musicians ensured that her style was passed on to the next generation of blues artists.

Forced Into Retirement

In addition to watering down her music, the record labels prevented Minnie from reaping the economic benefits of her success. One of her protegés, Brewer Phillips, conveyed that Minnie claimed to have been "messed around in the music" and gave him the advice, "You can learn to play, but don't let them take your money." In 1958 Minnie and third husband Little Son

Joe returned to Memphis, and lived in poverty. Aside from an occasional live radio spot, Minnie was no longer performing; her last performance was at a memorial for her friend and fellow musician, Bill Broonzy, in 1959. She had a stroke in 1960, Joe died in 1961, and shortly thereafter Minnie suffered another debilitating stroke which left her confined to a wheelchair for the last thirteen years of her life. Her sister, Daisy, cared for Minnie during her remaining years. Sadly, the woman who contributed so much to the early blues scene was ill and destitute at the end of her life. However, word of her predicament spread through the music community. Several artists held benefits to raise money for her care and the magazines *Living Blues* and *Blues Unlimited* helped to spread the word about Minnie's need, generating monetary support from fans.

Memphis Minnie died August 6, 1973, in Memphis. She is buried in New Hope Cemetery in Walls, Mississippi, in an unmarked grave. Posthumously, *Blues World* described Minnie's 1934 recording, *Early Rhythm & Blues*, as "the seminal electric sound guitar, bass, piano, drums which eventually cohesed into the style heard round the world." She was among the first musicians to be inducted into the Blues Foundation Hall of Fame, in 1980.

Selected discography

Hoodoo Lady, Columbia, 1933.
Early Rhythm & Blues, Biograph, 1934.
I Ain't No Bad Gal, Indigo, 1988.

Sources

Books

Garon, Paul, and Beth Garon, *Woman With Guitar: Memphis Minnie Blues*, Da Capo, New York, 1992.
Harrison, Daphne Duval, *Black Pearls: Blues Queens of the 1920s*, New Brunswick, Rutgers University Press, 1987.

On-Line

http://www.blueflamcafe.com/Memphis_Minnie.html
http://www.p-dub.com/thang/minnie.html
http://www.roadhouseblues.com/bipages/ bioMinnie.htm
http://www.surrealism-usa.org/pages/memphis.htm
http://www.wordesterphoenix.com/archive/music

—Christine Miner Minderovic

Reggie Miller

1965—

Professional basketball player

Reggie Miller is a talented man who comes from a very talented family in Riverside, California. One of five siblings, Miller is the second of two Millers to win an Olympic gold medal; the first was his older sister Cheryl, who earned her gold medal while playing for the United States women's basketball team during the 1984 Summer Olympics. Reggie won his medal in the 1996 Summer Olympics as a member of Dream Team III, the United States men's basketball team. His older brother, Darrell, was an outfielder for Major League Baseball's California Angels. Miller's other sister, Laura, played varsity volleyball at California State-Fullerton.

A 13-year National Basketball Association veteran, all with the Indiana Pacers, Miller is considered one of the league's most feared three-point shooters. On March 18, 2001, he hit his 2,000th three-point shot against the Sacramento Kings. In the same game, he also surpassed the 21,000-point plateau. Through the 2000-2001 NBA season, Miller averaged 19.5 points per game and scored 21,319 points.

As a youngster, Miller was plagued by a hip deformity that caused severely splayed feet, according to Indys-

tar.com. For the first four years of his life he wore leg braces to correct the birth defect and doctors wondered if he would ever walk unassisted. But he persevered, and by the time he was five, Miller was walking normally. Despite the struggle that could prove inspirational for many people, he rarely discussed this portion of his life. Growing up in an athletic family had its advantages for Miller, who worked diligently to beat them in pickup games in the driveway.

Miller played exceptionally well during high school but always stood in the shadows of his other talented siblings. His sister, Cheryl, is considered one of the greatest women's basketball players in the history of the game, while older brother, Darrell was an outstanding catcher and outfielder prospect. Miller was out to make his own name, as he starred at Riverside Polytechnical High School from 1979 to 1983. His abilities caught the attention of nearby UCLA, which wanted to recruit the slender, silky shooter. By the time he finished his college career, Miller had amassed 2,095 career points, ranking second in the school's history behind only the legendary Kareem Abdul-Jabbar.

Averaging more than 20 points per game during his senior season at UCLA, Miller was regarded as the

At a Glance . . .

Born Reginald Wayne Miller on August 21, 1965, in Riverside, CA; son of Saul and Carrie Miller; married Marita Stavrou. *Education*: Attended UCLA, 1983-87.

Career: Indiana Pacers, guard, 1987-; TV host, Indianapolis; co-author, *I Love Being the Enemy: A Season On The Court With The NBA's Best Shooter and Sharpest Tongue*, 1995.

Awards: NBA All-Star, 1990, 1995, 1996, 1998; All-NBA Third Team, 1995, 1996; won world championship gold medal, 1994; won Olympic gold medal, 1996; became the first Pacer to start in an NBA All-Star game, 1995; first player in NBA history to hit 100 three-pointers in eight consecutive seasons, 1989-97; first player in Pacers' history to top 15,000 career points; has 2,307 career treys going into the 2001-2002 season.

Addresses: Indiana Pacers, 300 E. Market St, Indianapolis, IN 46204.

purest shooter in the game. With shooting guard John Long aging, Miller was the logical choice for the Indiana Pacers, who chose him in the NBA Draft. But the home folks preferred Steve Alford, a local boy who played his college basketball at Indiana University. With the 11th overall pick, Pacers coach Jack Ramsay nabbed Miller and not Alford, who was taken by the Dallas Mavericks, much to the chagrin of the fans.

Although he was the Pacers' career leading scorer, Miller didn't get much notoriety until the team made a playoff run in 1994. With each team that the Pacers played, Miller's reputation grew. Even in a seven-game series loss to the Knicks, Miller's performance was most memorable: he scored 25 points in one quarter. On June 1, 1994, Miller hit five three-point shots against the Knicks to set a NBA playoff record. He also flashed the "choke" sign to film director Spike Lee, who was sitting courtside at Madison Square Garden. The incident has established Miller as one of the league's most notorious "trash-talkers." Another playoff run ended in the 1995 Eastern Conference Finals, this time the Pacers lost to the Orlando Magic.

Miller's "newfound" fame garnered him a spot on Dream Team II, the U.S. men's basketball team playing for gold at the World Basketball Championship. He

joined fellow NBA stars, Shaquille O'Neal, Alonzo Mourning, Shawn Kemp and Larry Johnson as they won the gold. Miller averaged 20 points per game and hit sixty percent of his three-point shots. He was also a member of Dream Team III, which included Grant Hill, Penny Hardaway, and David Robinson as they took home the gold in the 1996 Summer Olympics.

Off the court, Miller hosted a weekly TV show aimed at teenagers in Indianapolis. His topics ranged from homelessness to teen pregnancy. He has been heavily involved in the community. Miller explained to the *Gary Post-Tribune*, "People may think I'm a jerk, but that's just on the court. Off the court, I want to help." Miller also suffered a loss, when his home burned down. It was ruled arson, and the case remains unsolved. He has written his autobiography, *I Love Being the Enemy: A Season On The Court With The NBA's Best Shooter and Sharpest Tongue*.

Pacers' coach Larry Brown resigned after the 1996-1997 season and was replaced by legendary Boston Celtic and Indiana State star Larry Bird. That spring, the Pacers pushed the Chicago Bulls, led by Michael Jordan, to the brink, but lost again in seven games. In the 1998-1999 season, the Knicks eliminated the Pacers in the Eastern Conference Finals for a fourth time, this time. For the 10th year in a row, Miller was the Pacers' leading scorer, but still hadn't reached the NBA Finals.

The 1999-2000 season proved to be Miller's most memorable. He helped the Pacers advance to their first NBA Finals appearance against the Los Angeles Lakers. Miller had worked well with Jalen Rose, but the Lakers' Shaquille O'Neal and Kobe Bryant proved too much for the neophyte Pacers. In August of 2000, Miller signed a new three-year contract for $36 million and there was more change: Bird resigned and Pacers president Donnie Walsh hired new coach Isiah Thomas, another basketball legend with Indiana ties. In Thomas' first season, the Pacers fought the eventual Eastern Conference champion Philadelphia 76ers hard but lost in the first round. Still, Miller has remained upbeat about playing for Thomas and just playing altogether.

"I still get nervous before games," Miller told Yahoo Sports. "Looking down at the opposing two-guard, I still get excited for the rivalry no matter which it is. I always think I'm going to have my hands full, and I want to make sure they have their hands full." Through the years, Miller has established himself as one of the NBA's best players. According to the *New York Daily News*, "Reggie Miller's talent is more than his shot, even more than his mouth....Miller posesses in abundance that quality sportwriters crave more than any other: charisma."

Sources

Books

Newsmakers 1994, Issue 4, Gale Research, 1994.
Who's Who Among African Americans, 14th Edition, Gale Group, 2001.

Periodicals

Gary Post-Tribune, March 31, 1991.
Indianapolis Star, May 15, 1997.
New York Daily News, May 10, 1994; May 27, 1994; May 30, 1994; June 6, 1994.

On-Line

www.espn.com, May 5, 2001
www.indystar.com
Learning Network, www.infoplease.com/ipsa/A010 9140.html
www.nda.com
Reggie Miller.com, through Athlete's Direct.com
www.washingtonpost.com
Yahoo Sports Canada, November 3, 2001, www.ya hoo.com

Sam Mills

1959—

Former professional football player, assistant coach

From most descriptions Sam Mills sounds like the type of person you'd love to have over to the house for a barbecue or to watch the game. He is good-natured, outgoing, and can take a joke with the best of them. And it is good that he can, because no one would think a five-foot-nine-inch linebacker would make it to the National Football League (NFL), let alone have the enormous impact he had on teammates, coaches and to their regret, those he tackled. Most players at his position are considerably taller. For Mills, however, that would serve as motivation to become one of most feared defenders in the history of the game.

Born June 3, 1959 to Sam Sr. and Juanita Mills, Mills was the ninth of 11 children growing up in a housing project in Long Branch, New Jersey. Money was tight in the Mills home so he played football on a parking lot with broken glass. However, the family survived by remaining close-knit and very liberal with love. He moved away from the projects when one of his half-sisters bought a nearby house. His parents would later buy a modest house close to his sister. Mills excelled in football and wrestling at Long Branch High School and later attended Montclair State University, earning a bachelors of science in industrial technology and setting school records on the football field as a fearless line-backer.

The fact that he made it that far on the football field was impressive in its own right. Being shorter than other football players would put most at a serious disadvantage, not only in the eyes of the opponent, but in those of the coaches as well. After his final game at Montclair

Mills was signed as a free agent with the Cleveland Browns in 1981, but was cut after the coach found some bigger players at his position. He joined the Toronto Argonauts of the Canadian Football League, and during training camp, became their leading tackler. Again, he was cut due to lack of height. "It's like this," said Frank Glazier, Mill's high school coach, in a 1988 *Sports Illustrated* article. "No scout, no coach at a big college or in the pros wants to take a chance on a linebacker who is five-nine. If the kid doesn't pan out, the guy's job is on the line. Somebody above him is going to say 'Who got me this five-nine linebacker?' Or the head coach will look at some film where his team gets beat on a pass and say 'What, we couldn't find a six-two linebacker?' The kid's gone, and the guy who found him is gone too."

In 1983 someone took a chance and Mills landed a spot on the Philadelphia/Baltimore Stars of the now-defunct United States Football League. Mills wasted no time commanding the defense and stunting opposing offenses. Linebacking is not easy. It requires strength, amazing speed, the ability to hit very hard, and a keen sense of offensive schemes, designs and plays. Seconds before a play starts, the linebacker can view formations and call to his teammates to switch positions accordingly. The linebacker usually has the first chance to stop a runner or tackle a receiver on short- to mid-range passes. Mills, despite his lack of height, did so extremely well. In his first three seasons he was a three-time All-USFL selection and helped the Stars win league titles in 1983 and 1984. He made 592 tackles and recovered 10 fumbles, never missing a game and

At a Glance . . .

Born June 3, 1959 in Long Branch, NJ; Married Melanie; children: Sam III, Marcus, Larissa and Sierra (adopted.) *Education:* Montclair State, bachelor's of science in industrial technology, 1980.

Career: Professional linebacker, Philadelphia/ Baltimore Stars, USFL, 1983-85; New Orleans Saints, 1986-94; Carolina Panthers, 1995-97, pro scout/ defensive assistant, 1998-.

Awards: Named Kodak All-American his senior year at Montclair State, 1980; holds school records in career tackles (501), single-season tackles (142) and single-game tackles (22); three-time defensive player of the year by the New Jersey Collegiate Football Writers Association; member, Panthers Hall of Honor, New Orleans Saints Hall of Fame, Louisiana Hall of Fame; named to five Pro Bowls.

Addresses: c/o The Carolina Panthers, 800 S. Mint St, Charlotte, NC 28202.

played *every* defensive down. More importantly, the USFL experience provided him with a chance to prove himself in the NFL. Mills told *Sport Magazine,* "I was so psyched to make good plays. I was afraid that if the Denver team ran through me, I would be released Monday morning. I was trying to wind down because I was the signal caller. I wound up having a great game. Playing that game was like running for the elevator and no one shut the door on me."

Sports Illustrated writer Michael Bamberger assessed the diminutive defender's size. "Football people talk about Mills' lack of height—he is all of an inch or so shorter than average American adult male—as if it were a physical handicap. Mills is built along the lines of Mike Tyson....He weighs 230 pounds, which is average for an NFL linebacker. He can bench-press 400 pounds, after having been stuck for years at 395." "He has extraordinary strength and drive, and extraordinary humanity," Jim Finks, general manager of the Saints, told *Sports Illustrated.*

In 1986 the USFL folded. Head coach Jim Mora took the top job for the New Orleans Saints in the NFL and brought Mills with him. Mills played nine seasons for the Saints and would start a trend where, with age and experience, he would only get better. In his first season,

he finished with 92 tackles, earning the respect of his teammates. In his final season with the Saints in 1994 he finished with a career-high 115 tackles. He was 37, which, by NFL standards, is a rarity. During his Saints' tenure he was named to four Pro Bowls, an all-star-type exhibition game featuring the NFL's best positional players. He signed a two-year contract with the Carolina Panthers in 1996. He was named to his fifth Pro Bowl that season. When he retired from playing in 1997, Mills' stats were staggering: 12 NFL seasons, 1,319 tackles, 20.5 quarterback sacks, 11 interceptions and four touchdowns in 181 games with 173 starts. He also had not missed a start in 50 games.

And while Mill's ability to tackle and defend are what brought him success and notoriety, those around him marvel at his attitude. He also served as a mentor to younger players while with the Saints and Panthers. His tireless work ethic glowed among his teammates.

Mills is painted as a man of severe humility. He was twice cut in the pros. And even before he had the chance to endure that, he was making $13,500 per year as a high school wood shop and photography teacher in New Jersey. He was born hairless, impoverished and with poor eyesight. Yet, through years of hard work, extreme physical training, drive and determination, Mills turned a less-than-encouraging start into a prominent professional football career, one where he earned the admiration of fans, and the respect of teammates and opponents.

In 1999 Mills accepted an assistant coaching/scouting position with the Panthers. Having secured a viable career option after his playing days was something he started while in New Orleans. There, in the offseason, he worked as a trainee at a car dealership owned by the team's owner. Even then, as he pointed out in *Sport Magazine,* he had the foresight to realize what was truly important. "I know what it's like not to make much money. I have to prepare for my family's future. If I don't prepare, the blame is on me."

Sources

Periodicals

Sports Illustrated, August 11, 1997, pg. 64; December 12, 1988, pg. 66.
Sport Magazine, February 1992, pg. 20.
The Sporting News, August 7, 1995, pg. 40.

On-line

www.gastongazette.com
www.lasportshof.com

—John Horn

Albert L. Murray

1916—

Novelist, essayist, biographer, philosopher

A well-known author and essayist, Albert L. Murray has been called, according to Malcolm Jones, Jr. in *Newsweek*, one of the "most influential cultural figures" of the twentieth century. Murray's writings cover a variety of subjects, most notably his focus on African-American culture and music. Although most clearly identified as a spokesperson for African-American culture and widely acknowledged as one of black America's foremost thinkers, Murray himself rejected that label, pointing out that his skin is brown, not black (he prefers the designations "Negro" or "colored"), and that all Americans, black and white, share a common culture. He has called himself simply an American writer. According to Murray, that common culture is most eloquently expressed in blues and jazz music; somewhat like writer Amiri Baraka, who characterized black Americans as a "blues people," Murray identified a "blues idiom" that gives Americans the spirit and wit to overcome adversity.

In novels, essays, travel narratives, poems, and other forms, Murray has expressed his ideas with at least three mutually reinforcing levels: he writes, in the broadest sense, about the blues, in a style that resembles the blues, creating works that embody what he sees as a blues aesthetic of survival, perseverance,

and a positive spirit in the face of difficulty. The writer who has created this complex style took much of a lifetime to forge it; he did not publish his first book until his sixth decade.

Albert Lee Murray was born to a single mother in Nokomis, Alabama, on May 12, 1916. He was taken in and raised by a couple in the Magazine Point neighborhood of nearby Mobile, and his teachers recognized him as uncommonly intelligent while he was still a young child. Murray was sent to the Mobile County Training School, an institution whose strong-willed and oratorically gifted teachers were the source of an influence Murray has often acknowledged.

Attended Tuskegee Institute

Murray moved on to the flagship of the pre-integration system of black higher education in the South: the Tuskegee Institute. He studied the classics of European literature and received a bachelor's degree in education there in 1939. Of special influence during this time were the works of Austrian novelist Thomas Mann, who incorporated the music of classical composers Beethoven and Wagner into his mode of storytelling.

At a Glance . . .

Born Albert Lee Murray in Nokomis, Alabama, June 12, 1916; raised in Mobile, Alabama area. Married Mozelle Menefee, May 31, 1941, one child. *Education*: Graduated from Mobile County Training School; Tuskegee Institute, B.S. in education with much literature study, 1939; postgraduate work, University of Michigan, 1940, Northwestern University, 1941; New York University, M.A., 1948; University of Paris, Paris France, postgraduate study, 1950. *Military service*: U.S. Air Force, 1943-62; reached rank of major.

Career: Writer and educator. Taught at Tuskegee Institute, 1940s-50s; trained Tuskegee Airmen during World War II; moved to New York City, early 1960s; published numerous essays, 1960s; published first book, *The Omni-Americans*, a collection of essays, 1970; published trilogy of semi-autobiographical novels: *Train Whistle Guitar*, 1974; *The Spyglass Tree*, 1991; *The Seven League Boots*, 1996; worked with Count Basie on Basie's autobiography, early 1980s; published several volumes of essays and musical criticism; numerous visting lectureships at various colleges and universities, 1970s-90s.

Selected Awards: Lillian Smith Award for fiction, for *Train Whistle Guitar*, 1974; ASCAP Deems Taylor Award for musical criticism, for *Stomping the Blues*, 1976; National Book Critics' Circle Lifetime Achievement Award, 1996; numerous honorary doctoral degrees.

Address: 45 W. 132nd St., New York, NY 10037.

After doing graduate work at the University of Michigan and Northwestern University, Murray returned to Tuskegee, teaching English there for many years and also joining the U.S. Air Force. He became one of the trainers of the Tuskegee Airmen who distinguished themselves during World War II. Murray himself spent time in the great capitals of Europe during a stretch when he was stationed in Morocco; he studied at the University of Paris for a time. While stationed in the northeastern United States he completed an M.A. at New York University in 1948.

After retiring from the military with the rank of major in 1962, Murray moved with his wife and family to New

York's Harlem neighborhood and turned to writing in earnest. His first book, *The Omni-Americans* (1970), collected essays he had published during the 1960s. In these writings Murray emphasized the idea of an American culture composed of a unique mixture of elements, taking sharp issue both with black separatists and with the predominant white sociological writings of the day that emphasized only grim pathologies in the black experience. Murray then published the travel narrative *South to a Very Old Place* (1972), an account of a trip he made to his hometown of Mobile, with side visits to Tuskegee, Memphis, and other locales; the book, containing vivid descriptions of Mobile's black community, embodied Murray's original and very musical prose style.

Penned Autobiographical Trilogy

Murray's other writings of the 1970s included the first novel of an eventual autobiographical trilogy, *Train Whistle Guitar* (1974), which depicted the coming-of-age of an intelligent Mobile youth named Scooter. The other two works of the trilogy followed Scooter to Tuskegee (*The Spyglass Tree*, 1991), and into a swing-era jazz band (*The Seven League Boots*, 1996); Murray considered himself a fiction writer foremost. For many years, however, music came to the fore in his writing.

In such books as *The Hero and the Blues* (1973) and *Stomping the Blues* (1976), the second of which won the music industry's Deems Taylor Award for music criticism, Murray expressed his ideas about the place of blues and jazz in American culture. According to him, the "blues hero" is not simply a musician but the embodiment of black experience and values. Murray also regarded improvisation within a framework of a communal tradition as critical to the spirit of confrontation that resulted in the improvement of the conditions of black life in America. In other works, such as *The Blue Devils of Nada* (1996), he argued that the blues animated the spirit of American life itself, offering inspiration not only to African Americans beset by racism, but to anyone troubled by the lack of meaning in modern life.

A passage from *The Blue Devils of Nada* illustrates Murray's unique style, seemingly composed by turns of Southern downhome speech and European didactic argument. In this passage, he argues that a complete realization of the blues attitude towards life is not only necessary for blacks but for any group of people. He says that, "a fully orchestrated blues statement" is "a fundamental device for confrontation, improvisation, and existential affirmation: a strategy for acknowledging the fact that life is a lowdown dirty shame and for improvising or riffing on the exigencies of the predicament." In general, Murray states, suffering is a given, but can be overcome. "To protest the existence of dragons (or even hooded or unhooded Grand Dragons for that matter) is not only sentimental but naive," he concluded.

Worked with Count Basie

Murray put his interest in music to work in practical realms in the 1980s, taking a decade off from his own writings to work with jazz bandleader Count Basie on his autobiography, *Good Morning Blues* (1985). He helped found and served on the board of directors of the Jazz at Lincoln Center concert series, a major institution that presented jazz as an art form comparable to classical symphonic music or opera. In the 1990s, approaching his 80th year, Murray once again began to write prolifically despite being slowed by a series of spine operations.

In addition to the second and third Scooter novels and *The Blue Devils of Nada*, Murray published a volume of poetry, *Aubades: Epic Exits and Other Twelve Bar Riffs* (2001), a new book of essays, *From the Briarpatch File* (2001), a collection of letters he had exchanged with his Tuskegee contemporary Ralph Ellison, and an art exhibition catalogue devoted to the work of his friend Romare Bearden. Late in life, Murray was feted with a parade of honorary doctoral degrees, one of them from his alma mater of Tuskegee. He was presented with a Lifetime Achievement Award from the National Book Critics' Circle in 1996.

Selected writings

The Omni-Americans, 1970 (essays).
South to a Very Old Place, 1972 (travel narrative).
The Hero and the Blues, 1973 (music criticism).
Train Whistle Guitar, 1974 (novel).
Stomping the Blues, 1976 (music criticism).
Good Morning Blues: The Autobiography of Count Basie, as Told to Albert Murray, 1985.
The Spyglass Tree, 1991 (novel).
The Seven League Boots, 1996 (novel).
The Blue Devils of Nada, 1996 (music and philosophy).
(Editor, with John F. Callahan) *Trading Twelves: Selected Letters of Ralph Ellison and Albert Murray*, 2000.
Aubades: Epic Exits and Other Twelve Bar Riffs, 2001 (poetry).
From the Briarpatch File, 2001 (essays).

Sources

Books

Contemporary Novelists, 7th ed., St. James, 2001.
Contemporary Southern Writers, St. James, 1999.

Periodicals

African American Review, Summer 1993, p. 287; Spring 1999, p. 168.
American Heritage, September 1996, p. 68.
New Republic, February 3, 1992, p. 39.
Newsweek, February 5, 1996, p. 60.
Publisher's Weekly, February 26, 1996, p. 78; September 24, 2001, p. 91; October 1, 2001, p. 46.

On-line

Contemporary Authors Online, The Gale Group, 2001. Reproduced in *Biography Resource Center*, Gale, 2001, http://www.galenet.com/servlet/Bio RC

—James M. Manheim

Nas

1973—

Rap musician, actor

Not yet thirty years old, Nas has released five successful albums, launched his own record label, a fashion company, and appeared in several films. With his music, Nas bas become known for, according to Len Righi of the *Morning Call*, his "ability to look outside the immediate circumstances of his life" and address larger issues.

Nas was born Nasir Jones on September 14, 1973, in Queens, New York. His father, Olu Dara, a jazz and blues trumpeter, chose the name Nasir for his son because of its Arabic meaning: "helper" or "protector." Nas was raised by his mother, Fannie Ann Jones.

Growing up in New York City's tough Queensbridge housing projects, "it sometimes seemed to [Nas] his whole world was ill and being eaten away," wrote Christopher John Farley in *Time*. "Drugs were devouring minds, crime was destroying families, poverty was gnawing at souls." In May of 1992, both Nas's brother, Jungle, and best friend were shot on the same night. Although his brother lived, Nas's friend did not survive his injuries. "That was a wake-up call for me," Nas told *Time*.

Released Debut Album

Two years after his wake-up call, Nas released his debut album, *Illmatic*. Nas worked with a number of top hip-hop producers, and his hard work paid off. *Entertainment Weekly* said of the album: "his witty lyrics and gruffly gratifying beats draw listeners into [his neighborhood's] lifestyle with poetic efficiency." Farley, writing in *Time*, noted that the record "captures the ailing community he [Nas] was raised in—the random gunplay, the whir of police helicopters, the homeboys hanging out on the corner sipping bottles of Hennessey."

Setting himself apart from other gangsta rappers, Nas did not typically glorify violence in his music, but, rather, his songs evoke sadness and outrage. Farley noted in *Time* that Nas performs on the album with "submerged emotion" and describes urban tragedy dispassionately, much "like an anchorman relaying the day's grim news." *The New York Times* declared that, on the album, Nas "imbues his chronicle with humanity and humor, not just hardness....[He] reports violence without celebrating it, dwelling on the way life triumphs over grim circumstances rather than the other way around."

At a Glance . . .

Born Nasir Jones on September 14, 1973, in Queens, NY; son of Fannie Ann Jones and Olu Dara (jazz trumpeter).

Career: Rap musician, actor. Albums include: *Illmatic*, 1994; *It Was Written*, 1996; *I Am*, 1999; *Nastradamus*, 1999; *Stillmatic*, 2001; films include: *Belly*, 1998; *Ticker*, 2001; *Sacred Is the Flesh*, 2001.

Awards: Youth Summit Award, Hip-Hop Youth Summit, 2002.

Addresses: *Office*—c/o Sony Music Entertainment, Rap artist, 550 Madison Ave, New York, New York, United States 10022 (212) 833-8000.

Nas's sophomore album, *It Was Written*, was released in 1996, selling more than a million copies. Again, Nas worked with several hip-hop producers, including top selling Dr. Dre. With this album, however, Nas faced criticism that the songs were amoral, contained rough language, and included episodes of violence. Critics were also frustrated by the album's contradictions. The hit single "If I Ruled The World (Imagine That)," for example, depicts paradise as a "better livin' type of place to raise our kids in." However, this world is also one in which cocaine comes uncut, allowing higher profits on the drug. In a *Rolling Stone* review, Mark Coleman commented that Nas "possesses a phenomenal way with words and some savvy musical sense." Coleman continued, "It's a pity he doesn't put his verbal dexterity and powers of observation to better use....When Nas finally aligns his mind with his mouth, he'll truly be dangerous."

Music critic Toure, writing in the *New York Times*, noted a strong musical link between Nas and his father, Olu Dara. Though the two musicians came from very different backgrounds and subscribed to different musical schools, Toure wrote, "Nas's music is characterized by a laid-back cool, with a penchant for medium-pace tempos and relatively sparse tracks, all of which are hallmarks of his father's music." Nas's father, who had a trumpet solo on his son's first album, told Toure, "His aggressive is cool. Not like 'I'm angry! I'm mad!' It's cool. And that's the way my music is." Vernon Reid, a guitarist who has played with Dara, also noted similarities between father and son, saying in the *New York Times*: "Both have a finely tuned sense of irony, which I think is evident in Nas's lyrics and Olu's playing." Reid continued, "There's a kind of cockeyed way of looking at the world. A raised eyebrow. Sly.

They're seeing what's going on underneath the surface."

Appeared in First Film

In 1998 Nas made his feature film debut, appearing in *Belly*. Co-starring with fellow rapper DMX, the two hip-hop stars played best friends. Although they both come from the same violent neighborhood, these two friends want very different things out of life. Tommy, played by DMX, is willing to do whatever it takes to attain money, power, and women. Nas's character, Sincere, wishes only to provide for his girlfriend and their child. To do so, he has partnered with Tommy in a world of crime, violence, and drugs. Sincere, however, has begun to reconsider his ways. In the end, according to *Seattle Post-Intelligencer* reviewer Paula Nechak, both characters arrive at the same conclusion: "Life is what you make it and knowledge and self-respect are everything."

Critics, although praising the stylistic ability of the film's director, Hype Williams, skewered the film for its lack of originality. The *Seattle Times* criticized the acting skills of both rap stars, saying that Nas and DMX "couldn't mutter their way out of an unzipped starter jacket." Nechak, however, concluded in the *Seattle Post-Intelligencer*: "There is a real rite of passage these two young men go through in order to find themselves, and for once the payoff isn't death."

I Am, Nas's third album, was released in 1999. Here Nas collaborated with such stars as Sean "Puffy" Combs, Lauryn Hill, and Aaliyah. With numerous radio-friendly tracks on the album, a number of music critics accused the rapper of selling out. *The Record* noted that *I Am* seemed "tailored for mass consumption," and the *San Francisco Chronicle* suggested that several tracks "are too generic for Nas' delivery, leaving his vocals sounding ungrounded." Nas's talent had not waned however. According to the *San Francisco Chronicle*, "Nas continues to drop jaws and tingle ear canals with his complex and challenging wordplay." Rather, some critics felt that Nas, in producing so mainstream an album, had done a disservice to his talent. *The Record* concluded that "the commercial advance requires an artistic step backward."

Later that year, Nas released his fourth album, *Nastradamus*. Again, critics lamented the too-polished style of the album. *New York Times* critic Soren Baker observed, "It's as if in graduating from the ghetto, he's misplaced the gritty edge that made him a hero."

Feuded With Jay-Z

Perhaps Nas regained some of his edge when he began a feud of words with rapper Jay-Z. Jay-Z's album, *The Blueprint*, featured the track "Takeover." Here Jay-Z referred to Nas as "garbage," saying, "That's why your—l-a-a-a-me!—career's come to an end." Nas retaliated with an underground parody of the Jay-Z hit "Izzo." The feud was further fueled by several tracks on Nas's 2001 album, *Stillmatic*. Here Nas accused Jay-Z of usurping rhymes from the late Notorious B.I.G., criticized Jay-Z's preference for Hawaiian shirts, and even attempted a bit of armchair psychoanalysis. Hip-hop fans in both the United States and Europe were fascinated by the feud, choosing sides and, according to the *New York Times*, "debating each rapper's use of puns and metaphors." The feud came to an end in early 2002. Jay-Z, after receiving a call from his mother asking him to stop, telephoned a New York City radio station and publicly apologized for "Super Ugly," his response to Nas's *Stillmatic* tracks.

Nas has formed his own record label, Nas and Ill Will Records. He has also launched a clothing line—Esco. In 2001 he co-starred with Steven Segal in the action film, *Ticker*. Although he has branched out into business and film, Nas remained devoted to music. "Music is in my blood," he told the *New York Times*. "I could have chosen to do a lot of other things. I could have been a scientist, a lawyer. But this is where I'm comfortable at, right here."

Selected works

Albums

Illmatic, Columbia, 1994.
It Was Written, Columbia, 1996.
I Am, Columbia, 1999.
Nastradamus, Columbia, 1999.
Stillmatic, Ill Will, 2001.

Films

Belly, 1998.
Ticker, 2001.
Sacred Is the Flesh, 2001.

Sources

Books

Contemporary Musicians, Volume 19. Gale Research, 1997.
Who's Who Among African Americans, 14th ed. Gale Group, 2000.

Periodicals

Entertainment Weekly, April 22, 1994, p. 58; July 26, 1996, p. 56.
Florida Times Union, January 18, 2002, p. WE11.
The Independent Sunday (London, England), January 6, 2002, p. 9.
Los Angeles Times, November 21, 1999, p. C8; December 23, 2001, p.F71.
Morning Call (Allentown, PA), January 12, 2002, p. A40.
New York Times, Oct. 6, 1996, sec. 2; January 6, 2002, p. L1.
The Record (Bergen County, NJ) April 23, 1999, p. 8.
Rolling Stone, September 16, 1996, pp. 83-84; December 26, 1996, pp. 194-95.
San Francisco Chronicle, April 18, 1999, p. 42.
Seattle Post-Intelligencer, November 4, 1998, p. C3.
Seattle Times, November 4, 1998, p. F3.
Star-Ledger (Newark, NJ), January 23, 2002, p. 58.
Time, June 20, 1994, p. 62; July 29, 1996, p. 79.

On-line

All Music Guide, http://allmusicguide.com
Biography Resource Center, Gale Group, 2001, http://www.galenet.com/servlet/BioRC
Internet Movie Database, http://www.us.imdb.com
Sony Music, http://www.music.sony.co.artistinfo/nas/

—Jennifer M. York

Ben Ngubane

1941—

South African politician

South African post-apartheid politics have been characterized both by intense optimism and continuing frustrations. The images of apartheid falling, Nelson Mandela leaving prison after nearly three decades, and the country's first democratic elections in 1994, are still powerful motivators as the country goes forward. However, in no way is the progress easy. South Africans struggle daily with the backlash of decades of racism, tribal differences, and a blood-stained history. Continuing political violence, poverty, and health issues, particularly AIDS, color every South African's life. In addition there are numerous political factions vying for power. Even before Mandela's presidency, these factions have consistently impeded the progress of the new South African democracy with their infighting and often violent actions. From the official political parties to the traditional tribal groups, each faction has their own agenda. It takes an astute leader with compassion for the needs of the people and savvy to the ways of politicians to make government work under such circumstances. One member of the post-apartheid government that is uniquely qualified for just such a role is Ben Ngubane. *African Business* described Ngubane as "one of those rare politicians who doesn't have any real enemies."

From Teacher to Doctor to Politician

Baldwin Sipho "Ben" Ngubane was born on October 22, 1941 at the Inchanga Roman Catholic Mission at Camperdown in the KwaZulu-Natal province. He attended school at St. Francis College in Marianhill, a mission school just outside of Durban. After graduating in 1960 he continued at St. Francis as a Latin teacher for two years. He left teaching to pursue medical training, earning a medical degree from the Durban Medical School in 1971. This was augmented with diplomas in tropical medicine in 1982 and Public Health in 1983, both earned at the University of Witwatersrand. He rounded out his education with a Masters in family medicine and primary health from the Natal Medical School in 1986.

While pursuing his medical career, he joined the Inkatha National Cultural Liberation Movement and in 1977 became a member of its central committee. Like Nelson Mandela's African National Congress (ANC), the Inkatha Movement's ultimate goal was the liberation of South African people from the oppression of the apartheid government. However, there were key differences in their respective approaches. At that time the ANC was officially banned by the government and was operating in exile. The Inkatha movement, based in KwaZulu-Natal, South Africa, was considered a 'loyal opposition' party by the apartheid government. Among its philosophies were the preservation of traditional culture and customs, and movement towards liberation in a non-violent manner. At the time it also had a very strong leaning towards Zulu nationalism. Because the Inkatha movement initially tried to work with in the dictates of the apartheid government, many South Africans, exiled and not, viewed Inkatha as a collaborator of the government, not to be trusted.

The apartheid leaders quickly saw the Inkatha movement as a way to combat the ANC and other opposition leaders and manipulated the movement accordingly. Mistrust between the ANC and Inkatha began to grow. Ngubane would later tell *Focus*, "The original sin here was the ANC's refusal to make room for traditional African society within the liberation struggle. Inkatha contributed a great deal to that struggle but our role was denied and denigrated."

Ascended Party Ranks

Meanwhile, Ngubane was working his way up the ranks of Inkatha and the KwaZulu government, eventually becoming Minister of Health in 1991. However, his medical training had as much of an impact on his activities as did his political leanings. From 1978 on, Ngubane was very active in the South African Red Cross. He became a Regional Councilor for the organization in 1978 and throughout the 1980s represented South Africa at international Red Cross congresses. During the devastating floods in KwaZulu-Natal in the early 1980s, Ngubane was instrumental in implementing Red Cross services. Because of these actions he received a citation for dedicated service. During these busy decades Ngubane also managed to find time to begin a family and pursue his interests, which include education and sports. He also bore witness to the horrors of political and civil unrest that characterized South Africa during this time—student uprisings, politically motivated massacres, and widespread corruption.

After the freeing of Mandela by F.W. de Klerk and the formal reinstatement of the ANC as a political party in 1991, Ngubane became heavily involved in the negotiations that would lead to the 1994 multi-party democratic elections. At this time Inkatha formed the Inkatha Freedom Party (IFP). By this time the rift between the ANC and Inkatha was massive. Violence between members of the two parties was endemic and untold thousands lost their lives.

Even as Ngubane and other IFP leaders worked with the ANC and other party leaders, a violent campaign was being waged by IFP followers angry at the ANC's central role in the negotiations. During these negotiations, Ngubane's behavior cemented his reputation as gracious, moderate, and decisive. Of Ngubane's style, one political rival told *African Business*, "He has an unsettling aptitude to get to the crux of the matter with uncanny speed and accuracy."

Became Minister of Arts in KwaZulu-Natal

In 1994 elections were finally held and (as expected) the ANC came out the winners with 62% of the vote. Nelson Mandela became president and, true to his vision of a united South Africa, appointed Ngubane to Minister of Arts, Culture, Science and Technology. His performance in this role garnered national approval. Of his tenure, the *Mail and Guardian* wrote, "with his medical and cultural background he has made real impact," and described him as "likeable and knowledgeable." Highlighting the ongoing problems between the IFP and the majority party, *Mail and Guardian* continued, "He is the only Inkatha Freedom Party member who deserves a place in the Cabinet on merit."

Two years into Ngubane's five-year term, the IFP called him back to KwaZulu-Natal to assist with provincial legislature. A year later, in 1997, he was appointed to the Premiership of KwaZulu-Natal. Of his departure from national government, *African Business* wrote, "regret was genuine in all shades of political opinion." KwaZulu-Natal was rife with crime and unrest upon his appointment. One of his first commitments to the people was to promote peace and reduce the crime rate. Statistics prove he succeeded. He told *African Business* how this was accomplished, "More visible security was a key move." However, emphasizing his beliefs in leading by example, he continued, "What has also helped greatly is the tone of the rhetoric coming down from the politicians. [The government] is no longer permissive." As he worked to combat the social and economic problems of KwaZulu-Natal, Ngubane also sustained his role as an IFP leader becoming the national chairman of the party.

As premier, Ngubane's commitment to improving education came into focus. In discussing what he viewed as the futility of the labor initiatives of the ANC majority government he told *Focus* in an interview, "What we actually need is training, training, and more training. Not just excellence in higher education but perhaps even more important, training for artisans, plumbers, mechanics and other intermediate skills." During his two years as premier he also tackled problems of productivity, finance, development, and IFP-ANC relations. In the same interview, he said, "IFP-ANC talks are important: we must work together to lower tension and increase tolerance." Of the magnitude of his tasks he told *African Business*: "There are people who tell me that change on such a big scale takes time. I remind them that time is something we do not have a lot of," adding with characteristic decisiveness, "We have a challenge, and we will face it now."

In 1999 Mandela stepped down and Thebo Mbeki was elected president. Again the ANC took the majority of the votes. Ngubane left his premiership of KwaZulu-Natal and was once again appointed Minister of Arts, Culture, Science and Technology. Of this transition the *Mail and Guardian* alluding to political finagling, wrote, "the IFP ousted him from [the premiership] and transferred him back to Arts in the national government. The official reason for his removal was that he had presided over poor matric results. Speculation was that the real reason was his refusal to back a Casino bid involving IFP sympathizers."

Focus on Science and Technology

In the years since Ngubane returned to national government, he has spent much of his energy on science and technology. In 2000 he became the chair of the Commonwealth Science Council, an international organization that promotes the advancement of science in the 54 countries that make up the voluntary Commonwealth organization. In the same year he became chair of ComNet, another Commonwealth organization that promotes computer, Internet, and web technology for its member nations. Under his leadership, South Africa has embarked upon the development of an international astronomy program and the building of one of the world's largest telescopes. However, according to the *Mail and Guardian's* 2001 grading of South Africa's politicians, Ngubane has failed miserably on the Arts and Culture front. "The theater industry is a sad story of downsized theatres, closed mainstream performing arts companies, procrastination and poor departmental decisions." It continued, "Ngubane's department has been criticized for a lack of progress in delivering new jobs and income-generating opportunities in [crafts and cultural tourism]."

As a medical doctor and a politician, a respected national and international leader and a member of the much-maligned IFP party, Ngubane has had to balance many roles. History has recorded his success in his execution of these positions. However, nothing is ever easy in politics. Critics and opponents are forever there to document and exploit missteps and failures. Yet, as *African Business* wrote, "he is one of those uncommonly found public figures who is well-liked across party lines." In a country with such a complex historical, cultural, and political identity, this alone is an accomplishment to be celebrated.

Sources

Periodicals

African Business, November, 1997, p. 28.

Mail and Guardian, (South Africa), June, 1999; November 12, 1999; December 22, 1999; December 22, 2000; December 20, 2001.

On-line

www.ebooks.whsmithonline.co.uk/Encyclopedia
www.gov.za/profiles/ngubane.htm
Focus,   http://www.hsf.org.za/focus_10/F10_ben_
  ngu bane.htm

—Candace LaBalle

Richard Dean Parsons

1948—

Corporate executive

Richard Parsons has become one of the most prominent figures in American business, without rising through the usual ranks required to reach a high-level corporate position. Named president of Dime Savings Bank of New York in 1988 even though he had no previous experience in the banking industry, he masterminded a turnaround at the bank in just a few years. In the early 1990s he became president of Time Warner Inc., making him one of the most highly ranked African Americans in the corporate United States. In 1999, when AOL and Time Warner merged, parsons became the co-chief operating officer, a position shared with Bob Pittman. In 2001 Parsons was named the successor to AOL Time Warner's CEO, Gerald Levin, who was retired in May of 2002.

Hard work has been a crucial component of the Parsons success story, a value he claims to have learned from his father. As he told *Ebony*, "I have never missed a single day of work in my life. Never. Not one." Also fueling his rise were connections he has made with important people over the years. "A gregarious and thoughtful man, Mr. Parsons has risen by winning the affection and loyalty of influential mentors," wrote Laurence Zuckerman in the *New York Times*.

Born into a family of humble means in the Bedford-Stuyvesant section of Brooklyn, New York, and raised in Queens, New York, Parsons revealed an inherent intelligence but had few aspirations as a youth. He graduated high school at the age of 16, then devoted much of his attention to sports as a student at the

University of Hawaii. He played varsity basketball there, and was also the social chairman of his fraternity. His journey to future success was given some impetus by his girlfriend at the time, Laura Bush, who became his wife in 1968.

"Left to my own devices, I don't feel any compulsion to strive," he told the *New York Times* in 1990. "My wife became my focus and the person to whom I owed my best." His plans to become a fighter pilot were redirected to law school largely due to Bush's influence. According to *Ebony*, Parsons said that "the woman I was dating [Bush] told me, 'You like to argue so much you ought to become a lawyer and get paid for it.'"

At Union University of the University of Albany Law School, Parsons helped pay his way through school by working part-time as a janitor and later as an aide in the State Assembly. He graduated number one in his class of more than 100 students at the age of 23, then received the highest marks among 3,600 lawyers who took the state bar examination in 1971.

Career Shaped by Rockefeller

Beginning his legal career as an aide on New York governor Nelson Rockefeller's legal staff, Parsons made a very favorable impression on the governor. Governor Rockefeller rewarded Parsons's solid performance by keeping him on his staff when he became vice president under President Gerald Ford in 1974. President Ford also used his services, first as a general council and then as associate director of the domestic council. In the latter post, Parsons focused on drug issues.

Rockefeller's influence on Parsons remained strong and prompted him to become a Republican whose views were liberal on social issues and conservative on economic ones. It also brought Parsons to the attention of high-ranking people who later sought his services. As Parsons said in the *New York Times* in 1994, "becoming a part of that Rockefeller entourage ... created for me a group of people who've looked out for me ever since." Parsons own concern for the underprivileged has been clearly shown by his work as chairman of the Wildcat Service Corporation, which has provided on-the-job instruction for people whose previous crimes, drug addiction, or poverty have made it difficult to find work.

By the mid-1970s Parsons was noted as a rising star among black professionals, and he was profiled in *Black Enterprise's* "Under 30 & Moving Up" series in 1975. When departing Deputy Attorney General Harold R. Tyler, Jr., became a partner at a well-established New York City law firm in 1977, he asked Parsons to come on board. Parsons became a partner in just two years at Patterson, Belknap, Webb & Tyler, a move that typically demanded seven years. In his 11 years with the firm, he made his mark in both corporate law and civil litigation. Among his clients were such high-profile figures as Happy Rockefeller and the cosmetics queen Estee Lauder.

Critical to the next chapter in the Parsons success story was his work with the Dimes Saving Bank of New York, which he provided with legal counsel for about six years while with Patterson, Belknap, Webb & Tyler. Just when he seemed poised to become the first black to head a major law firm, shock waves rippled through the New York corporate world in 1988 when Parsons was appointed chief operating officer of the Dime by chairman and CEO Harry Albright, Jr. Before being offered the position, Parsons had never even considered entering the banking business. As he later told *Black Enterprise,* "My wife talked me into it. She said I needed the change."

Parsons's appointment made him the first black to manage a lending company the size of Dime Savings Bank. "It's a statement by and to corporate America that there are no more areas where African Americans haven't succeeded," he told the *New York Times* in 1990. Some top officials at the bank questioned his appointment, both because of his lack of experience in the banking industry and his previous work in government that made him likely to leave the company for the political arena. Parsons answered these reservations by promising to devote his full attention to his new $525,000-a-year post. Over the years Parsons has, however, admitted the possibility of entering politics later in life. "It's a venue to which I could see myself returning at some point in time," he told the *New York Times* in 1994, referring to public service as the "highest calling, large and important work."

Parsons began working at Dime during a difficult period. The bank had suffered a series of losses due to the drastic devaluation of New York City real estate in the late 1980s, and during the previous year it had lost $92.3 million. Parsons also had to deal with an onslaught of unhappy regulators. Under his tutelage the bank staged a remarkable comeback, largely through his massive overhauling of the bank's management systems and work force. In just a few years he reduced the Dime's $1 billion in bad debts to $335 million.

During that time he also earned the respect of the staff for his fair treatment. "Colleagues say Parsons' management style helped smooth the painful layoffs that he had to make," wrote Fonda Marie Lloyd and Mark Lowery in *Black Enterprise.* "They credit him with keeping employees informed every step of the way, at one point even producing several videos that were distributed to employees." When Albright departed the Dime, Parsons became chairman and CEO. With the bank now on solid financial ground, he engineered a merger with Anchor Savings Bank to create Dime Bancorp in early 1995. The merger created the fourth largest thrift institution in the nation and the largest on the East Coast, with assets worth $20 billion.

Politics Differed From Most Blacks

In 1993 Parsons was criticized by other blacks for supporting Rudolph Giuliani in the New York City mayoral race, instead of the incumbent Democrat, black mayor David Dinkins. This political stance was consistent with his rejection of the Democrats' philosophy. According to an article in *Black Enterprise,* Parsons feels that the Democrats believe in taking from one group to give to another one, while the Rockefeller Republicans espouse a policy of equipping a group with skills so that they can achieve what they need on their own. "You can't give something to somebody to have," said Parsons in the same article. "Then, they don't value it. Value is associated with hard work."

After Giuliani was elected, he named Parsons to be head of his transition council. Peter J. Powers, New York City's First Deputy Mayor at the time, complemented Parsons's leadership skills in the *New York Times,* noting that Parsons "really knows how to bring people together and find common ground." Mayor Giuliani later asked Parsons to become his deputy mayor for Economic Development. Although Parsons refused that position, he consented to work as chairman of the city's Economic Development Corporation.

Admiration for Parsons's skills in the business world resulted in his being courted as a board member for a number of leading companies and institutions, including Time Warner Inc., Philip Morris, Tristar Pictures, Howard University, and the Metropolitan Museum of Art. His involvement with Time Warner resulted in his developing close ties with important company executives such as Robert W. Morgado, the chairman of the Warner Music Group, and Michael J. Fuchs, chairman of HBO. Parsons was asked to become the new president of Time Warner by its chairman, Gerald M. Levin, in the fall of 1994. In the *Washington Post,* Levin called Parsons "an exceptional business leader with the broad experience, financial acumen and the knowledge of our business that will strengthen and solidify our corporate management."

Parsons accepted the presidency for a reported salary of several million dollars a year. The position placed him second in command over the entire Time Warner holdings in magazine and book publishing, music, film entertainment, theme parks, and cable television. Meanwhile, he answered complaints from colleagues at the Dime that he was deserting them. "This opportunity with Time Warner is a once in a lifetime one. It was either you go for it, or it's gone forever," claimed Parsons in *Black Enterprise.* "It's not a bad time for me to make a move. I know the bank is in good hands."

The Parsons appointment was not without controversy at Time Warner. He was again entering an industry that was new to him, and some doubted his qualifications. Parsons also inherited a number of problems when he assumed his new post in January of 1995. Time Warner's record division was experiencing difficulty, and company officials were suspicious about the designs of Edgar Bronfman of the Seagram Companies, which owned 15 percent of the company's stock. The conglomerate was also saddled with significant debt. Chief among his tasks since joining Time Warner have been the restructuring of the company's financial and administrative operations, as well as evaluating the responsibilities of artists regarding explicit displays of sex and violence.

Role of Race Downplayed

Some considered the Parsons appointment at Time Warner to be a significant achievement for black executives, one that helps pave the way for them to enter the highest positions in business. "There are a number of other black executives who have elevated positions in corporate America," said Parsons in *Black Enterprise.* "The process is rolling forward, even if it isn't moving as fast as some of us would like." Despite his distinction as a high-ranking black in business, Parsons downplays the racial aspects of his success. He has claimed that race was never a "defining character" in his life. "I don't do anything differently than I would otherwise because I have that responsibility to my family," he told the *New York Times* in 1994. "Whether I was an African-American, an Arab-American, a Jewish-American, or some other American, there are a lot of people who I cannot let down, so you have to live your life a certain way to be a role model to the people who are important to you."

After a year-long governmental review, Internet company America Online (AOL) and Time Warner merged in 2001. Parsons was named CEO for AOL Time Warner. *The Atlanta Journal-Constitution* wrote, "His designation as chief executive of the $36 billion media empire proves that African-Americans can not only perform in positions of commercial leadership but can wildly surpass all expectations." Known for his excellent mediation skills and his ability to put others at ease, Parsons told *The Atlanta Journal-Constitution* that he is "a lunch pail manager" who will display "an in-the-trenches style of leadership. I like to be with the troops."

Sources

Atlanta Journal-Constitution, January 22, 2002, C3.

Black Enterprise, October 1994, pp. 68-70, 72, 76, 77; January 1995, p. 15.

Business Week, November 14, 1994, pp. 38, 39.

Ebony, June 1988, pp. 156, 158.

Emerge, February 1995, p. 69.

Financial Times, December 8, 2001, p. 13.

Los Angeles Times, January 13, 2001, p. C1; December 6, 2001, p. C1.

New York Times, May 8, 1990, p. D5; August 26, 1990, p. D5; July 7, 1994, p. D4; October 31, 1994, pp. D1, D6.

Observer, (London, England) December 9, 2001, p. 4.

Wall Street Journal, May 8, 1990, p. B10; January 30, 1995, pp. B1, B3.

Washington Post, November 1, 1994, p. D5; December 6, 2001, p. EO1.

—Ed Decker and Christine Miner Minderovic

Ma Rainey

1886-1939

Blues singer

Ma Rainey was one of the most significant female blues singers to have emerged from the south during the 1920s. Often referred to as "The Black Nightingale" and the "Songbird of the South," she mostly came to be known as the "Mother of the Blues." Music historians often identify Rainey as a classic blues singer but her roots laid solidly in the raw style of southern country blues that evolved out of the traveling minstrel and vaudeville shows popular in the south at the end of the 19th century and at the beginning of the 20th century. Some music historians also consider Ma Rainey as the link between the male- dominated country blues that originated in the south and the female-dominated urban blues that developed in the north. Her style of blues can be heard in later blues and gospel singers such as Ethel Waters, Billie Holiday, and Mahalia Jackson. Her best known songs include "See See Rider" (CC Rider), "Jelly Bean Blues," and "Boll Weevil Blues."

Born on April 29, 1886 in Columbus, Georgia, Gertrude Melissa Nix Pridgett was the second of five children born to Thomas and Ella (Allen) Pridgett, who were minstrel and vaudeville performers. Gertrude was used to the traveling and performing life and made her first solo performance in 1900 at a talent show in her hometown, at the Springer Opera House. A couple of years later, in 1902, when the family was in St. Louis, Gertrude heard for the first time, a woman sing the blues. Touched by the emotional content, attracted to the largely melancholic, improvisational elements of the "blues," as well as to the unique structure of the music, from then on Gertrude herself began singing the blues, and has been credited as the first woman to have incorporated this style of singing into the vaudeville tradition.

In 1904 Gertrude married William "Pa" Rainey, a minstrel song and dance man. She adopted the name Ma Rainey, and together they toured the south. The pair were billed as Rainey & Rainey or Ma & Pa Rainey, Assassinators of the Blues, and performed with the Rabbit Foot Minstrels where they befriended a young Bessie Smith. Ma & Pa Rainey also were part of Tolliver's Circus and Musical Extravaganza and various other tent shows and black variety shows. Essentially, Ma Rainey adopted the blues as her own, and was instrumental in popularizing the blues style. Her blues described woeful tales, a wide variety of love tales, humorous situations, and tales of endurance. When

At a Glance . . .

Born Gertrude Malissa Nix Pridgett on April 26, 1886, in Columbus, Georgia; daughter of Thomas Pridgett and Ella Allen; married William "Pa" Rainey (comedy performer), February 2, 1904; died on December 22, 1939, in Rome, Georgia.

Career: Performed in local stage show, 1900; toured South with husband William "Pa" Rainey, 1904; member of Fat Chappelle's Rabbit Foot Minstrels; performed at various tent shows and variety shows including Tolliver's Circus and Silas Green from New Orleans minstrel show; made recording debut for Paramount label,1923; recorded with various sideman for Paramount, until 1928; worked with revue show, Bandanna Babies, 1930; retired from music, 1935; became theater owner and manager.

Awards: Blues Foundation Hall of Fame, inducted, 1983; Rock 'n Roll Hall of Fame, inducted, 1990.

Rainey came to town, the people went wild and lined up to see her. After Ma and Pa's marriage broke up, Ma continued on her own, further developing her characteristic style. Her voice was a deep contralto, at times raspy, and she sang with a jug band—kazoos, jugs, banjos, and perhaps a musical saw.

In the early 1920s Rainey was a featured performer with the TOBA (Theater Owners Booking Association), an organization that was instrumental in promoting black artists. In 1923, at the age of 37, she signed a recording contract with Paramount. By this time Rainey had been performing for about 25 years and had already earned, on her own, the billing that Paramount gave her: "Discovered At Last, 'Mother of the Blues.'" Although Rainey was extremely popular in the south, until she began recording with Paramount, she was virtually unknown in the north. As the public acquired phonographs and radios, more people heard Rainey. She traveled north, performing in large theaters in Detroit, Chicago, and Pittsburgh, and for a time, billed herself as Madame Rainey. She was also billed as the "Paramount Wildcat" and after becoming famous, Rainey displayed her wealth in the form of a necklace made of gold coins and was sometimes referred to as "Gold Necklace Woman of the Blues."

Rainey's recording career ended early in 1928. During the six years that she was under contract to Paramount she recorded about 100 songs. In addition, due to Rainey's success, Paramount evolved from a small recording business that was a subsidiary of a furniture company to a major recording label. While recording for Paramount, Rainey worked with a more sophisticated jazz band and collaborated with several well-known blues artists, such as Coleman Hawkins, Fletcher Henderson, and Louis Armstrong. She also collaborated with the Rev. Thomas Dorsey, the godfather of gospel music, who at one time was known as Georgia Tom.

During the 1920s Rainey's only serious rival was Bessie Smith, although Ida Cox and Sippie Wallace were also considered to be close contenders. Although each of these female blues artists was unique, they were constantly compared with each other because of their similar background and down-home, gutsy, and raw singing style. Aside from her driving blues style, Rainey's brand of distinction lay with the fact that she was very outspoken on women's issues and served as a role model for other African-American female performers, urging them to become economically independent. It is also interesting to note that both Rainey and Smith arranged their own music, composed, and managed their own bands. At the height of Rainey's career, she was making around $2,000 a week, which was a considerable sum of money at that time.

Not regarded as a particularly physically attractive woman, Rainey compensated with her wardrobe and her seductive demeanor, wearing bright, flashy sequined gowns and feathered headdresses. Even more provocative was the fact that she openly admitted to being bisexual. Once, in 1925, Rainey was arrested and spent a night in jail in Chicago for throwing an "indecent party." The party was so noisy that neighbors called the police, who arrived to a room full of naked women engaged in "intimate" situations. For the promotion of the song, "Prove It On Me," recorded in 1928, Ma was featured flirting with two women and was wearing a man's suit. The lyrics reflect her openly bisexual feelings: "Went out last night with a crowd of my friends/They must have been women, 'cause I don't like no men."

Rainey's career was greatly affected during the Depression. In 1935 she retired from the business and returned to Columbus, Georgia, where she lived with her brother, Thomas Pridgett, a deacon at the Friendship Baptist Church. With money that she had earned during her career, Rainey built and operated two theaters in Georgia: the Lyric Theater in Rome, and the Airdome Theater in Columbus. During her life, Rainey was a foster mother to seven children. The Mother of the Blues died of a heart attack on December 22, 1939. She was buried in a family plot in the Porterdale Cemetery in Columbus, Georgia. Rainey was inducted into the Blues Foundation's Hall of Fame in 1983 and into the Rock 'n Roll Hall of Fame in 1990. In 1994, the United States also featured Rainey on a postage stamp. Those who want to experience a slice of Rainey's life can see August Wilson's play, *Ma Rainey's Blackbottom*, which made it to Broadway in the 1980s.

Selected discography

Mother of the Blues, Dutch Fontana, 1965.
The Immortal Ma Rainey, Milestone, 1967.
Ma Rainey's Black Bottom, Riverside, 1975.
Black Bottom, Yazoo, 1990.
Complete Recorded Works: 1928 Sessions, Document, 1994.

Sources

Books

Davis, Angela Y. *Blues Legacies and Black Feminism: Gertrude 'Ma' Rainey, Bessie Smith, and Billie Holiday,* Pantheon, 1988.
Harrison, Daphne Duval. *Black Pearls: Blues Queens of the 1920s.* Rutgers University Press, 1988.

Lieb, Sandra R. *Mother of the Blues: A Study of Ma Rainey.* University of Massachusetts Press, 1981.
Stewart-Baxter, Derrick. *Ma Rainey and the Classic Blues Singers.* Stein and Day, 1970.

On-line

http://www.blueflamecafe.com/Ma_Rainey.html
http://www.blues.org/history/
   womenhistory.marainey.html
http://www.eyeneer.com/America/Genre/Blues/
   Profiles/ma.rainey.html
http://www.gawomen.org/honorees/long/
   raineyg_long. htm
http://www.lambda.net/[]maximum/rainey.html
http://library.thinkquest.org/10320/Rainey.htm
http:///.lclark.edu/[]cowan/marainey.htm

—Christine Miner Minderovic

Stephanie Ready

1975—

Professional basketball coach

Stephanie Ready, one of the first females to coach men professionally, doesn't see herself as special, unique or different. She saw herself as a coach, one who works to teach and improve her players. Ready told NBA.com, "Coaching men or women, athletes are always trying to get better. When you're coaching at the highest levels, you will find the more competitive athletes will do whatever it takes to win and also to improve their skills individually. In that sense I really don't think there's much difference coaching men and women."

Ready is doing something that very few women are doing at any level of basketball. She is an assistant coach for the National Basketball Developmental League's Greenville Groove. Ready is assistant coach to Milton Barnes, a former college assistant coach himself for the University of Detroit, Kent University, and the University of Minnesota. Barnes told *Contemporary Black Biography,* "The thing that I like about Stephanie is that she understands and knows the game of basketball. She also knows how to get it across to the players and that's what separated her from any other coaches that I had interviewed for the job."

A native of Takoma Park, Maryland, Ready was a standout basketball and volleyball player at Coppin State. Ready also ranked in the top-10 on the career list at Coppin State in steals (2nd), assists (4th), points (8th) and rebounds (10th). Ready graduated cum laude from Coppin State with a bachelor's degree in psychology in 1998. Ron "Fang" Mitchell, the men's basketball coach, hired Ready to coach the women's volleyball team. Mitchell was also the person that urged Ready to pursue coaching basketball and hold off on graduate school.

Hired two weeks before the start of the season, Ready began working with the team and soon the Lady Eagles' 129-match losing streak was snapped. At the time, Ready was one of the youngest Division I volleyball coaches in the country and she kept the position for three years, until she resigned during the spring of 2001. Mitchell called upon Ready again, but this time he wanted her to assist him on the bench—for Coppin State's men's team. She became only the third woman ever to coach Division I men's basketball; Jennifer Johnston of Oakland University in Michigan, and Bernadette Mattox, who coached at the University of Kentucky from 1990 to 1995 under former coach Rick Pitino, were the others. Of the three, Ready was the

At a Glance . . .

Born 1975 in Takoma Park, MD. *Education:* Coppin State University, Baltimore, MD, graduated cum laude, psychology, 1998.

Career: Coppin State University, women's volleyball coach, 1998-2000, asst. coach, men's basketball, 2000-01; NBDL, Greenville Groove, assistant coach, 2001-.

Address: *Team*—Greenville Groove, BI-LO Center, 650 N. Academy St., Greenville, SC, 29601-2246.

only woman who was allowed to recruit off-campus. "It was a no-brainer," Mitchell told blackvoices.com, of his decision to hire Ready. "She's very detail-oriented and one of the most organized people I've had a pleasure to work with."

In many circles, Ready's hiring has been perceived as a publicity stunt. It appeared that the NBDL matched Ready with Greenville to attract interest to the new league, which is comprised of mostly former college stars and players who previously played overseas. Before Ready resigned her coaching position from Coppin State in August of 2001, she had received a ringing endorsement from Mitchell, who had spoken to NBDL senior director of basketball Karl Hicks and Rob Levine. After researching Ready, Levine told blackvoices.com, "I don't think the NBDL is constrained by the folks who are going to be skeptics. We want to be a league that breaks old paradigms and provides opportunities."

Though there are doubters, those who favor Ready's advancement far outweigh them. "We don't have time to worry about who's coaching us," Greenville Groove guard Merl Code commented to *USA Today.* "Coach Ready is there to help us and we want to let her help." To Barnes, Ready has been a great help and he appreciates her basketball aptitude. "Coach Ready

knows the game of basketball, has a proven track record at the collegiate level of basketball that helped her to develop her skills, and she comes highly recommended," Barnes told meacfans.com. Upon being hired, Ready assisted Barnes in assembling the players' manuals, which included various offensive and defensive strategies, along with team rules.

While Ready has been consumed with her preparation as a coach, she also understood her position as a role model. Ready appeared on NBC's *Today Show,* and *Ebony* magazine named her one of "The 56 Most Intriguing Blacks of 2001" along with Shaquille O'Neal, Kobe Bryant, and Michael Jordan. Still, it all comes down to coaching for Ready, who might someday consider coaching in the NBA or WNBA. Mitchell told meacfans.com, "I saw something special in her when she was a student-athlete and she's lived up to that as a coach." Though the rise has been meteoric, Ready felt fortunate to be experiencing the challenge. "I feel like I'm on a whirlwind, but I'm not complaining," Ready told blackvoices.com. "This is a great opportunity to do what I love in a league in the NBA family that will show people that little girls can grow up and do the same thing that little boys have a chance to do."

Sources

Periodicals

Baltimore Sun, August 16, 2001.
Bergen Record, October 17, 2001.
USA Today, November 30, 2001.

On-line

BlackVoices.com
Inthecrease.com
MEACfans.com
NBA.com
Onnidan.com Online

Other

Additional information for this profile was obtained in an interview conducted with *Contemporary Black Biography,* on November 2, 2001.

Don Rojas

1949—

Journalist, business executive

Don Rojas is an internationally respected journalist and intellectual. As the founder of *The Black World Today,* the only internet portal dedicated to serving the black community worldwide, he is also considered a visionary. With a career that stretches from Caribbean politics to European journalism to American business, Rojas is a fascinating figure and a role model to aspiring African American journalists.

Though his roots are in the West Indies—a group of Caribbean island nations not far off the coast of Venezuela, South America—Rojas attended college in the United States at the University of Wisconsin, Madison. There he studied journalism and communications before embarking on an illustrious career shaped by both his liberal political leanings and his commitment to providing high-quality journalism aimed at African-American and minority audiences. Two of his early jobs illustrate his dual aims. One of his first positions was assistant director of communications for the National Urban League. Following his stint there Rojas became an assistant editor at a Baltimore, Maryland based African-American newspaper. Baltimore would eventually become his permanent home.

In the late 1970s Rojas temporarily returned to his native West Indies where he served as editor-in-chief of the national newspaper of the island nation of Grenada. At that time a Marxist government has assumed power—the People's Revolutionary Government of Grenada—led by charismatic Prime Minister Maurice Bishop, "We Leader" to the people of Grenada. Rojas became the press secretary to Bishop and was at the forefront of Grenadian politics during the early 1980s political uprisings which culminated in the imprisonment and murder of Bishop and the intervention of the United States military. Prior to this political instability, Rojas successfully organized the first conference of Caribbean journalists and the first conference of Caribbean intellectuals, both held in Grenada. Rojas left Grenada in 1983. Since then, Rojas has edited several books about Grenadian revolution and the events leading to Bishop's death.

Rojas next move took him to Prague in the former country of Czechoslovakia. There, in the mid-eighties, he served as an executive for the International Organization of Journalists. His job entailed assisting member journalists and other media workers in North America and the Caribbean. During this time Rojas organized the first tour of Eastern Germany, Czechoslovakia, and the Soviet Union exclusively for African-American journalists. His work on the international front of journalism afforded him the opportunity to become the only black journalist to cover the 1985 summit meeting between U.S. president Ronald Reagan and Soviet leader Mikhail Gorbachev.

Rojas returned stateside in the early 1990s and took on the position of executive editor and assistant to the publisher for the New York *Amsterdam News.* At the time, the *Amsterdam News* was the largest black owned newspaper aimed at a black audience in the country. This position would give Rojas powerful leverage in the black communities and among those businesses and politicians who wanted access to this audience. Unfortunately, as he would later find out, because

At a Glance . . .

Born in October 1949; married Karen Codrington; three children. *Education:* Studied Journalism and Communications, University of Wisconsin at Madison.

Career: Communications For a New Tomorrow LLC, founder, president, CEO, which owns two major Internet portals: The Black World Today and The Black World Radio Network, 1996-; NAACP, communications director, 1993; *New York Amsterdam News,* executive editor and assistant publisher, early 1990s; International Organization of Journalists, Prague, Czechoslovakia, executive, mid 1980s; national newspaper of Grenada, West Indies, editor-in-chief, 1979-83; Press Secretary to Grenadian Prime Minister, Maurice Bishop, 1979-83; National Urban League, assistant director, Communications; *Afro-American* newspaper of Baltimore, assistant editor.

Awards: The Black World Today nominated for Webby Award, 1998; Rojas named one of the "Silicon Alley Dozen," 1999; Recognized for Outstanding Contribution to Journalism, The Institute of Caribbean Studies.

Addresses: *Home*—Baltimore, MD; *Office*—The Black World Today, 729 E. Pratt Street, Suite 500, Baltimore, MD 21202, Phone (410) 539-6547, Fax: (410) 521-9993; *Email*—donrojas@tbwt.net.

some groups considered the *Amsterdam News* alternatively anti-Semitic and dangerously liberal, this position, along with his role in Grenada, would come to be used against him.

In 1993 the newly appointed head of the National Association for the Advancement of Colored People (NAACP), Dr. Ben Chavis, selected Rojas to serve as his communications director. As one of the most powerful positions in the NAACP, the communications director is responsible for all public relations and communications, both within the organization and with the public. Because there were many within and without the NAACP that wanted to see Chavis ousted, Rojas's appointment almost immediately began to be used against Chavis. Rojas was called out as being a "dangerous leftie," according to www.zmag.org His role in the revolutionary government of Grenada was also used to show his unfitness for the NAACP. The Jewish community, long supporters of the NAACP were concerned about his past at the New York *Amsterdam*

News, because of the perceived anti-Semitic leanings of the paper. Chavis's position was doomed almost from the start and his term was ended after only 16 months.

Following his tumultuous tenure as communications director of the NAACP, Rojas settled soundly in Baltimore, Maryland with his wife Karen Codrington and their three children. There he began a career in the private sector. In 1996 having surmised the potential of the Internet as a news medium, Rojas founded the first black-oriented Internet portal, *The Black World Today,* (www.tbwt.net) becoming its president and CEO. According to the website, *The Black World Today* is just one part of Rojas's multimedia company called Communications for a New Tomorrow, "dedicated to the reporting and dissemination of relevant news, views and useful information about people of color communities around the world." In 1998 *The Black World Today* was nominated for a Webby Award, the cyberworld's version of an Academy Award. It was in the running against communication powerhouse sites CNN and *Time.*

Running *The Black World Today* has not always been an easy endeavor. According to *The Industry Standard Magazine,* in 1999 Rojas faced serious difficulties in obtaining investments to keep the site running. Many factors were pointed to in explanation; Rojas' lack of business savvy was one. "I'm not a businessman by training or propensity," he admitted to the magazine. Another is that investors want to know there is potential for revenue when funding a site. A spokesperson for the New York New Media Association, an internet investment group who chose to award $1.2 million in funding to bikini.com rather that *The Black World Today* said of Rojas, "He was smart and articulate, but he didn't have his revenue stream crystallized." Finally, many saw the inability to gain funding as yet another example of a business world afraid to invest in a black-targeted venture. "We don't want to point fingers or say 'They're all a bunch of racists,'" Rojas told the magazine, "But there's a trivialization of a growing market here."

As of 2002, *The Black World Today* is still a leader in black-oriented websites. Funding, while still a struggle has materialized and the company continues to grow. There is hope for Rojas that he may accomplish his dream that "apart from my family, TBWT would be the greatest achievement of my adulthood," as he remarked to *The Industry Standard Magazine.* He has already won over the site's enthusiasts and cultural critics with honest, informative reporting and an esteemed staff of writers and editors.

Sources

Periodicals

Green Left Weekly, December 6, 1995.
Industry Standard Magazine, July 12, 1999.

On-line

The Institute for Caribbean Studies, www.icsdc.org/
The Black World Today, www.tbwt.net
www.znet.org

—Candace LaBalle

Roxanne Shante

1969—

Rap musician, psychologist

During its infancy, rap music was strictly a male domain filled with male deejays, male rappers, and male sensibilities. Full of misogynistic, sexist, and downright obscene lyrics to describe women, rap music did not provide a forum for women to respond. That is, not until 14-year-old Roxanne Shante took notice. In response to a popular song, "Roxanne, Roxanne," in which three male rappers denigrate a beautiful woman who won't give them the time of day, Gooden recorded an "answer record" called "Roxanne's Revenge." With that 1984 recording Gooden, "not only proved that females could rock the mic, but at the tender age of fourteen she also provided the first rap critique of sexism in the black community," wrote Aida Croal in "Talking Back: Women in Hip-Hop," published on www.Africana.com. In doing so, she laid the groundwork for the female hip-hop and rap musicians that followed, from Queen Latifah to Lil' Kim.

Lolita Shante Gooden was born on November 9, 1969, in Long Island, New York. There, she grew up in the Queensbridge housing projects. A well-known anecdote in rap music history describes how Gooden fell into rapping. "Roxanne, Roxanne," recorded by a group called UTFO was ruling the airwaves on New York's "Rap Attack" radio show. It was a raw, explicit anthem that held no punches in its dissing of women. One day Gooden was walking near her home and passed three neighborhood guys—also rappers—and she overheard them discussing the fact that UTFO was pulling out of a local show. Gooden approached the group and offered to record an "answer" song that would get back at UTFO. One of the three, producer

Marlon "Marley Marl" Williams took her up on the offer and "Roxanne's Revenge" was recorded. In rap as explicit as anything male rappers put out, the squeaky-voiced Gooden uses expletives like punctuation, coming down hard on UTFO.

The song became an instant hit locally. DJ Mr. Magic, host of "Rap Attack," had as many requests for "Roxanne's Revenge" as it did for the song that inspired it. With this success, Roxanne Shante was born. She began performing the song at local showcases and her fame soon spread. "People everywhere wanted to hear this frank young girl with the foul mouth," wrote *The Herald* of Glasgow, Scotland. One of those people was Dana Goodman of Pop Art Records. Sensing a megahit, he produced a record of the song and it hit music stores and national airwaves blaring. Gooden, still a high school student, was suddenly famous. She had to stop attending classes because of crowds of fans who gathered outside of her classroom door. This sudden stardom surprised Gooden, "It wasn't like I wanted to be a rapper; it was just luck and timing," she told London's *The Independent Sunday*, adding, "which is something I'm pretty good at."

Despite the novelty of this "answer record," and despite the fact that teenaged Shante was swearing and using sexual imagery as raunchy as any male rapper, the fact that she was a talented rapper helped Gooden become more than a one-hit wonder. She was a natural at freestyling, pulling a rhyme out of nothing and making it work onstage. She has credited this skill to her childhood fascination with black comics. Of Nipsey

At a Glance . . .

Born Lolita Shante Gooden on November 9, 1969, in Long Island, NY; married with two children. *Education*: Master's degree in Psychology.

Career: Rap musician. Released single, "Roxanne's Revenge," at age 14, 1984; albums: *Bad Sister*, 1989; *The Bitch is Back*, 1992; toured extensively, late 1980s and early 1990s; retired from music; criminal psychologist in New York, NY, currently.

Russell, she told *The Independent Sunday*, "We used to watch him and you'd come outside the next day and see if you could do the same thing. Eventually, I got so good at it I was able to pursue a career from it, making records in five or 10 minutes, just going in and doing it."

Following the national release of "Roxanne's Revenge," Gooden began to tour non-stop and wouldn't stop for nearly four years. She worked with other rappers, including Marley Marl and Mr. Magic, forming the Juice Crew Allstars. At one point she was playing three gigs in as many states in a single day. At the same time, she was conducting interviews, meeting with press, and making records. Pop Art released *Def Mix Volume 1: Roxanne Shante* in 1985, which, in addition to "Roxanne's Revenge," included titles like "Bite This" and "To the Other MCs." A series of 12-inch vinyl records and singles followed. However, it wasn't until 1989 that Gooden recorded her first full-length album, *Bad Sister*, followed by her second album, *The Bitch is Back* in 1992.

Gooden's schedule was grueling. She didn't even take time off to have her first child, a son named Kareem. He was born on the road when Gooden was 15 and he toured with her for his first few years of his life. However, Gooden's hard work was paying off—she was earning lots of money. But, as a minor, her earnings went to her mother, who had no experience dealing with the recording industry, leaving Gooden to fight for credit and royalties for much of her own work. "She didn't know too much about the record business;

she was just happy that they were giving her money," Gooden explained to *The Independent Sunday*. Eventually Gooden got fed up, and, while still in her early twenties, she retired from the music business.

By 1992 Gooden was married and had a second child. She went on to college, eventually earning a master's degree in Psychology. Settled in an upscale neighborhood of Queens, New York with her family, this female pioneer of rap with a penchant for bad language, became a criminal psychologist for New York State, working with convicts up for parole. She emerged from her domestic life long enough to record a song on a 2000 release by British techno artist Mekon, who had to hire a private detective to find her. Despite the bad taste the record industry left in her mouth, Gooden had few regrets. She told *The Independent Sunday*, "I like the fact that hip-hop taught me a lot. Hip-hop and the entertainment industry prepared me for life itself."

Selected discography

Def Mix Volume 1: Roxanne Shante, Pop Art Records (vinyl album).
Bad Sister, Cold Chillin' Records, Reprise/Warner, 1989.
The Bitch is Back, Livin' Large/Tommy Boy Records, 1992.
Roxanne Shante's Greatest Hits, Cold Chillin' Records, 1995.

Sources

Periodicals

The Herald, (Glasgow, Scotland), January 2, 2002, p. 11.
The Independent Sunday, (London, England), August 27, 2000, p8.

On-line

www.Africana.com/DailyArticles/index_20000713.htm
www.allmusic.com
www.globaldarkness.com
www.oldschoolhiphop.com

—Candace LaBalle

George Irving Shirley

1934—

Opera singer, educator

The first black member of the U.S. Army Chorus, George Shirley went on to become the first African-American tenor placed under contract by the Metropolitan Opera. Throughout his career, Shirley has performed in the world's most prestigious opera houses and been accompanied by the most distinguishes orchestras in the world. In addition to performing and recording, he has also worked as a music educator.

Shirley was born on April 18, 1934, in Indianapolis, Indiana. He grew up in a musical household. Shirley's father, Irving Ewing, played guitar, piano, and violin, and his mother, Daisy Shirley, sang. At age of five, Shirley entered a radio contest, singing a popular Bing Crosby song. As a prize, he was given the first recording of himself. When his parents moved to Detroit, Shirley continued to sing in church and school. He also played baritone horn in a community band. In addition, Shirley attended the Ebersol School of Music for six years. As a youth, Shirley never considered a career in opera. Rather, he was interested in music education.

Shirley attended Wayne State University, earning his B.S. degree in music education in 1955. He spent a year in Wayne State's graduate program, and taught school before joining the army in 1956. Shirley and his high school sweetheart, Gladys Lee Ishop, were married on June 24, 1956.

Made Operatic Debut

Shirley considered joining the army band program, but then he decided to audition for the U.S. Army Chorus.

The audition was successful, and Shirley became the first black member of the famed touring and performing ensemble. He spent three years with the Army Chorus, also singing regularly with the choir at Vermont Avenue Baptist Church in Washington, D.C. In 1959 Shirley heard from an Army Chorus friend, Ara Berberian, who also later developed an operatic career, that the Turnau Opera Company was looking for a tenor to perform at a summer resort in New York's Catskill mountains. Shirley was hired and he made his operatic debut Johann Strauss's *Die Fledermaus*.

Shirley caught the attention of Boris Goldovsky, a renowned opera conductor, and Goldovsky urged him to attend the Tanglewood Music Center. Goldovsky also suggested that Shirley participate in his summer opera school. With Goldovsky's encouragement, Shirley entered and won the American Opera Auditions in Cincinnati. Shirley was then offered the chance to sing in Milan and Florence. It was in Milan that he made his European debut, taking on the role of Rodolpho in Puccini's *La Bohème*.

Shirley returned to America, claiming first prize in auditions at New York's Metropolitan Opera in 1961. He was the first black tenor to win this competition. The prize entailed a $2,000 scholarship and the chance to perform at the Metropolitan Opera House. Following a performance on the television show, *The Bell Telephone Hour*, and he made his debut with Metropolitan Opera in October of 1961, appearing in the role of Ferrando in Mozart's *Così Fan Tutte*.

At a Glance . . .

Born born on April 18, 1934, in Indianapolis, IN; son of Irving Ewing and Daisy Shirley; married Gladys Lee Ishop, 1956; children: Olwyn, Lyle. *Education*: Wayne State University, B.S., 1955., graduate study, 1955-56.

Career: Opera singer, educator. Detroit Board of Education, music teacher, 1955- 56; debut as Eisenstein in *Die Fledermaus*, Woodstock, New York, 1959; Italian debut as Rodolfo at Teatro Nuovo, Milan, 1960; New York City Opera debut as Rodolfo, 1961; Metropolitan Opera, leading tenor, 1961-73; Glyndebourne debut as Tamino, 1966; Royal Opera, Covent Garden, London, leading tenor, 1967-79; Alwa in *Lulu*, Santa Fe, 1973; University of MD, voice professor, 1981-87; Deutsche Opera, West Berlin, leading tenor, 1983; University of MI, voice professor, director of Vocal Arts Division, 1987-; Staten Island Community College; Morgan State College, Baltimore, Artist-in-Residence.

Memberships: National Association of Teachers of Singing; American Guild of Musical Artists; AFTRA; National Association of Negro Musicians; Wayne State University Alumni Association; board of directors, University of MI Musical Society; Alpha Phi Alpha; Phi Mu Alpha; Phi Kappa Phi; Omicron Delta Kappa; Pi Kappa Lambda.

Awards: National Arts Club award, 1960; Grammy Award, for performance in recording of Mozart's *Così Fan Tutte*, 1968; named one of Distinguished Scholar-Teachers, University of MD, 1985-86; Alumni Association Award, Arts Achievement Award, Black Alumni Achievement Award, Wayne State University; honorary degrees: Wilberforce University, H.D.H., 1967; Montclair State College, L.L.D., 1984; Lake Forest College, D.F.A., 1988.

Addresses: *Office*—School of Music, University of Michigan, Ann Arbor MI 48109 (734) 764-5595. *Email*—gis@umich.edu. *Agent*—Ann Summers International, Box 188 Station A, Toronto M5W 1B2 (416) 362-1422.

Joined the Metropolitan Opera

While in New York, Shirley began studying with Cornelius Reid. When the Metropolitan Opera placed him under contract, he became the first black singer to perform under contract at the Met. Shirley remained a regular performer there for the next 11 years. During this time, he won major roles in more than twenty operas, including Adorno in *Simon Boccanegra*, Fenton in *Falstaff*, Rodolpho in *La Bohème*, and Don Jose in *Carmen*. Shirley also appeared regularly at the New York City Opera, Opera Society of Washington, D.C., the Santa Fe Opera, and the Spring Opera in San Francisco. He also performed abroad, appearing in *Don Giovanni* at Covent Garden in London and in *The Magic Flute* at the Glyndebourne Festival. In addition, Shirley performed with such renowned orchestras as the New York Philharmonic, the Philadelphia Orchestra, and the Boston Symphony.

Shirley found himself facing a professional setback in 1972. He had been asked to substitute for the Italian tenor Franco Corelli at the Metropolitan Opera. At the opening of the fall season, Shirley took the stage in the title role of Gounod's *Roméo et Juliette*. Although he was vocally prepared for the role, he did not feel mentally ready. The performance was sharply criticized *New York Times*, and Shirley's confidence was shaken. It was only after a period of self-examination that Shirley was able to return to the stage.

After recording several successful performances, Shirley found himself in demand once again. In 1975 he sang in the American premiere of Cavalli's *L'Egisto*. He also appeared at London's Royal Opera, taking on the role of Loge in *Das Rheingold*. For this 1976 performance, Shirley worked under the direction of Colin Davis. In 1977, Shirley appeared in the role of Romilayu at the New York City Opera's world premiere of Kirchner's *Lily*, and also appeared in Stravinsky's *Oedipus Rex* with the Houston Symphony. Also in 1977, he debuted at Milan's prestigious opera house, La Scala, taking on the role of Pelléas in Debussy's *Pelléas et Melisande*.

Shirley has been featured regularly with the Deutsche Opera of Berlin, joining them on a 1988 tour of Japan and, in 1990, singing the role of Pluto in Offenbach's *Orpheus in the Underworld*. Also in 1990, he sang in the premiere of Richard Strauss's *Friedenstag* at Carnegie Hall and performed as soloist with the Mormon Tabernacle Choir on CBS radio.

Won Grammy Award

Shirley has recorded for several record labels, including RCA, Columbia, Decca, Angel, Vanguard, and Phillips Records. He has also recorded tenor arias for Music Minus One records' Laureate Series. In 1968 he received a Grammy Award for his performance in the prize-winning recording of Mozart's *Così Fan Tutte*.

In addition to performing and recording, Shirley has worked as a professor of voice and a member of the artist faculty of the University of Michigan since 1987. He has also served as director of the university's Vocal Arts Division. He has also worked as adjunct professor of voice at Long Island Community College, artist-in-residence at Morgan State College, humanist-in-residence at Howard University, and professor of voice at the University of Maryland from 1980 to 1987. Shirley and Therman Bailey, a New York singer and voice teacher, have formed an organization, Independent Black Singers, to assist young aspiring singers.

In 1999 Shirley appeared at the Glimmerglass Opera in Cooperstown, New York. For this performance, he took on the role of Eumete in the Monteverdi opera, *Il Ritorno d'Ulisse*. That same year, he joined the Chicago Symphony Orchestra, narrating *Three Places in New England* by Charles Ives. This was not Shirley's first work as a narrator, however. A 1996 recording featured his narration of two James Forsyth poems: "Spirit of St. Louis" and "Ruth."

Throughout his career, Shirley has achieved many firsts. He was Detroit's first black high school music teacher, the first African-American member of the U.S. Army Chorus, the first black tenor to win the Metropolitan Opera Auditions, and the first African-American tenor to sing under contract at the Metropolitan Opera. Also, in many of the theaters in which he has performed, Shirley was the first black to sing major operatic roles. Shirley has appeared in over eighty operas.

Sources

Books

Abdul, Raoul. *Blacks in Classical Music*. Dodd, Mead, 1977.
Baker's Biographical Dictionary of Musicians. 8th ed. Revised by Nicholas Slonimsky. G. Schirmer, 1992.
The Complete Marquis Who's Who, Marquis Who's Who, 2001.

Hitchcock, H. Wiley, ed. *New Grove Dictionary of American Music*. Macmillan, 1986.
International Dictionary of Opera. 2 vols. St. James Press, 1993.
Notable Black American Men, Gale Research, 1998.
Ploski, Harry A., and Williams, James. *The Negro Almanac*. 5th ed. Gale Research, 1989.
Roach, Hildred. *Black American Music*. 2nd ed. Krieger Publishing Co., 1992.
Southern, Eileen. *Biographical Dictionary of Afro-American and African Musicians*. Greenwood Press, 1982.
Southern, Eileen. *The Music of Black Americans*. 3rd ed. Norton, 1997.
Who's Who in America. 44th ed. Marquis, 1986.

Periodicals

Amsterdam News, November 4, 1995.
Black Perspective in Music, Spring 1981, pp. 73-90.
Ebony, January 1966, pp. 84-91.
Opera News, January 1971, pp. 6-13; December 1976, p. 7.
The Washington Post Magazine, July 29, 1979, pp. 10-13.

On-line

Biography Resource Center, Gale Group, 2001, http://www.galenet.com/servlet/BioRC
Ann Summers International, http:\\www.sumarts.com (February 14, 2002).
University of Michigan, http:\\www.music.umich.edu/faculty/shirley.george.html (February 14, 2002).

Other

Additional material for this profile was obtained from an e-mail from George Shirley to Darius Thieme, February 1998; a letter from Shirley to Darius L. Thieme, February 16, 1998; and an interview with Shirley conducted by Darius L. Thieme, February 16, 1998.

—Darius L. Theime and Jennifer M. York

Supremes

Rhythm and blues group

The first girl group signed with Motown Records, the Supremes achieved widespread popularity and scored twelve number-one hits. Although the Supremes experienced several changes in their lineup, the group achieved their greatest success with Diana Ross as lead singer and Mary Wilson and Florence Ballard as backing vocalists. According to *Black Issues Book Review*, the Supremes "heralded the success of other sister-girl groups…connecting with listeners nationwide, regardless of color."

Diana Ross, Mary Wilson, and Florence Ballard, were teenagers in Detroit when they formed a quartet called the Primettes in the late 1950s. The young women attempted to audition for Berry Gordy, head of Motown Records, but he considered them too young. So instead, the Primettes recorded—both as a featured group and as back-up singers—for Lupine Records, a local Detroit label. The Primettes continued their efforts to gain a contract with Motown, however. Barbara Martin, the fourth member of the group left in 1961, and the Primettes become a trio. They signed a contract with Motown and changed their name to the Supremes. They released their first album, *Meet the Supremes*, in 1963.

For the group's first six singles, either by Berry Gordy or Smokey Robinson acted as producer, but none of these early singles performed very well. For their next single, the Supremes, although they reportedly did not like the song, recorded "When the Lovelight Starts Shining Through His Eyes." The song was written and produced by brothers Eddie and Brian Holland and Lamont Dozier, known as Holland-Dozier- Holland.

Scored First String of Hits

The Supremes' first consecutive string of hits were all written and produced by the Holland-Dozier-Holland team. This string began in July of 1964 with "Where Did Our Love Go," and was followed by "Baby Love," "Come See About Me," "Stop! In The Name of Love," and "Back in My Arms Again." With Ross on lead vocals, the Supremes produced a brand of pop/rock that, with a good beat for dancing, complemented by striking melodies and memorable lyrics, captured the attention of American teenagers. Within a few years, the group was also playing the nightclub circuit and singing for more mature audiences.

The fall of 1965 found the Supremes in great demand for television appearances, and the trio was featured on variety shows hosted by Ed Sullivan, Dean Martin, Sammy Davis, and Red Skelton, in addition to several "Hullabaloo" shows. The glamorous look of the Supremes began to take shape in 1965. On-stage, the girls had previously worn little makeup and knee-length dresses, but they now began wearing their signature wigs, heavy false eyelashes, and glamorous gowns. The Supremes toured the Far East, and upon their return, made their first Las Vegas appearance. By the end of the year, "I Hear a Symphony" was added to their list of chart-topping hits. The "symphony" heard in the background was provided by members of the Detroit Symphony Orchestra.

In 1966, still working with Holland-Dozier-Holland, the Supremes began another string of hits that continued into the next year. "My World Is Empty Without You" and "Love Is Like an Itching in My Heart," their first two songs of the year, reached the top ten. Those songs were followed by four straight number ones: "You Can't Hurry Love," "You Keep Me Hangin' On," "Love Is Here and Now You're Gone," and "The Happening."

At a Glance . . .

Born Florence Ballard (original member) on June 30, 1943, in Detroit, MI, died February 22, 1976, in Detroit; born Diana Ross (original member) on March 26, 1944, in Detroit; born Mary Wilson (original member) on March 4, 1944, in Detroit; born Barbara Martin (original member), left group, 1961. Born Cindy Birdsong (replaced Ballard, 1967) on December 15, 1939, in Camden, NJ; born Jean Terrell (replaced Ross, 1970) on November 26, c. 1944, in Texas; Also in group: born Scherrie Payne; Lynda Laurence; Susaye Green; Karen Jackson.

Education: (Wilson) New York University, A.A., 2001.

Career: Group formed in Detroit as vocal quartet the Primettes, 1950s; disbanded, 1977.

Awards: Rock and Roll Hall of Fame, inducted, 1988; received star on Hollywood Walk of Fame, 1994.

Name Changed to Feature Ross

Motown's most popular singing group, the trio's schedule of live appearances had become extremely demanding by mid-1967. In live performances, the group was now being billed as "Diana Ross and the Supremes." Where the group had once been presented as a unified trio, Ross was now presented as the leader of the Supremes. Wilson and Ballard both felt crushed by this change, and tension arose within the trio.

Florence Ballard, was removed from the Supremes in 1967, and replaced by Cindy Birdsong, who had worked as a backup singer in Patti LaBelle's group, the Blue Belles. Motown explained Ballard's departure on exhaustion, saying that the girls' demanding schedule had taken its toll. In a lawsuit Ballard later accused Motown, as well as present and future Supremes, of forming a conspiracy to oust her from the group. Some saw Ballard as a victim of Berry Gordy's greed and Diana Ross's ambition, and others felt that she had brought about her own downfall through her behavior and unrealistic expectations. Ballard was unable to launch a solo career, and she died of cardiac arrest in 1976.

Initially, Motown had promoted the group in such a way as to downplay the individuality of the group's members—least until the Supremes became a launching pad for Ross's rise to individual stardom—so most casual fans of the group were probably unaware of the personnel change. With Ross clearly featured as the group's lead singer, the Supremes achieved two more top pop hits, 1968's "Love Child" and "Someday We'll Be Together" in 1969. During the 1968 Christmas season, the Supremes, along with the Temptations, co-hosted Motown's first television special, *T.C.B.: Taking Care of Business*. In addition to several albums, this collaboration with the Temptations produced the number-two pop hit, "I'm Gonna Make You Love Me,"which featured the lead vocals by Ross and Eddie Kendricks.

"Reflections," the first song released by the Ross-Wilson-Birdsong lineup, reached number two, and their next song, "In and Out of Love," made the top ten. Reflective of Motown's lack of concern with the group's individual members, "Reflections" according to Mary Wilson, was recorded when Ballard was still a member of the group. In fact, Wilson's and Ballard's vocals were not included on "Love Child" or "Someday We'll Be Together."

Ross Left the Supremes

When Ross decided to leave the group in favor of a solo career, the Supremes held a series of farewell shows at the Frontier Hotel in Las Vegas in January of 1970. Highlights from these performances were recorded for the double-album set, *Farewell*. In addition to a medley of their mid-1960s hits, Ross led the group through a variety of show tunes and pop songs.

Ross went on to a successful career as a solo artist and film star. The Supremes went through a succession of personnel changes. Ross was replaced by Jean Terrell, who had been discovered in 1968 by Berry Gordy. The Terrell-Wilson-Birdsong edition of the Supremes proved the most popular post-Ross combination, producing such hits as "Stoned Love," which charted in the top ten in 1970; "Nathan Jones" in 1971, which reached the top twenty; and "Floy Joy" in 1972.

In 1973 Terrell left the group to get married. The Supremes did not release any albums until 1975, when Scherrie Payne joined the group. The Supremes officially disbanded in 1977. However, Wilson toured the United Kingdom the following year, performing with Karen Ragland and Karen Jackson as the Supremes. In 1988 the group, in their Ross-Wilson-Ballard incarnation, was inducted into the Rock and Roll Hall of Fame. Upon their induction *Rolling Stone* said of the Hall of Famers: "The Supremes embodied the 'Motown sound' that kept America dancing throughout the Sixties." Furthermore, the citation concluded, the Supremes "set a gorgeous new standard for Top Forty pop."

Launched Controversial Reunion Tour

The announcement that Diana Ross and the Supremes would launch a reunion tour in 2000 was followed

The Original Supremes, circa 1960s

almost immediately by controversy. Due to money squabbles, the "Return to Love" tour did not include original Supreme Mary Wilson or Cindy Birdsong, who had replaced Ballard. Where Ross was offered $20 million to do the tour, Wilson was offered $2 million, and Birdsong was offered less that $1 million. Feeling such offers unfair, Wilson and Birdsong declined. Instead, Scherrie Payne and Lynda Laurence, who had joined the group after Ross had left the Supremes, were recruited for the tour. The tour was not nearly as successful as it was controversial. At most venues, less than half of the tickets were sold. Gary Bongiovanni, a concert magazine writer, told *People Weekly* that the public felt the tour "wasn't a real Supremes reunion." The tour also suffered from frequent cancellations before it was canceled in July of 2000.

Selected discography

As the Supremes

Meet the Supremes, Motown, 1963.
Where Did Our Love Go, Motown, 1964.
A Bit of Liverpool, Motown, 1964.
Supremes Sing Country, Western and Pop, Motown, 1965.
We Remember Sam Cooke, Motown, 1965.
More Hits by the Supremes, Motown, 1965.
Merry Christmas, Motown, 1965.
Supremes at the Copa, Motown, 1965.
I Hear a Symphony, Motown, 1966.
Supremes a Go Go, Motown, 1966.
Supremes Sing Holland, Dozier, Holland, Motown, 1967.
Right On, Motown, 1970
(With the Four Tops) *The Magnificent Seven, Motown*, 1970
New Ways but Love Stays, Motown, 1970.
(With the Four Tops) *The Return of the Magnificent Seven*, Motown, 1971.
Touch, Motown, 1971.
(With the Four Tops) *Dynamite*, Motown, 1971.
Floy Joy, Motown, 1972.
The Supremes, Motown, 1972.
Anthology, Motown, 1974.
The Supremes, Motown, 1975.
High Energy, Motown, 1976.
Mary, Scherrie & Susaye, Motown, 1976.
At Their Best, Motown, 1978.

As Diana Ross and the Supremes

Supremes Sing Rodgers and Hart, Motown, 1967.
Diana Ross and the Supremes Greatest Hits, Motown, 1967.
Reflection s, Motown, 1968.
Diana Ross and the Supremes Sing and Perform "Funny Girl," Motown, 1968.
Diana Ross and the Supremes "Live&" at London's Talk of Town, Motown, 1968.
Diana Ross and the Supremes Join the Temptations, Motown, 1968.
Love Child, Motown, 1968.
(With the Temptations) *TCB*, Motown, 1968.
Let the Sunshine In, Motown, 1969.
(With the Temptations) *Together*, Motown, 1969. /L *Cream of the Crop*, Motown, 1969.
(With the Temptations) *On Broadway*, Motown, 1969.
Diana Ross and the Supremes Greatest Hits, Volume 3, Motown, 1970.
Farewell, Motown, 1970.

Sources

Books

Betrock, Alan, *Girl Groups: The Story Of A Sound*, Delilah Books, 1982.

Bianco, David, *Heat Wave: The Motown Fact Book*, Pierian Press, 1988.
Contemporary Black Biography Volumes 27, 28. Gale Group, 2001. *Contemporary Musicians*, Volume 6. Gale Research, 1991.
Hirshey, Gerri, *Nowhere To Run*, Times Books, 1984.
Turner, Tony, with Barbara Aria, *All That Glittered: My Life With The Supremes*, Dutton, 1990.
Wilson, Mary, *Dreamgirl: My Life As A Supreme*, St. Martin's, 1986.
Wilson, Mary, *Supreme Faith: Someday We'll Be Together*, Harper & Row, 1990.

Periodicals

Black Issues Book Review, March 2001.
Entertainment Weekly, January 10, 1992.
Jet, March 28, 1994; July 24, 2000; May 28, 2001.
People Weely, July 17, 2000.
Rolling Stone, November 11, 1988.

On-line

Biography Resource Center, Gale Group, 2001, http://www.galenet.com/servlet/BioRC

—David Bianco and Jennifer M. York

The Temptations

Rhythm and blues group

First formed in 1961, The Temptations are one of the few surviving groups from the days when Motown reigned the airwaves. In forty years, the group has dealt with numerous changes in the group's lineup and the ever-changing tastes of popular music. Despite such changes, The Temptations have managed to maintain their style, sound, and popularity.

It was in 1961 that two members of the Primes, Eddie Kendricks and Paul Williams, and three members of the Distants, Otis Williams, Elbridge Bryant, and Melvin Franklin decided to form a group. Although both the Primes and the Distants were popular in their local Detroit, neither group had produced a national hit. The quintet decided on the name, the Elgins. But the group soon learned that the name of a high-quality watch had already been adopted by another music group. Finally, the group decided to call themselves the Temptations. "You can see today that it was the perfect name," wrote Otis Williams in his book *Temptations*. "It was about style and elegance but also suggested romance and, frankly, sex." From their earliest days, Williams added, the group made a conscious effort to cultivate an image of sophistication. Williams wrote, "In our songs and in our moves, we were subtler and more romantic than some other guys, who were always grunting and sweating and carrying on."

Signed to Motown Records

The Temptations auditioned for Berry Gordy, and, impressed by their harmonizing, Gordy immediately offered them a contract on the spot. Now a fixture of Motown Records' roster, the group played at numerous Detroit clubs, earning an enthusiastic following. The also sang backup for many Motown stars, in addition to touring with the Motortown Revue. After none of the group's first seven singles produced a hit, Gordy briefly renamed the act the Pirates. Gordy had hoped the 1962 name change would change their luck, but the group was relieved their releases as the Pirates, "Mind Over Matter" and "I'll Love You Till I Die," also flopped. Williams explained in *Temptations*, "We'd have died for a hit, but if it meant going through life in pirate uniforms, no thanks!"

Elbridge Bryant left the group in 1964, due to personality conflicts, and he was replaced by David Ruffin, a Detroit singer who had enjoyed some solo success. Ruffin possessed an athletic stage presence, performing spins, cartwheels, and splits. The addition of Ruffin brought an exciting new dimension to the act. The Temptations then began working with Cholly Atkins, choreographer for Gladys Knight and the Pips, Frankie Lymon and the Teenagers, the Cadillacs, and other

At a Glance . . .

Born Otis Williams (original member) on October 30, 1949, in Texarkana, TX; born Melvin Franklin (original member) on October 12, 1942, in Montgomery, AL, died 1995; born Paul Williams (original member) on July 1, 1939, in Birmingham, AL, died on August 17, 1973, in Detroit, MI; born Edward James Kendricks (original member) on December 17, 1939, in Birmingham, AL, died on October 5, 1992; Elbridge Bryant (original member). Born David Ruffin (replaced Bryant, 1964) on January 18, 1941, in Wyanot, MS, died of a drug overdose on June 1, 1991; born Dennis Edwards (replaced Ruffin, 1968) on February 3, 1943, in Birmingham, AL; born Richard Street (replaced Paul Williams, 1971) on October 5, 1942, in Detroit, MI; Ricky Owens (replaced Kendricks, 1971); born Damon Otis Harris (replaced Owens, 1971) on July 3, 1950, in Baltimore, MD; Glenn Leonard; Ron Tyson; Louis Price; Ollie Woodson; Theo Peoples; Harry McGillberry; Terry Weeks; Barrington Henderson.

Career: Originally formed as the Elgins, Detroit, MI, 1961; name changed to The Temptations, 1961; albums include: *Meet the Temptations*, 1964; *The Temptations Sing Smokey*, 1965; *Temptin' Temptations*, 1965; *The Temptations Greatest Hits*, 1966; *Temptations Live!*, 1967, 1969; *Temptations Greatest Hits*, Volume II, 1970; *All the Million-Sellers*, 1981; *The Temptations 25th Anniversary*, 1986; *To Be Continued*, 1986; *Together Again, 1987*; *Phoenix Rising*, 1998; *Ear-Resistable*, 2000; *Awesome*, 2001.

Awards: Grammy Award, Best R&B Performance by a Group, for "Cloud Nine," 1969, for "Papa Was a Rolling Stone," 1972; Grammy, Best R&B song and Best R&B instrumental performance, for "Papa Was a Rolling Stone," 1972; American Music Award, Best Vocal Group, 1974.

Addresses: *Office*—c/o Motown Record Corporation, Hollywood, CA 90028.

successful groups. Atkins developed many of the Temptations's trademark dance steps.

The group finally achieved national success with the 1964 single, "The Way You Do the Things You Do."

Written and produced by Smokey Robinson, the song peaked at number 11 on the pop charts. Motown, capitalizing on this success, released *Meet the Temptations* that same year. The album included "The Way You Do the Things You Do," and its B side, "Just Let Me Know," along with all of the group's previously unsuccessful singles.

Scored First Number One

The following year, the Temptations had their first number-one hit, "My Girl." Also that year, the group worked with producer Norman Whitfield, and the end result was one of their most popular songs. "Ain't Too Proud to Beg" marked the start of a long and successful collaboration. "Norman Whitfield could and did produce soft, smooth ballads with the best of them but, stylistically speaking, he was headed into another realm," wrote Otis Williams in *Temptations*. "His backing tracks crackled with more intricate percussion, wailing, almost rock-style guitars, and arrangements that featured us as five distinct singers instead of one lead singer fronting a homogenized doo-wop chorus....[He] took us in new directions without losing the heart of our sound."

The Temptations remained one of the most popular acts in America for several years. They played the hottest nightclubs and appeared on numerous television shows, including *The Ed Sullivan Show*. The group also joined with the Supremes for a series of recordings and television appearances that broadened both groups' appeal. A special four- headed microphone was designed specifically for them, allowing members enough distance from each other so that, even when executing complicated moves, they were in no danger of stepping on each other.

Success, however, brought its own set of problems. Some members proved unable to handle their wealth and fame. Ego clashes often flared within the group, and the late 1960s and early 1970s saw several changes in the group's roster. David Ruffin left to pursue a solo career in 1968 and was replaced by Dennis Edwards. Edwards's career with the group was fitful; he was asked to leave in 1974 and replaced by Louis Price, but returned briefly in 1979, only to be turned out in favor of Ollie Woodson. Edwards returned to the group a third time in 1986. In 1970 Eddie Kendricks decided to go solo, and he was replaced by Ricky Owens of the Vibrations. Owens was almost immediately dismissed in favor of Damon Harris, who stayed with the group until 1974. Harris was then replaced by Glenn Leonard, who was, in turn, replaced by Ron Tyson in 1982. Paul Williams, with his worsening alcoholism and related health problems, was asked to leave the group in 1971; his spot was filled by Richard Street. Williams committed suicide two years later.

Pioneered Psychedelic Soul

At the same time that the group was undergoing these rapid roster changes, the Temptations and producer Whitfield still managed to pioneer the "psychedelic soul" movement. Characterized by an electric funk sound and socially conscious lyrics, this new musical trend yielded several big hits for the Temptations, including "Cloud Nine," "Ball of Confusion," and "Papa Was a Rolling Stone." Whitfield persisted with the movement long after psychedelic soul had run its course, and the once-creative relationship between the Temptations and their producer became stagnant. Otis Williams reported in *Temptations* that Whitfield began minimizing the singers' contributions: "On some tracks our singing seemed to function as ornamentation for Norman's instrumental excursions. When we started reading articles where writers referred to us as 'the Norman Whitfield Choral Singers,' we really got mad."

Fans of the group were disappointed as well, and record sales fell dramatically. The Temptations sought more artistic control, but Berry Gordy was deaf to their requests. Frustrated, the group severed its ties with Motown in 1976.

It was now the age of disco, and many Motown acts faded away. A two-year contract with Atlantic failed to help the Temptations out of their slump. In 1979 they renegotiated a return to Motown. Shortly thereafter, the classic Motown sound came back into vogue and the Temptations were once again in demand. Ruffin and Kendricks briefly rejoined the group for a tour, but personality conflicts soon resurfaced, and the Temptations quickly returned to a five-man lineup. After their appearance on the *Motown 25* television special, they teamed with the Four Tops for a "T 'n T Tour" that ran worldwide for nearly three years.

The early 1990s saw the deaths of several Temptations. On June 1, 1991 David Ruffin, who had left the group in 1968, died of a drug overdose. Ruffin's ex-wife, Sandra, told *People Weekly*, "The only downfall he had was the drugs. He was really trying, but after 24 years with the drugs, he just couldn't conquer it" The following year, Eddie Kendricks, one of the group's original members, died of lung cancer. Another original member, Melvin Franklin, died in 1995. Franklin had left the group in 1994, due to failing health. After suffering a series of brain seizures in February of 1995, Franklin was hospitalized, dying of heart failure a month later. Otis Williams was now the only living, original member of the Temptations.

This decade also saw further changes in the Temptations's roster. Ali Woodson, a member since 1983, left the group to pursue a solo career. Theo Peoples joined the group in the early 1990s. Temptation Ron Tyson had seen Peoples perform at a St. Louis jazz club, and invited Peoples to audition. Peoples told the *St. Louis Post-Dispatch* that the new members of the group try to sound as much like the original members as possible, maintaining a consistent Temptations sound. "But maybe we also interject a little of ourselves," he added.

Filed Lawsuit Against Former Member

When former member Dennis Edwards began performing under such names as Dennis Edwards & the New Temptations or Dennis Edwards & the Temptations Review, Williams, along with Franklin's estate, filed suit against Edwards, claiming trademark infringement. Edwards told the *St. Louis Post-Dispatch* "I need a piece of the name in order to make people remember me." In 1999 a federal judge issued a permanent injunction preventing Edwards from performing under any variation of the group's name.

In 1998 the Temptations released *Phoenix Rising*. Like the mythological figure of the phoenix, Williams told the *St. Louis Post-Dispatch*, "We've always been able to rise out of the ashes. That's what The Temptations have always been about." In the fall of 1999, the album was certified platinum by the Recording Industry Association of America. *Phoenix Rising* was the group's first album to ever be officially certified platinum. "This is tremendously gratifying after so many years," Williams told *Billboard*.

Also in 1998, the story of the Temptations came to life on the small screen when NBC aired a two-part mini-series. Based on Williams's book, *Temptations*, the mini-series was also co-produced by Williams. "Everywhere I would go from Hollywood to Europe, people would ask me when we were going to do a show like this," Williams told the *Seattle Post-Intelligencer*.

In November of 2001 the Temptations released *Awesome*. The group's lineup now included Williams, Tyson, Harry McGillberry, Terry Weeks, and Barrington Henderson. There have been a total of 19 members over the years. "I always compare the Temptations to a great sports franchise," Williams told the *Seattle Post-Intelligencer*. "Great players will come and go but the team endures. We are a team that has endured against tremendous odds and we will continue to endure. The Temptations are forever."

Selected discography

Albums

Meet the Temptations, 1964
The Temptations Sing Smokey, 1965.
Temptin' Temptations, 1965.
The Temptations Greatest Hits, 1966.
Temptations Live!, 1967, 1969.
Temptations Greatest Hits, Volume II, 1970.
All the Million-Sellers, 1981.

The Temptations 25th Anniversary, 1986.
To Be Continued, 1986.
Together Again, 1987.
Phoenix Rising, 1998.
Ear-Resistable, 2000.
Awesome, 2001.

Albums with Diana Ross and the Supremes

Diana Ross and the Supremes Join the Temptations, 1968.
TCB, 1968.
Together, 1969.
On Broadway, 1969.

Sources

Books

Contemporary Musicians, Volume 3. Gale Research, 1990.

Dalton, David and Lenny Kaye, *Rock 100*, Grosset & Dunlap, 1977.

Hardy, Phil and Dave Laing, *Encyclopedia of Rock*, McDonald, 1987.

Miller, Jim, editor, *The Rolling Stone Illustrated History of Rock and Roll*, Rolling Stone Press, 1976.

Williams, Otis, and Patricia Romanowski, *Temptations*, Putman, 1988.

Periodicals

Atlanta Journal-Constitution, October 30, 1998.
Billboard, May 3, 1986 October 14, 1992; August 20, 1994; November 22, 1997; January 9, 1999; November 6, 1999.
Dallas Morning News, November 1, 1998.
Jet, March 13, 1995; January 18, 1999; August 16, 1999.
Los Angeles Times, July 15, 1996.
Morning Call (Allentown, PA), February 9, 2002.
Newsweek, January 27, 1986.
People, August 25, 1986; September 1, 1986.
People Weekly, June 17, 1991.
Seattle Post-Intelligencer, October 30, 1998; February 1, 2002.
Seattle Times, November 1, 1998.
St. Louis Post-Dispatch, March 4, 1998; March 14, 1999; July 1, 1999; October 7, 2000; June 3, 2001.

On-line

Biography Resource Center, Gale Group, 2001, http://www.galenet.com/servlet/BioRC

—Joan Goldsworthy and Jennifer M. York

Big Mama Thornton

1926-1984

Blues singer, songwriter, musician

Willie Mae Thornton, known popularly as "Big Mama" because of her broad girth, was not only a successful singer/songwriter in her own time, but also influenced later performers such as Elvis Presley and Janis Joplin. She herself was influenced by the famous blues singers of the 1920s and 1930s like Bessie Smith, Memphis Minnie, and Ma Rainey. She was a popular performer famous for exuberant shows. "Her booming voice, sometimes 200-pound frame, and exuberant stage manner had audiences stomping their feet and shouting encouragement in R&B theaters from coast to coast from the early 1950s on," according to the *Encyclopedia of Pop Rock & Soul*. She received no formal training, either for voice, or for the instruments she played, like the harmonica and the drums. She was a true musician and was able to watch others play and then try things out until she got them right.

Born December 11, 1926 in the country outside Montgomery, Alabama, Thornton was one of seven children of a minister. She began her music career singing alongside her mother in her father's church choir and also playing harmonica, an instrument she picked up at a very early age, in small shows around the countryside. When, in 1940, her mother died Thorn-

ton was forced to go out and work. Only 14 years old, she took a job scrubbing floors at a local saloon and it was there that she had her first opportunity to sing in public when the regular singer suddenly quit her job one night leaving the place with no entertainment. After her first successful attempt at singing in public, Thornton entered a small talent show in which she won first prize, and it was there that she came to the attention of Sammy Green. Green asked her to join his Hot Harlem Review and Thornton was soon after seen touring with the vaudeville troupe, dancing and singing across the South.

In 1948 she stopped touring and settled in Houston, Texas having signed a five-year contract with Don Robey to be his nightclub singer, singing with Louis Jordan's band. There she met such famous musicians as Junior Parker, Lightning Hopkins, Lowell Fulson, and Gatemouth Brown. They all helped influence her building style, and it was while living in Houston that Thornton released her first recording under the name Harlem Stars. It was at this time too that Thornton learned how to play the drums. According the *Rolling Stone*, Thornton said, "I got tired of everybody messin' up, so I just started bangin'." Brought more firmly into

At a Glance . . .

Born Willie Mae Thornton on December 11, 1926, in Montgomery, AL; died on July 25, 1984, in Los Angeles, CA of a heart attack.

Career: Sammy Green's Hot Harlem Review, 1941; first recording as Harlem Stars, 1950; Johnny Otis band, early 1950s; recorded "Hound Dog," 1953; toured with Junior Parker and Johnny Ace, 1953-54; toured with Gatehouse Brown, 1956; wrote and recorded "Ball and Chain," 1961; Monterey Jazz Festival, 1964 & 1966; "From Spirituals to Swing," Carnegie Hall, 1967; *Black, White, and Blue,* PBS, 1967; *Della,* New York, 1969; *Rock I,* Toronto, 1970; *The Dick Cavett Show,* 1971; *Midnight Special,* 1974; performed at two state penitentiaries, 1975; American Folk Blues Festival in Europe, 1965; signed with Arhoolie label, 1965; Kool Newport Jazz Festival, 1980; "Blues Is a Woman," Avery Fisher Hall, 1980.

Awards: San Francisco Blues Festival Award, 1979; Blues Foundation's Hall of Fame, inducted, 1984.

the blues world by this release, she was signed onto the Peacock label, which had her heading to Los Angles to perform with Johnny Otis, the famous pop music bandleader.

She toured with Johnny Otis's Rhythm and Blues Caravan throughout the early 1950s. In 1952 they went to New York to perform at the Apollo, it was while there that Big Mama got her nickname, given to her after the first performance because she was six feet tall, was rather large, and had an immense, earthy voice. The name stuck. At the same time she was touring she recorded around thirty songs of her own.

In 1953 she recorded "Hound Dog," the song later made famous by Elvis Presley. Johnny Otis, asked Jerry Lieber and Mike Stoller to write a song specifically for Thornton and that song was "Hound Dog." It quickly went up the R&B charts to number one and was the song that made Thornton a big star. *Notable Black American Women* quoted Ian Whitcomb describing Thornton singing the song, "When Big Mama sings 'Hound Dog' she's slow and easy and also menacing, smiling like a saber-tooth tiger, her black diamond eyes glinting fiercely. Then, with the band in full roar, she leaves her chair to ambulate off in a swaying promenade that has a certain military regality, and the whole house cheers like royal subjects."

Three years later Elvis Presley recorded the song and it became an enormous hit for him. Thornton, in the meantime, always thought she'd never received the credit she should have for the song. Although written by Lieber and Stoller, it was her additions to the song that made it the hit it is today but she received only one check for $500 for the song and never saw another penny that the popular song pulled in. *Rolling Stone* quoted her as having said, "Didn't get no money from them at all. Everybody livin' in a house but me. I'm just livin.'"

After the release of "Hound Dog" in 1952, Thornton went on tour with some of her old friends, first with Junior Parker and Johnny Ace from 1953 to 1954, and then with Gatemouth Brown in 1956. After her tours finished she moved to Los Angeles and started playing harmonica and drums in some of the local clubs as the popularity of blues began to decline. In 1961 Thornton was brought into the limelight again with her release of the song "Ball and Chain."

Although she struggled a bit professionally during her life, Thornton was well received at such festivals as the Monterey Jazz Festival, the Newport Folk Festival, and the Ann Arbor Blues Festival. She also toured Europe with the American Folk Blues Festival in 1964. When she returned she signed a contract with the Arhoolie label in 1965, with whom she stayed until the 1980s. In 1979 she took part in the San Francisco Blues Festival, despite poor health, and gave there what critics called the performance of a lifetime. To recognize her contributions to the blues music scene, Thornton was awarded the San Francisco Blues Festival Award. Thornton appeared on many television shows throughout her life, and in 1980 she was seen onstage at the Newport Jazz Festival in a program "Blues Is a Woman" alongside other veteran female singers.

Thornton was known to be a heavy drinker and her notorious hard living finally took its toll in the 1970s and the 1980s, but Thornton performed in her lively fashion almost to the end, always dressed in nun's clothes. Her robust frame was gone as well as she lost most of her weight in later years. Even after a serious car accident in 1981 for which she required major surgery, she performed at a cabaret in Pasadena, California though she was unable to walk or stand during the performance. She died on July 25, 1984 in a boarding house in Los Angeles, California of a heart attack and complications from cirrhosis of the liver.

After a lifetime of performing, Thornton was inducted into the Blue's Foundations Hall of Fame in 1984. In the year 2000 Thornton was remembered in a dance show called "Sweet Willie Mae." Andrea E. Woods, who was the choreographer of the show, wanted to celebrate the freedom she found in Thornton's music. "What makes Willie Mae Thornton's music so intense and personal," Woods told the *Winston-Salem Journal,* "is that she owns the music." Thornton was also part of an exhibit at the Woman's Museum in Dallas, her recording of "Hound Dog" playing continuously in a room dedicated to female musicians. Also, the Fund for Women Artists website has a page dedicated to The Big Mama Thornton Project, a collaboration for a play based on Thornton's life. These are high honors for a woman who died penniless and alone, and ones that will most likely be repeated as more and more people discover a woman who helped make Blues and R&B the popular forms of music they are today.

Selected discography

Big Mama Thornton in Europe, Arhoolie, 1965.
Big Mama Thornton with the Chicago Blues Band, Arhoolie, 1967.
Big Mama Thornton: Ball N' Chain, Arhoolie, 1968.
Big Mama Thornton: Saved, Pentagram Records, 1970(?).
She's Back, Backbeat Label, 1970(?).
The Complete Vanguard Recordings, Vanguard, 1975.
Sassy Mama, Vanguard, 1975.
Jail, Vanguard, 1975.
Big Mama Swings, Vanguard, 1975.
Quit Snoopin' 'round My Door, Ace Records, 1984(?).

Sources

Books

Almanac of Famous People, 6th edition, Gale Research, 1998.
Contemporary Musicians, Volume 18, Gale Research, 1997.
Notable Black American Women, Book 2, Gale Research, 1996.

Periodicals

Business Wire, November 4, 1998.
Ebony, July 2001.
Entertainment Weekly, February 19, 1993, p. 64.
The Gazette (Colorado Springs, CO), May 13, 2001, p. T&B1.
The Observer (London, England), June 8, 1997, p. 13.
Rolling Stone, September 13, 1984, p. 43.
Winston-Salem Journal (Winston-Salem, NC), November 12, 2000, p. E1.

On-line

www.blueflamecafe.com/Big_Mama_Thornton.html
www.bluenight.com
www.blues.org/history/womenhistory/bigmama.html
www.busyfingers.com/fundwomen/bigmama.html
Contemporary Authors Online, The Gale Group, 2000.
www.epinions.com
www.greenmanreview.com/bigmamathornton.html
www. home.wanadoo.nl/rock_and_roll/bigmama.htm
www.jaybross.com/bio/bmama.html
www.roadhouseblues.com/biopages/bioBigMama.htm
www.tsha.utexas.edu/handbook/online/articles/print/TT/fthpg.html
www.who2.com/williemaethornton.html

—Catherine Victoria Donaldson

Cornel West

1953—

Scholar, educator, social critic, writer

Professor of religion and Afro-American studies at Harvard University, Cornel West has dazzled a vast array of audiences from scholars and activists to students and churchgoers with his analytical speeches and writings on issues of morality, race relations, cultural diversity, and progressive politics. A keeper of the prophetic African-American religious tradition, West taught the philosophy of religion at both Union Theological Seminary, Yale Divinity School, and Princeton before landing his position at Harvard.

As a scholar, activist, and teacher of religion, West juggles his theological concerns with his political convictions. While teaching religion at Yale, for instance, he was arrested for participating in a protest rally. West's blend of philosophy and an "on-the-streets" politics reflected his passion and commitment to his main goal: namely, "uphold[ing] the moral character of the black freedom struggle in America," as he was quoted as saying in *Emerge.*

Thought of as "our black Jeremiah" by Henry Louis Gates, Jr., chair of Harvard University's African American Studies Department, West served dual roles as prophet and intellectual both within and beyond the black community in the United States. His writings, which reflect the theories of early American historian Sacvan Bercovitch, combine a dual castigation for moral failure with an optimism that insists on the possibility—through struggle—of making real a world of higher morality.

In a 1991 book written with West, African American social critic, bell hooks, wrote that "the word 'prophetic' has emerged as that expression which best names both West's intellectual project, his spiritual commitment, and his revolutionary political agenda." Their book, *Breaking Bread: Insurgent Black Intellectual Life,* draws its title from West's own model for an effective—and sorely-needed—relevant black intellectual community.

West envisions the most effective role for the black intellectual as a "critical, organic catalyst" in what he calls the "insurgency model." In this model, intellectuals would challenge the status quo, voicing opposition to an inherently racist civil authority. The rebellion would then lead to the creation in the long term of a "post-(not anti-) Western civilization" and the revitalization in the short term of institutions that foster insightful critical thought and serve the cause of black insurgency.

At a Glance . . .

Born Cornel Ronald West, June 2, 1953, in Tulsa, OK; son of Clifton L., Jr. and Irene (Bias) West; divorced twice; married third wife; children: Clifton Louis. *Education:* Harvard College, A.B. 1973; Princeton University, M.A., 1975, Ph.D., 1980. *Politics:* Democratic Socialists of America (DSA). *Religion:* Baptist.

Career: Assistant professor of philosophy of religion at Union Theological Seminary, 1977-83 and 1988, Yale Divinity School, 1984-87, and University of Paris VIII, spring 1987; director of Afro-American Studies and professor of religion at Princeton University, 1989-94; Professor of Religion and African-American Studies, Harvard University, 1994-; involved in Theology in the Americas movement; joined Democratic Socialists of America, 1982; served on national political committee for seven years; became honorary chairperson.

Addresses: *Office*— Barker Center, 2nd floor, Department of African-American Studies, Harvard University, Cambridge, MA, 02138, FAX (617) 496-2871. *Publisher*—Beacon Press, 25 Beacon St., Boston, MA 02108.

West defined his vision in *Breaking Bread,* noting, "The central task of postmodern black intellectuals is to stimulate, hasten, and enable alternative perceptions and practices by dislodging prevailing discourses and powers."

Early Life: Family, Church, and Friends in Struggle

In his autobiographical introduction to his book *The Ethical Dimensions of Marxist Thought,* West describes the various academic, political, and personal influences on his life, attributing most significance to his experience in "my closely knit family and overlapping communities of church and friends." West was born on June 2, 1953, in Tulsa, Oklahoma, the grandson of the Reverend Clifton L. West, Sr., pastor of the Tulsa Metropolitan Baptist Church. West's mother, Irene Bias West, was an elementary school teacher (and later principal), while his father, Clifton L. West, Jr., was a civilian Air Force administrator. From his parents, siblings, and community, young West derived "ideals and images of dignity, integrity, majesty, and humility." These values, presented in Christian narratives, sym-

bols, rituals, and moral examples, provided him "existential and ethical equipment to confront the crises, terrors, and horrors of life." West suggests that the basis for his "life vocation" lies in three essential components of that Christian outlook, which he viewed most clearly in the example of Martin Luther King, Jr. These were "a Christian ethic of love-informed service to others, ego-deflating humility about oneself owing to the precious yet fallible humanity of others, and politically engaged struggle for social betterment."

In *Ethical Dimensions,* West examined his own experiences and those of his ancestors against a broad historical backdrop. His views on what he calls the "Age of Europe" are informed by his descendence from seven generations of Africans who were "enslaved and exploited, devalued and despised" by Euro-Americans, and three more generations who were "subordinated and terrorized" by the legal racist practices of Jim Crow laws in the South. He recounted that both of his parents were born into a place and time—Louisiana during the Great Depression—when Jim Crow laws of segregation were thriving. West viewed himself, however, as the product of the post-World War II eclipse of this "Age of Europe," when European cultural domination of the world ended. Still closer to home, West sees himself as a child of the "American Century"—what American editor and publisher Henry Luce defined as the period of unprecedented economic prosperity in the United States—and a youth of the time that witnessed the overturning of discriminatory segregationist laws in the United States.

West's community of friends and family participated actively in the struggle to overturn these racist laws. His earliest political actions included marching with his family in a Sacramento civil rights demonstration and coordinating with three other Sacramento high school students a strike to demand courses in black studies. In his youth, West admired "the sincere black militancy of Malcolm X, the defiant rage of the Black Panther Party, and the livid black theology of James Cone [a noted writer and professor of religion at Union Theological Seminary]."

Robert S. Boynton highlighted in the *New York Times Magazine* the role the Panthers played in refining West's progressive international perspective: they taught him the importance of community-based struggle; introduced him to the writings of Ghanaian anticolonial philosopher Kwame Nkrumah; and acquainted him with the principles of critical Marxist thought, which called for the achievement of a classless society. Still, West recalled in his introduction to *Ethical Dimensions* that he never fully agreed with these groups and thinkers, since he longed for more of the self-critical humility found in the life and work of Martin Luther King, Jr. In addition, he considers himself a "non-Marxist socialist," since he champions his Christianity over Marxism and believes that religion and socialism are reconcilable doctrines.

Developed Skills of Critical Thinking and Political Action

At age 17, West enrolled in Harvard as an undergraduate. By taking eight courses per term as a junior, he was able to graduate one year early, achieving magna cum laude in Near Eastern languages and literature. While there, he once wrote a spontaneous 50-page essay to work through the differences between Immanuel Kant and George Wilhelm Friedrich Hegel's conceptions of God. He even dreamed of philosophical concepts taking form and battling one another. According to Boynton, government professor Martin Kilson called West "the most intellectually aggressive and highly cerebral student I have taught in my 30 years [at Harvard]."

West credited his time at Harvard with fueling a reexamination of his world views; over those three years, he surveyed his own thoughts and actions and pursued a rigorous study of new ideas. In class, he developed a passionate interest on the effects of time and culture on philosophical thought and historical actions. Outside of class, he participated in a "breakfast program" group in the Massachusetts village of Jamaica Plain, took weekly trips to Norfolk State Prison, and worked with the Black Student Organization, which was responsible for the 1972 takeover of Massachusetts Hall to both protest Harvard's investments in Gulf Oil and show support for liberation forces operating in the southwest African country of Angola. But West attributed his greatest intellectual influences on political matters to a variety of philosophers such as nineteenth-century Serbian political writer Svetozar Markovic. He continued, however, to recognize the limits of "book knowledge" and to value dedication in action.

After Harvard, West began pursuing a doctorate in philosophy at Princeton University. There, he discovered that the values most precious to him were those of individuality and democracy. In the introduction to *Ethical Dimensions,* he defined individuality as "the sanctity and dignity of all individuals shaped in and by communities," and explained democracy as a way of living as well as a way of governing. The work of Richard Rorty, a philosopher at Princeton, also impressed West. West called Rorty's attention to history "music to my ears" and subsequently developed his own vision of Rorty's favorite philosophical tradition—American pragmatism—in his 1989 book *The American Evasion of Philosophy: A Genealogy of Pragmatism.* In this book, West defined his own version of pragmatism, called "prophetic pragmatism," which he believes is vital in promoting the formation of a democracy that both recognizes and extols the virtues of individual morality, autonomy, and creativity. Philosopher K. Anthony Appiah, writing in *Nation,* considered the book "a powerful call for philosophy to play its role in building a radical democracy in alliance with the wretched of the earth" and deemed West possibly "the pre-eminent African-American intellectual of our generation."

Into the Limelight: A Career in Teaching and Writing

West's books began to be published in the early 1980s, but he wrote many of them in the late 1970s. During his mid-twenties, he left Princeton, returned to Harvard as a Du Bois fellow to finish his dissertation, and then began his first tenure-track teaching job as an assistant professor of philosophy of religion at Union Theological Seminary in New York City. While a Du Bois fellow, West married and had a son, Clifton. Both this marriage and a later one ended in divorce.

While teaching at Union, West concerned himself with "the major national progressive multiracial and religious activity in the country in the 1970s." He also traveled to Brazil, Jamaica, Costa Rica, Mexico, Europe, and South Africa, where he saw and involved himself with intellectual and political progressive movements "reminiscent of our 1960s." In the early 1980s, West encountered Michael Harrington's Democratic Socialists of America (DSA), an organization that shaped the version of democratic socialism he would subsequently promote. West described the DSA in *Ethical Dimensions* as "the first multiracial, socialist organization close enough to my politics that I could join."

West wrote *The Ethical Dimensions of Marxist Thought* during his time at Union, but it wasn't published until 1991. In the book, he traced Karl Marx's intellectual development to reveal how Marx incorporated the growing consciousness of history in modern thought with values of individuality and democracy. West combined his interests in Marxism and religion in his 1982 book *Prophesy Deliverance! An Afro-American Revolutionary Christianity,* in which he shows the potential in prophetic Christianity—and especially in aspects of the black church—for meaningful opposition to racism and oppression.

In 1984 West assumed a post at the Yale Divinity School that eventually became a joint appointment with the institution's American Studies Department. He participated in a campus drive for clerical unionism and against Yale's investments in South African companies and was arrested and jailed during one campus protest. West viewed his political actions at Yale as "a fine example for my wonderful son, Clifton," who had become a progressive student body president in his predominantly black middle school in Atlanta. The Yale administration punished West by canceling his leave and requiring him to teach a full load of two courses in the spring of 1987.

Before his leave was canceled, West had already arranged to teach African-American thought and American pragmatism at the University of Paris, so in order to fulfill his responsibilities to both schools, he commuted to Paris for his three courses there while teaching his two courses at Yale. He also served as the American correspondent for *Le Monde diplomatique* at Yale. In 1988, West returned to Union; one year after that move, he accepted a position at Princeton University as professor of religion and director of the Afro-American Studies program. West continued to write and edit books on philosophy throughout the 1980s and early 1990s. In his 1985 publication *Post-Analytic Philosophy,* which he edited with John Rajchman, West reflected on the crisis in American philosophy. *Prophetic Fragments,* an essay collection published in 1988, is considered a tome of contemporary cultural criticism, addressing such subjects as theology, sex, suicide, and violence in America today. In 1991's *Breaking Bread: Insurgent Black Intellectual Life,* co-authors West and bell hooks limit themselves to the problems of creating black male-female dialogue and an effective black intellectual community while suggesting practical solutions to communication problems.

The Power of Diversity

West's impassioned and insightful writings make a resounding appeal for cross-cultural tolerance and unity, while urging individuals to recognize the power of diversity within a society. As a member of the editorial collective for the journal *Boundary 2: An International Journal of Literature and Culture,* West draws on his research to relate Marxist thought to cultural politics of difference, including differences in race, gender, sexual orientation, and age. And out of a desire to contribute to the building of coalitions across different communities, he writes a column for the progressive Jewish journal *Tikkun.* Finally, in an effort to reach out to still wider audiences, West provides commentary on contemporary subjects for popular journals, such as his essay on the 1992 Los Angeles riots for the *New York Times Magazine.*

West continues his exploration of race relations and cultural diversity in his 1993 book *Race Matters,* which his publisher, Beacon Press, promotes as a "healing vision for the crisis of racial politics today." Appealing to a "broader audience" than some of his earlier works, West's message "remains ... uncompromising and unconventional," according to Ellis Cose in *Newsweek.* "He sees salvation in a renewal of love, empathy and compassion, in a radical redistribution of power and wealth—and in facing difficult truths."

As Boynton indicated, West's inimitable drive to keep on teaching and writing is so strong that West feels as though if he were to stop, he would "just explode." Resolute in his belief that people of color must struggle now for a better future, he persists in his quest to create an effective, black, progressive leadership. West ends his introduction to *Ethical Dimensions* with a call to action: "The future of U.S. progressive politics lies in the capacity of a collective leadership to energize, mobilize, and organize working and poor people. Democratic socialists can play a crucial role in projecting an all-embracing moral vision of freedom, justice, and equality, and making social analyses that connect and link activists together....America's massive social breakdown requires that we come together—for the sake of our lives, our children, and our sacred honor."

Moved Into the Twenty-first Century

West is devoted to celebrating African-American citizens who have left an indelible mark on people of all cultures and races, and continues to address issues that affect the lives of all people. Since his move to Harvard, West has published several more books including *The Future of the Race* and *The African American Century: How Black Americans Have Shaped Our Country,* both co-authored with his colleague Henry Louis Gates, Jr. The latter is a book that is comprised of approximately 100 biographies of prominent African Americans, including some obscure notables such as the first black woman aviator, Bessie Colman. For the book, the authors wrote, "At the dawn of the 21st century ... we cannot imagine a truly American culture that has not, in profound ways, been shaped by the contributions of African Americans."

In 1996 West, along with feminist and economist, Sylvia Ann Hewlett, created the Task Force of Parent Empowerment, and later, West and Hewlett co-authored *The War Against Parents: What We Can Do For America's Beleaguered Moms and Dads* and *Taking Parenting Public: The Case For A New Social Movement,* which was edited by Hewlett. Both books address how American government policies and the American media work against families. West and Hewlett have called for a Parent Bill of Rights.

West decided to try something new. He recorded a CD that included rap and spoken word, *Sketches of My Culture.* While the CD may not have measured up to a rap critic's "picks," West was harshly criticized by Harvard President, Larry Summers, President Clinton's treasury secretary. Summers suggested that West pay attention to more scholarly pursuits and inferred that West allowed grade inflation. West was also criticized for leading a committee for Al Sharpton's presidential campaign, should he decide to run. In addition, Summers commented that West should be publishing books that would be reviewed by academic journals rather than in the *New York Times.* According to *The Economist,* the incident "spiraled into a full-blown tempest" which caused West, along with Henry Louis Gates, Jr. and Kwame Anthony Appiah, to consider quitting and going elsewhere. Summers and West have since made peace. Gates, who turned Harvard's fledgling African American Studies department into a robust and thriving department that can boast of having the country's top black intellectuals and has had record number of students enrolled said, "One of Professor West's great gifts is that he can engage in conversation with almost anyone, whatever their ideology. His keen-edged analysis forces us to remember what he has to say. There's no one from whom I've learned more than Cornel West. One of the most important things that he has to teach, I think, is that being a Black intellectual doesn't have to mean mindless, pompous cheerleading."

Selected works

Albums

Sketches of My Culture, 2001.

Books

Black Theology and Marxist Thought, Theology in the Americas, 1979.
Prophesy Deliverance! An Afro-American Revolutionary Christianity, Westminster Press, 1982.
(Coeditor) *Theology in the Americas,* Orbis Books, 1982.
(Coeditor) *Post-Analytic Philosophy,* Columbia University Press, 1985.
Prophetic Fragments, Eerdmans, 1988.
The American Evasion of Philosophy: A Genealogy of Pragmatism, University of Wisconsin Press, 1989.
(Coeditor) *Out There: Marginalization and Contemporary Cultures,* 1990.
(With bell hooks) *Breaking Bread: Insurgent Black Intellectual Life,* South End Press, 1991.
The Ethical Dimensions of Marxist Thought, Monthly Review Press, 1991.
Beyond Eurocentrism and Multiculturalism, Common Courage Press, 1993.
Race Matters, Beacon Press, 1993.
Future of the Race, 1997.
(with Sylvia Ann Hewlett) *The War Against Parents: What We Can Do For America's Beleaguered Moms and Dads,* 1998.
Cornel West: A Critical Reader, 2001.

Contributor of articles to periodicals, including *Monthly Review, Yale Journal of Criticism: Interpretation in the Humanities, Critical Quarterly, Nation, October, Tikkun, New York Times Book Review,* and *New York Times Magazine.* American correspondent for *Le Monde diplomatique,* 1984-87; member of editorial collective *Boundary 2: An International Journal of Literature and Culture.*

Sources

Books

Bercovitch, Sacvan, *The American Jeremiad,* University of Wisconsin Press, 1978.
hooks, bell, and Cornel West, *Breaking Bread: Insurgent Black Intellectual Life,* South End Press, 1991.
West, Cornel, *The American Evasion of Philosophy: A Genealogy of Pragmatism,* University of Wisconsin Press, 1989.
West, Cornel, *The Ethical Dimensions of Marxist Thought,* Monthly Review Press, 1991.

Periodicals

Commonweal, December 20, 1985, p. 708.
The Economist, January 5, 2002.
Emerge, March 1993.
Essence, June 1996, p. 42.
Nation, April 9, 1990, pp. 496-8.
National Review, January 28, 2002.
Newsweek, June 7, 1993, p. 71.
New York Times Magazine, September 15, 1991.
The Progressive, January, 1997, p. 26.
Publishers Weekly, March 30, 1998, p. 60; October 16, 2000, p.57.
Religious Studies Review, April 1992, p. 103.
Time, January 14, 2002, p. 14.
Voice Literary Supplement, December 1988, pp. 3-4.

—Nicholas S. Patti and Christine Miner Minderovic

Clarence Williams

1893(?)-1965

Jazz musician, publisher

Clarence Williams was one of the premier music publishers of his time. He claimed to be the originator of jazz, and while this has not been proven true, it can be said that Williams did make a major impact in the development of jazz. He was also a very successful, though sometimes shady, businessman and entrepreneur.

Williams was born in 1893 (some accounts say 1898) in Plaquemine, Louisiana. His father was a hotel owner and a bass player. The family moved to New Orleans in 1906 and Williams began his career singing in the streets. At the age of twelve, Williams joined a minstrel show as a singer. He then became the show's emcee.

In 1915 Williams returned to New Orleans, particularly the Storyville District. He began to work as an organizer, record producer, and composer. He also started a suit cleaning service and ran a cabaret. Williams teamed up with famed bandleader and violinist Armand (A.J.) Piron to start and music publishing company.

In 1916 Williams wrote "Brown Skin, Who You For" and received $1,600, his first payment for a composition and considered the largest payout ever in New Orleans. The song, included a short play with words

some consider a precursor to rap music. During this time, many made the claim to be the creator of jazz music, Williams included. Tom Morgan at bluesnet.hub.org stated that Williams not only claimed to be the first person to use the word 'jazz' in a song but he had the title "The Originator of Jazz and Boogie Woogie" placed on his business card.

Williams worked with numerous jazz greats of the day including: Fats Waller, James P. Johnson, and Sidney Bechet. He and his partner, Piron, created a vaudeville act that had minimal success. While touring, the duo became acquainted with W. C. Handy. They were even on hand to perform in Handy's program when he switched venues in Atlanta.

The Storyville district closed, and Williams moved to Chicago. He opened a music store that was so lucrative, he opened two more stores. Many people began listening to black female blues singers, and Williams decided to capitalize on this. He married blues singer Eva Taylor, sold his stores and moved to New York in 1923. He opened his own music publishing company.

Though Williams performed with his wife, he is perhaps known more for his collaborations with renowned vocalist, Bessie Smith. The two had released many songs, of those "Gulf Coast Blues," "Baby Won't You Please Come Home," and "T'ain't Nobody's Bizness If I Do" are considered classics. Though the two were successful together, Williams wasn't honest with the singer. According to Tom Morgan, he fooled the singer into signing a contract with him instead of with Columbia Records, and he pocketed half of her recording fee. The teaming ended after a surprise visit by Smith and her boyfriend to Williams' office.

Williams became A&R director for Okeh Records. He helped to develop many new artists and advanced the careers of many jazz legends including Louis Armstrong. He also employed a number of talented people including arranger Don Redman and saxophone player Coleman Hawkins. As A&R director, Williams nurtured and groomed many artists by arranging sessions, supplying material and publishing compositions.

Williams was also producing and playing for himself. He recorded over 300 records with his band. Williams was a perfectionist, and if he didn't like how a session went, he'd record the music somewhere else under a pseudonyms, usually The Dixie Washboard Band or Bluegrass Footwarmers. According to basinstreet.com, Williams' music was "never sweet, coy or weak. It had a sturdy solid strength, a deep emotionality, an inner calmness that provided beauty and true art."

Williams also produced and composed the musical *Bottomland,* which also starred his wife, Eva. By the 1930s, swing had become popular and demand for his Dixieland style had waned. Williams switched his focus from performing and producing to mainly composing. According to Dick Stafford, a writer for www.musicweb.uk.net, Williams retired from full-time music after he sold his catalog to Decca Records. He lost his eyesight after an accident in 1956. He died nine years later in New York.

Williams' music represented the early jazz sound of New Orleans. He was a well-respected pianist and publisher. Many looked to Williams' work as a guide to what was in vogue at the time. Many of his songs have achieved lasting fame—though some of them he claimed credit for, he hadn't composed alone. According to allmusic.com, Williams "had a real ear for talent," and helped to make Okeh Records one of the preeminent record labels in the 1920s. He was an intriguing and highly profitable businessman. His nurturing of and collaborations with many of the top jazz musicians and singers of his time helped create the jazz heard and admired in both the late twentieth and twenty-first centuries. His name may have faded into obscurity but his sound has endured. Clarence Williams, though not the originator of jazz, can be considered one of its most influential pioneers.

Selected discography

Sides

"Brown Skin, Who You For."
"Royal Garden Blues."
"Jail House Blues."
"Charleston Hound."
"Cushion Foot Stomp."
"Gulf Coast Blues."
"Baby Won't You Please Come Home."
"T'ain't Nobody Bizness If I Do."

Sources

All Music Guide, www.allmusic.com
http://atj.8k.com/noartist/atjwilliams.html
http://basinstreet.com/Programs/Clarence Williams/
   index.htm
http://bluesnet.hub.org/readings/
   clarence.williams.html
http://www.edsite2.fsnet.co.uk/clarencewilliams.html
Jass.com, www.jass.com
http://www.musicweb.uk.net/jazz/2001/Oct01/
   Clarence_Williams.htm

—Ashyia N. Henderson

August Wilson

1945—

Playwright

August Wilson is one of America's most prolific writers, whose plays, like those written by Arthur Miller and Tennessee Williams, are produced throughout the country on a regular basis. He has won two Pulitzer Prizes, seven New York Drama Critics Circle Awards, and has earned twenty three honorary degrees. He has no particular method of writing his plays, but admits to relying on what he calls the "4 B's": the *Blues*; fellow playwright, Amiri *B*akara; author, Jorge Luis *B*orges, and painter, Romare *B*earden to tell what he needs to tell. Regarding Bearden, Wilson claimed, "When I saw his work, it was the first time that I had seen black life presented in all its richness, and I said, 'I want to do that—I want my plays to be the equal of his canvases.'"

Called "one of the most important voices in the American theater today" by Mervyn Rothstein in the *New York Times,* August Wilson has written a string of acclaimed plays since his *Ma Rainey's Black Bottom* first excited the theater world in 1984. His authentic sounding characters have brought a new understanding of the black experience to audiences in a series of plays, each one addressing people of color in each decade of the twentieth century. Although Wilson's "decade" plays have not been written in chronological order, the consistent, and key, theme in Wilson's dramas is the sense of disconnection suffered by blacks uprooted from their original homeland. He told the *Chicago Tribune* that "by not developing their own tradition, a more African response to the world, [African Americans] lost their sense of identity." Wilson has felt that black people must know their roots to understand themselves, and his plays demonstrate the black struggle to gain this understanding—or escape from it. Charles Whittaker, a critic for *Ebony* wrote, "Each of the eight plays he has produced to date is set in a different decade of he 20th century, a device that has enabled Wilson to explore, often in very subtle ways, the myriad and mutating forms of the legacy of slavery."

Most of the ideas for Wilson's plays have come from images, snippets of conversation, or lyrics from blues songs captured by his ever-vigilant writer's eye and ear. Virtually all of his characters end up singing the blues to show their feelings at key moments during his plays. The play *Fences* evolved from his seeing an image of a man holding a baby, and *Joe Turner's Come and Gone* from the depiction of a struggling mill hand in a collage by acclaimed black painter Romare Bearden, whom Wilson has cited as a particularly strong influence on his work. The blues have always had the greatest influence on Wilson, however. "I have always consciously been chasing the musicians," Wilson told interviewer Sandra G. Shannon in *African American Review.* "It's like our culture is in the music. And the writers are way behind the musicians I see. So I'm trying to close the gap."

Grew Up Poor in Pittsburgh

August Wilson grew up as the fourth of six children in a black slum of Pittsburgh, his home a two-room apartment without hot water or a telephone. Relying on welfare checks and wages from house cleaning jobs,

At a Glance . . .

Born Frederick August Kittell, April 27, 1945 in Pittsburgh, PA; son of Frederick August Kittel (a baker) and Daisy Wilson (a housekeeper); married Brenda Burton, 1969 (divorced, 1972); married Judy Oliver (a social worker), 1981 (divorced); married Constanza Romero (costume designer), 1988; children: Sakina Ansari (with Burton); Azula (with Romero). *Military service:* U.S. Army, 1962-63.

Career: Playwright. Worked as a sheet-metal worker, porter, toy-store stock worker, gardener, dishwasher, and short-order cook; published poems in *Black World* and *Black Lines*, 1971-72; co-founded Black Horizons on the Hill (theater company), Pittsburgh, PA, 1968; wrote scripts for Science Museum of Minnesota.

Awards: Pulitzer Prize, best drama, for *Fences,* 1987, and for *The Piano Lesson,* 1990; New York Drama Critics Circle Award for *Ma Rainey"s Black Bottom,* 1984, for *Fences,* 1987, and for *Joe Turner"s Come and Gone,* 1988; Tony Award, best drama, for *Fences,* 1986-87; American Theater Critics Award, 1986, 1989, 1990, 1991, 1992, 1998; Harold Washington Literary Award, 2001.

his mother, Daisy Wilson, managed to keep her children clothed and fed. August's father, Frederick August Kittel, a baker by trade, was a white German immigrant who never lived with the family and rarely made an appearance at the apartment. August Wilson officially erased his connection to his real father when he adopted his mother's name in the 1970s. David Bedford became Wilson's stepfather when the boy was a teenager, but the relationship between father and son was rocky. An ex-convict whose race prevented him from earning a football scholarship to college, Bedford would become a source for the play *Fences,* whose protagonist was a former baseball player blocked from the major leagues by segregation.

Learning to read at the age of four, Wilson consumed books voraciously. At first he read the Nancy Drew mysteries his mother managed to buy for the family, but by age 12 he was a regular at the local library. Despite his interest in the written word, August Wilson was an unexceptional student who developed a reputation for yelling answers out of turn in class. The mostly white parochial high school he attended also gave him a harsh dose of racism. When he turned in a well-written term paper on Napoleon, Wilson was accused of plagiarism by a teacher who would not believe a black child could do that well on his own. Wilson would often find notes on his desk reading "Nigger go home." At home, his family had to endure racial taunts when they moved to the mostly white Hazelwood area of Pittsburgh.

At age 15, sick of the racism that surrounded him, Wilson dropped out of school and began to educate himself, beginning in the "Negro" section of the public library. Reading works by Ralph Ellison, Richard Wright, Langston Hughes, Arna Bontemps, and other black writers, Wilson was caught up in the power of words. His fascination with language made him an avid listener, and he soaked up the conversations he overheard in coffee shops and on street corners, using the tidbits of conversations to construct stories in his head.

Poetry Writing an Early Focus

By his late teens, Wilson had dedicated himself to the task of becoming a writer. His mother wanted him to become a lawyer, but when her son continued to work at odd jobs, she got fed up with what she considered his lack of direction and kicked him out of the house. He enlisted in the U.S. Army, but somehow got himself discharged a year later. At age 20 he moved into a boarding house and began writing lines of poetry on paper bags while sitting in a local restaurant, gathering inspiration from tales swapped by elderly men at a nearby cigar store.

The symbolic starting point of Wilson's serious writing career came in 1965 when he bought a used typewriter, paying for it with twenty dollars that his sister gave him for writing her a rush term paper on Robert Frost and Carl Sandburg. Wilson immersed himself in the works of Dylan Thomas and John Berryman. He also loved Amiri Baraka's poems and plays because of their lively rhythms and street-smart language. Although some of Wilson's poems were published in some small magazines over the next few years, he failed to achieve recognition as a poet.

In the late 1960s, Wilson discovered the writings of Malcolm X and, according to Chip Brown in *Esquire,* took up the banner of cultural nationalism. "Cultural nationalism meant black people working toward self-definition, self-determination," Wilson told Brown. "It meant that we had a culture that was valid and that we weren't willing to trade it to participate in the American Dream." In 1969 Wilson and Rob Penny, a playwright and teacher, founded the black activist theater company Black Horizons on the Hill, which focused on politicizing the community and raising black consciousness. Black Horizons gave Wilson the chance to present his own early plays, mostly in public schools and community centers. Wilson never fully embraced the religion of black nationalism, however, which contributed to the failure of his first marriage to Brenda Burton, a member of the Muslim Nation of Islam.

Found a Voice

To find the voice that would make him famous as a playwright, Wilson needed to gain distance from his roots. This opportunity came in 1978 when he visited his friend Claude Purdy in St. Paul, Minnesota, and decided to stay there. Purdy urged Wilson to write a play and Wilson felt more ready than ever before. "Having moved from Pittsburgh to St. Paul, I felt I could hear voices for the first time accurately," he told the *New York Times.* In ten days of writing while sitting in a fish-and-chips restaurant, Wilson finished a draft of *Jitney,* a play set in a gypsy-cab station. He submitted the play to the Minneapolis Playwrights Center and won a $200-a-month fellowship.

Jitney and Wilson's next work, *Fullerton Street,* were produced at the Allegheny Repertory Theater in Pittsburgh. *Jitney* earned Wilson acceptance at the 1982 National Playwrights Conference, where he honed his rewriting skills. Now convinced that he was going somewhere, he quit his job writing scripts for the Science Museum of Minnesota so he could have more time to compose his own works. Financial support was provided primarily by his second wife, Judy Oliver, who was a social worker.

Wilson's breakthrough came with the combination of a good play, *Ma Rainey's Black Bottom,* and a supportive director, Lloyd Richards, artistic director of the Yale Repertory Theater. The play came to Richards's attention at the National Playwrights Conference in 1983. "The talent was unmistakable," Richards told Brown. *Ma Rainey's Black Bottom* began a long collaboration between the seasoned director and the novice playwright: Richards has gone on to direct all of Wilson's plays. He has also served as spokesperson and promoter for the publicity-shy Wilson, and as the father he never had. Wilson explained their relationship to Shannon: "Another way I look at it, since I love boxing, is that I am the boxer and he is the trainer. He's my trainer—'My boy August will get them.'"

Play Shown on Broadway

Ma Rainey's Black Bottom tapped the playwright's interest in the blues and its importance in American black history. He told *Newsday* in 1987, "I see the blues as a book of literature and it influences everything I do.… Blacks' cultural response to the world is contained in blues." His interest in blues singer Gertrude "Ma" Rainey went back to 1965, when he heard a recording by Bessie Smith, who had taken lessons from Rainey. Set in 1927, the play deals with how black singers were exploited by whites who took in the lion's share of profits generated by these entertainers. *Ma Rainey's Black Bottom* opened on Broadway at the Cort Theatre in 1984 and was a popular and critical success, running for 275 performances. In his review, Frank Rich of the *New York Times* called it "a searing inside account of what white racism does to its victims." Critics offered high praise of Wilson's true-to-life dialogue, although some complained that the play was too talky.

Wilson's next play, *Joe Turner's Come and Gone,* is about a freed black man who comes north to search for his wife, who disappeared during his enslavement. It focuses on the theme of African Americans moving from the agricultural South to a new set of hardships in the industrial cities of the North in the early twentieth century. *Joe Turner* expresses Wilson's belief that blacks would have been stronger if they had not migrated from country to city, since they came from agrarian roots in Africa. Although the play failed at the box office, many critics loved it. Rich's review in the *New York Times* in 1986 said that it was "as rich in religious feeling as in historical detail."

Wilson struck gold with *Fences,* which hit Broadway while *Joe Turner* was still playing there. Set in the 1950s, its subject is Troy Maxson, a trash collector whose dreams of playing professional baseball were thwarted by white racism. Maxson's bitterness leads him to deny his son the athletic success that was not possible for blacks in the past. The title demonstrates Wilson's concern with choices and responsibility, since fences can keep people in as well as out. Like all of Wilson's characters, Maxson is a complex man who, while having moral lapses, also worked hard to provide for his family. The play, which won the Pulitzer Prize and other awards, opened on Broadway in 1987 with James Earl Jones in the starring role.

When Wilson won the Pulitzer Prize for *The Piano Lesson* in 1990, he became the seventh playwright to win at least twice. A largely realistic play, *The Piano Lesson* focuses on a family conflict over an heirloom piano. Berniece Charles's slave ancestors were traded for the piano, and another family member carved African-style portraits of them on it. Later Berniece's father died reclaiming it. Now Berniece's brother Boy Willie wants to sell it to buy farmland, and the issue threatens to tear the family apart. A *Time* critic hailed it as Wilson's "richest" play yet.

In *Two Trains Running,* which opened in New York City in 1992, Wilson probed the turbulent era of the late 1960s, when racial strife and the Vietnam War convulsed the nation. While many critics considered the play overly metaphorical and lacking in a strong female character, Rich called it Wilson's "most adventurous and honest attempt to reveal the intimate heart of history" and "a penetrating revelation of a world hidden from view to those outside it." William A. Henry III added in *Time* magazine that it was "Wilson's most delicate and mature work."

"A Struggling Playwright"

Wilson's plays clearly demonstrate the tensions between blacks who want to hold onto their African heritage and those who want to break away from it. As a result of being pulled in different directions, violence often breaks out among blacks in Wilson's plays, yet that violence is often misdirected. Wilson dramatized this dilemma in *Ma Rainey's Black Bottom,* when the character Levee stabs a fellow musician who unintentionally stepped on his shoe, instead of attacking the white man who had stolen his music. When Cory Maxson threatens to assail his father with a baseball bat in *Fences,* he mocks his father's manhood and shows the futility of his past as a Negro baseball player. Wilson has devoted his career to dramatizing these tensions within the black community even while he upholds the dignity of the individuals who struggle with their past.

During the early 1990s, Wilson wrote *Seven Guitars,* a play that takes place during the post-World War II years. *Seven Guitars* features the story of a blues guitarist, who is murdered, and his circle of friends. The friends gather at the wake, and their stories are told in flashback form. Interestingly, Wilson often introduces characters in his plays that become the main characters in subsequent plays. In *Seven Guitars* King Hedley was "a cracked old man who sees ghosts" and becomes obsessed with fathering a child, a "new Messiah." Wilson's next play, *King Hedley II,* takes place in the 1980s. The character, King Hedley II is an ex-con who returns home and must deal with his past as well as figure out how to go "ligit." *King Hedley II* was first seen in the fall of 1999 at the Pittsburgh Public Theater and made it to Broadway in the summer of 2001, playing for twelve weeks. He has already constructed the framework for his next play whose main character, who was alluded to in *King Hedley II,* is a 366 year old mystical woman, Aunt Esther.

August Wilson has refused to give in to the temptations of Hollywood. He moved to Seattle in the early 1990s, where he has remained remarkably focused on his play writing. Wilson has said that he rarely watches television, goes to the movies, or even attends plays. His daily routine consists of writing longhand while sitting in restaurants starting around noon, then typing up his work at night, often until 4:00 a.m. Despite his success, Wilson told the *New York Times:* "I always tell people I'm a struggling playwright. I'm struggling to get the next play down on paper." Though the lives of many of his characters are bleak, he also has maintained a degree of optimism about the situation of people of color in the United States. "Black culture is still alive, still vital. The human spirit cannot and will not be broken."

Selected writings

Staged plays

Jitney, first produced at Allegheny Repertory Theatre, Pittsburgh, PA, 1982.
Fullerton Street, produced at Allegheny Repertory Theater.

Ma Rainey's Black Bottom, first produced at Yale Repertory Theater, New Haven, CT, 1984; produced on Broadway at Cort Theatre, October, 1984.
Fences, first produced at Yale Repertory Theater, 1985; produced on Broadway at 46th Street Theatre, March, 1987.
Joe Turner's Come and Gone, first produced at Yale Repertory Theater, 1986; produced on Broadway at Barrymore Theatre, March, 1988.
The Piano Lesson, first produced at Yale Repertory Theater, 1987; produced on Broadway at Walter Kerr Theatre, 1990.
Two Trains Running, first produced at Yale Repertory Theater, 1991; produced on Broadway at Walter Kerr Theatre, 1992.
Seven Guitars, first produced in 1996.
King Hedley II, first produced at Pittsburgh Public Theater, 1999.

Published plays

Ma Rainey's Black Bottom, New American Library, 1985.
Fences, New American Library, 1986.
Joe Turner's Come and Gone, New American Library, 1988.
The Piano Lesson, Dutton, 1990.
Three Plays (contains *Ma Rainey's Black Bottom, Fences,* and *Joe Turner's Come and Gone),* University of Pittsburgh Press, 1991.
Two Trains Running, Dutton, 1992.
Seven Guitars, Plume.

Sources

Books

Black Literature Criticism, Gale, 1992.
Contemporary Dramatists, 6th ed. St. James Press, 1999.
Shannon, Sandra G., *The Dramatic Vision of August Wilson,* Howard University Press, 1994.

Periodicals

African American Review, Vol. 27, No. 4, 1994, pp. 539-59; Spring 2001, p. 93.
American Theatre, September, 1996, p 14.
American Visions, August 2000, p. 14.
Chicago Tribune, September 16, 1984, p. 13.
Commonweal, July 13, 1990, p. 422.
Contemporary Literature, Spring 1999, p. 1.
Ebony, September 2001, p. 80.
Esquire, April 1989, pp. 116-27.
Essence, August 2001, p. 58.
Nation, June 11, 1990, p. 832; June 8, 1992, p. 799.
New Republic, May 21, 1990, pp. 28-30.
New Yorker, April 30, 1990, pp. 82-83.

New York Newsday, March 27, 1987, sec. 2, p. 11;
April 20, 1987, p. 47.

New York Times, October 22, 1984, p. C12; April
15, 1990, pp. B1, B8; April 14, 1992, pp. C13,
C17; June 3, 1992, pp. C1, C8.

New York Times Magazine, March 15, 1987, pp.
36-40, 49, 70; September 10, 1989, pp. 18-19,
58-60.

People Weekly, May 13, 1996, p. 63.

St. Louis Dispatch, January 6, 2002, pp. G1, D4.

Theater, Fall-Winter 1984, pp. 50-55.

The New Leader, June 3, 1996, p. 23; July, 2001, p.
45.

Time, April 23, 1990, p. 99; April 27, 1992, pp.
65-66; July 9, 2001, p.84.

—Ed Decker and Christine Miner Minderovic

Jacob Zuma

1942-

South African politician

Jacob Zuma, a native of South Africa's Zulu region and long-time member of the African National Congress, has spent a large part of his career shuttling between the two parties, who are often at odds over the course of South Africa's future. White South African rule and the segregationist politics of apartheid held the country in a vise grip from the late 1940s onwards. The country was characterized by bloody riots, political tortures, endless strikes, burning townships, and the immeasurable suffering of Black South Africans. Nelson Mandela, a leader in the anti-apartheid movement, was sentenced to life in prison by the government. As he languished there for over two decades he became a revered international symbol for human rights, freedom, and perseverance. When apartheid finally crumbled and the first democratic elections were held in 1994, Mandela became president of South Africa and his political party, the African National Congress (ANC) took a majority of the votes across the country.

But Black South Africa did not rise in unison to toss out apartheid together. Different political factions formed, each with their own agenda. One of the more contentious of those factions is the Inkatha Freedom Party (IFP). Based in Zulu tribal territory, the IFP stressed Zulu ethnicity and traditionalism. According to the South African government's official website, "Battles for turf between Inkatha and the ANC became a very destructive accompaniment to South Africa's transition to democracy." In a country with such a volatile history and as many varied ethnicities, Zuma's job has been to find a non-violent way to communicate between opposing factions.

Jacob Gedleyihlekisa Zuma was born April 12, 1942 in Inkandla, KwaZulu-Natal (then called Zululand). His name was created by his police officer father, from the sentence 'Ngeke ngithule umuntu engigedla engihlekisa'—meaning, 'I can't keep quiet when someone pretends to love me with a deceitful smile.' Breaking the sentence in two, his father gave Zuma the name Gedleyihlekisa while his brother became Ngekengithule. His father died when Zuma was just four years old. This loss meant that his mother had to take on the role of breadwinner, and Zuma would have to forego school to help support the family. The family moved closer to his mother's homeland and Zuma got his first job as a cattle shepherd. "I used to look after them very well. That was the first time I was praised for a job well done," he told the Saturday Argus. When the family moved once again to a township just outside of Durban,

At a Glance . . .

Born Jacob Gedleyihlekisa Zuma on April 12, 1942 in Inkandla, KwaZulu-Natal (then known as Zululand); *Education:* Mostly self-taught; attended night classes for a few years starting in 1955.

Career: Became a member of the militant wing of the ANC, the Umkhonto We Sizwe, 1962; arrested for conspiring to overthrow the government in 1963 and served 10 years in prison; upon release organized ANC in KwaZulu-Natal, 1973-75; exiled, 1975; ANC, National Executive Committee, 1977, chief representative in Mozambique, until 1984, Political-Military Committee, mid-1980s, head of underground structures, late 1980s, Intelligence Department, chief, 1987; chairperson of the Southern Natal, Executive Committee of Economic Affairs and Tourism in KwaZulu-Natal, 1994; ANC, national chair; KwaZulu-Natal, ANC chair, 1994; ANC, deputy president 1997; appointed deputy president of South Africa, 1999.

Memberships: ANC, 1958-; Government Business in the National Assembly, head, 1997-; South African National Aids Council, chair; University of Zululand, chancellor; Jacob Zuma Bursary Fund, patron, 1998-; Peace and Reconstruction Foundation, patron; Albert Luthuli Education and Development Foundation, patron.

Awards: Nelson Mandela Award for Outstanding Leadership, Washington DC, 1998; honorary doctorates from: University of Fort Hare, 2001; University of Zululand, 2001; Medical University of Southern Africa, 2001.

Addresses: *Mailing*—Private Bag X1000, Pretoria, South Africa, 0001. *Office*—Union Buildings, West Wing, 2nd Floor, Government Ave., Pretoria, South Africa; *E-mail*—Deputypresident@po.gov.za; *Press Agent*—Ms. Lakela Kaunda, lakela@po.gov.za.

his mother took a low-paying job as a domestic servant and Zuma held a variety of odd jobs.

Despite not being able to attend school, Zuma had an insatiable appetite to learn. Each day he pestered young school-going friends and relatives to teach him what they had learned. Eventually he taught himself to read and write, a fact that he would later use as a politician to "encourage those whose circumstances also did not allow them to go to school," as he told *Briefing.* "Education is education whether it is formal or not." The bit of formal training he did have came when his cousin agreed to take Zuma to night classes in 1955. The rest of his education has been on his own and he's done an exceptional job. "I have done everything the educated have done," he told *Briefing.*

In 1958 Zuma turned his energies from education of the books-and-paper variety to a different kind of schooling—that of politics, resistance, and activism. At seventeen he joined the ANC unbeknownst to most of his family members. This secrecy was necessary as the ANC as well as all other opposition groups had been banned by the government. In the early 1960s, in reaction to increasing oppression by the apartheid system, the ANC—long committed to non-violent resistance—created a militaristic wing, Umkhonto We Sizwe (Spear of the Nation). Zuma became an active member in 1962. Just a year later he was arrested along with 45 other recruits and convicted of conspiring to overthrow the government. He spent ten years in prison.

When Zuma was released in 1973 he returned directly back to his ANC activities. He is widely credited with establishing the underground ANC infrastructure in KwaZulu-Natal. In 1975 he was forced to flee South Africa and spent 15 years of exile living in many African countries including Mozambique, Swaziland, and Zambia. He continued working with the ANC and became a powerful player in its activities. Among his inner circle of friends was fellow ANC leader and exile, future South African president Thabo Mbeki. Zuma served in a number of high ranking positions in the exiled ANC including executive committee member, head of Underground Structures, and chief of the Intelligence Department at ANC headquarters in Zambia. During his exile, Zuma married Nkosazana Dlamini. Although they later divorced, they would serve together in the post-apartheid government.

Back in South Africa, the political front was changing. The continued work of the ANC, as well as that of the Black Consciousness Movement, and other opposition groups was having the desired effect on the apartheid government. Internationally, South Africa's treatment of its majority population represented the worst of civilization—inhumane, immoral, and shameful. It was in this environment in 1990 that then-president F. W. de Klerk lifted the ban on opposition groups and released political prisoners, most notably Nelson Mandela. Zuma was one of the first ANC leaders to return home.

In the intermediate years before the democratic elections that would make Mandela president, Zuma was instrumental in a number of political decisions. From negotiating the release of political prisoners and the return of exiles, to brokering peace in KwaZulu-Natal and promoting relations between the ANC and the IFP, Zuma left a definitive mark on the burgeoning democracy. He developed a support base in KwaZulu-Natal and according to the *Mail and Guardian,* even took on two wives and a traditional house according to Zulu custom.

In 1994 Mandela was elected president of South Africa. Zuma played a key role in this new political arena, both in the ANC and in KwaZulu-Natal politics. That year he was appointed national chairperson of the ANC, chairperson of the ANC in KwaZulu-Natal, and member of the Executive Committee of Economic Affairs and Tourism for the KwaZulu-Natal. He also ran an unsuccessful campaign for the premiership of the KwaZulu-Natal region. Though he is widely credited for increasing the peace and stability of the region and for building stronger ties between the ANC and the IFP, he has also come under criticism for dividing his time between ANC party issues and KwaZulu-Natal practical issues. The *Mail and Guardian* commented, "[Zuma] is suited to either task, but not both."

Despite the competing nature of his positions, Zuma did not shirk from the task, though he did acknowledge the extreme difficulty of obtaining lasting peace in KwaZulu-Natal. "The political violence has not come to an end," he told *Briefing* in 1998. Discussing the prospect for a co-operative pact between the IFP and the ANC, he stated, "We are still working on that.... We need to ask what the practical and fundamental issues are that we have to face … to come to terms with peace and stability."

Zuma found finally found some resolution of his dual roles when he was appointed deputy president of South Africa, following his old friend Thabo Mbeki's election to President in 1999. Because of his experience in KwaZulu-Natal and his proven skills as a peacemaker, he assumed the de facto role as governmental peace mediator. Whether dealing with trade unions, other political parties, or traditional leaders, it is generally agreed that Zuma is successfully applying his hard-earned talents. He has a well deserved reputation as hard working and loyal and he remains firmly committed to improving the lot of South Africa—its people, economy, and international standing. The *Mail and Guardian,* in evaluating the record of the Mbeki government in 2000, gave Zuma a B-minus, stating "his approach usually generates warmth, even among opposition [leaders]" and "within the presidency Zuma is seen as something of a gem." With crime, political violence, poverty, and AIDS still plaguing many South African citizens, it is fortunate that a man such as Zuma is onboard to lead the beleaguered nation into the 21st century.

Sources

Periodicals

Mail and Guardian (South Africa), June, 1999; December 22, 1999; December 22, 2000.
Saturday Argus (Cape Town, South Africa), September 11, 1999.

On-line

Official South African Government Website, www.gov.za
www.bbc.co.uk/hi/English/world/Africa/
www.hsf.org.za/Briefing_11/Jacob_Zuma.htm

—Candace LaBalle

Cumulative Nationality Index

Volume numbers appear in **bold**

Jackson, Maynard **2**
Jackson, Michael **19**
Jackson, Millie **25**
Jackson, Milt **26**
Jackson, Reggie **15**
Jackson, Samuel L. **8, 19**
Jackson, Sheneska **18**
Jackson, Shirley Ann **12**
Jacob, John E. **2**
Jakes, Thomas "T.D." **17**
James, Daniel Jr. **16**
James, Etta **13**
James, Juanita **13**
James, Rick **19**
James, Sharpe **23**
Jamison, Judith **7**
Jarreau, Al **21**
Jarvis, Charlene Drew **21**
Jay-Z **27**
Jazzy Jeff **32**
Jefferson, William J. **25**
Jeffries, Leonard **8**
Jemison, Mae C. **1**
Jenifer, Franklyn G. **2**
Jenkins, Beverly **14**
Jenkins, Ella **15**
Jerkins, Rodney **31**
Jeter, Derek **27**
Jimmy Jam **13**
Joe, Yolanda **21**
John, Daymond **23**
Johnson, Beverly **2**
Johnson, Charles **1**
Johnson, Charles S. **12**
Johnson, Dwayne "The Rock" **29**
Johnson, Earvin "Magic" **3**
Johnson, Eddie Bernice **8**
Johnson, George E. **29**
Johnson, Jack **8**
Johnson, James Weldon **5**
Johnson, John H. **3**
Johnson Jr., Harvey **24**
Johnson, Larry **28**
Johnson, Lonnie **32**
Johnson, Mat **31**
Johnson, Michael **13**
Johnson, Norma L. Holloway **17**
Johnson, Rafer **33**
Johnson, Robert **2**
Johnson, Robert L. **3**
Johnson, Robert T. **17**
Johnson, Rodney Van **28**
Johnson, Virginia **9**
Johnson, William Henry **3**
Jolley, Willie **28**
Jones, Bill T. **1**
Jones, Bobby **20**
Jones, Carl **7**
Jones, Caroline **29**
Jones, Cobi N'Gai **18**
Jones, Donell **29**
Jones, Elaine R. **7**
Jones, Elvin **14**
Jones, Ingrid Saunders **18**
Jones, James Earl **3**
Jones, Lois Mailou **13**
Jones, Marion **21**
Jones, Orlando **30**
Jones, Quincy **8, 30**
Jones, Star **10, 27**
Joplin, Scott **6**
Jordan, Barbara **4**
Jordan, June **7**
Jordan, Michael **6, 21**
Jordan, Montell **23**

Jordan, Vernon E. **3**
Josey, E. J. **10**
Joyner-Kersee, Jackie **5**
Joyner, Marjorie Stewart **26**
Joyner, Matilda Sissieretta **15**
Joyner, Tom **19**
Julian, Percy Lavon **6**
July, William **27**
Just, Ernest Everett **3**
Justice, David **18**
Kani, Karl **10**
Karenga, Maulana **10**
Kearse, Amalya Lyle **12**
Keith, Damon J. **16**
Kelly, Patrick **3**
Kelly, R. **18**
Kendricks, Eddie **22**
Kennedy, Adrienne **11**
Kennedy, Florynce **12, 33**
Keyes, Alan L. **11**
Keys, Alicia **32**
Khan, Chaka **12**
Khanga, Yelena **6**
Kilpatrick, Carolyn Cheeks **16**
Kimbro, Dennis **10**
Kimbro, Henry A. **25**
Kincaid, Bernard **28**
Kincaid, Jamaica **4**
King, B. B. **7**
King, Barbara **22**
King, Bernice **4**
King, Coretta Scott **3**
King, Dexter **10**
King, Don **14**
King, Gayle **19**
King, Martin Luther, Jr. **1**
King, Martin Luther, III **20**
King, Preston **28**
King, Woodie, Jr. **27**
King, Yolanda **6**
Kirby, George **14**
Kirk, Ron **11**
Kitt, Eartha **16**
Kitt, Sandra **23**
Knight, Gladys **16**
Knight, Suge **11, 30**
Komunyakaa, Yusef **9**
Kotto, Yaphet **7**
Kountz, Samuel L. **10**
Kravitz, Lenny **10**
Kunjufu, Jawanza **3**
L.L. Cool J **16**
La Salle, Eriq **12**
LaBelle, Patti **13, 30**
Lacy, Sam **30**
Lafontant, Jewel Stradford **3**
Lampkin, Daisy **19**
Lane, Charles **3**
Lane, Vincent **5**
Langhart, Janet **19**
Lanier, Willie **33**
Lankford, Ray **23**
Larkin, Barry **24**
Lars, Byron **32**
Larsen, Nella **10**
Lassiter, Roy **24**
Lathan, Sanaa **27**
Latimer, Lewis H. **4**
Lawless, Theodore K. **8**
Lawrence, Jacob **4, 28**
Lawrence, Jr., Robert H. **16**
Lawrence-Lightfoot, Sara **10**
Lawrence, Martin **6, 27**
Lawson, Jennifer **1**
Leary, Kathryn D. **10**

Leavell, Dorothy R. **17**
Lee, Annie Francis **22**
Lee, Barbara **25**
Lee, Canada **8**
Lee, Joie **1**
Lee-Smith, Hughie **5, 22**
Lee, Spike **5, 19**
Leffall, LaSalle, Jr. **3**
Leland, Mickey **2**
Lemmons, Kasi **20**
Lennox, Betty **31**
Leon, Kenny **10**
Leonard, Sugar Ray **15**
Lester, Julius **9**
Levert, Gerald **22**
Lewellyn, J. Bruce **13**
Lewis, Ananda **28**
Lewis, Byron E. **13**
Lewis, Carl **4**
Lewis, David Levering **9**
Lewis, Delano **7**
Lewis, Edmonia **10**
Lewis, Edward T. **21**
Lewis, John **2**
Lewis, Ray **33**
Lewis, Reginald F. **6**
Lewis, Samella **25**
Lewis, Shirley A. R. **14**
Lewis, Terry **13**
Lewis, Thomas **19**
Lewis-Thornton, Rae **32**
Lil' Kim **28**
Lincoln, Abbey **3**
LisaRaye **27**
Liston, Sonny **33**
Little, Benilde **21**
Little Richard **15**
Little, Robert L. **2**
Lloyd, Earl **26**
Lloyd, John Henry "Pop" **30**
Locke, Alain **10**
Lofton, Kenny **12**
Logan, Onnie Lee **14**
Long, Eddie L. **29**
Long, Nia **17**
Lorde, Audre **6**
Lott, Ronnie **9**
Louis, Errol T. **8**
Louis, Joe **5**
Love, Darlene **23**
Love, Nat **9**
Lover, Ed **10**
Lowery, Joseph **2**
Lucas, John **7**
Lyles, Lester Lawrence **31**
Lymon, Frankie **22**
Lyons, Henry **12**
Lyttle, Hulda Margaret **14**
Mabley, Moms **15**
Mabrey, Vicki **26**
Mac, Bernie **29**
Madhubuti, Haki R. **7**
Madison, Joseph E. **17**
Major, Clarence **9**
Mallett, Jr., Conrad **16**
Malone, Annie **13**
Malone, Karl A. **18**
Malone, Maurice **32**
Malveaux, Julianne **32**
Manigault, Earl "The Goat" **15**
Manley, Audrey Forbes **16**
Marable, Manning **10**
Marino, Eugene Antonio **30**
Marrow, Queen Esther **24**
Marsalis, Wynton **16**

Wilson, Charlie **31**
Wilson, Flip **21**
Wilson, Mary **28**
Wilson, Nancy **10**
Wilson, Phill **9**
Wilson, Sunnie **7**
Wilson, William Julius **20**
Winans, BeBe **14**
Winans, CeCe **14**
Winans, Marvin L. **17**
Winans, Vickie **24**
Winfield, Dave **5**
Winfield, Paul **2**
Winfrey, Oprah **2, 15**
Witt, Edwin T. **26**
Wolfe, George C. **6**
Wonder, Stevie **11**
Woodard, Alfre **9**
Woodruff, Hale **9**
Woods, Granville T. **5**
Woods, Tiger **14, 31**
Woodson, Carter G. **2**
Woodson, Robert L. **10**
Worrill, Conrad **12**
Wright, Bruce McMarion **3**
Wright, Deborah C. **25**
Wright, Louis Tompkins **4**
Wright, Richard **5**
Wynn, Albert R. **25**
X, Malcolm **1**
Yoba, Malik **11**
Young, Andrew **3**
Young, Coleman **1, 20**
Young, Jean Childs **14**
Young, Roger Arliner **29**
Young, Whitney M., Jr. **4**
Youngblood, Johnny Ray **8**
Youngblood, Shay **32**
Zollar, Jawole Willa Jo **28**

Angolan
Bonga, Kuenda **13**
Savimbi, Jonas **2**

Australian
Freeman, Cathy **29**

Bahamian
Ingraham, Hubert A. **19**

Barbadian
Arthur, Owen **33**
Clarke, Austin C. **32**
Flash, Grandmaster **33**
Foster, Cecil **32**
Kamau, Kwadwo Agymah **28**

Batswana
Masire, Quett **5**

Belizian
Jones, Marion **21**

Beninois
Hounsou, Djimon **19**
Kerekou, Ahmed (Mathieu) **1**
Mogae, Festus Gontebanye **19**
Soglo, Nicéphore **15**

Bermudian
Gordon, Pamela **17**
Smith, Jennifer **21**

Brazilian
da Silva, Benedita **5**
Nascimento, Milton **2**
Pelé **7**
Pitta, Celso **17**

British
Abbott, Diane **9**
Armatrading, Joan **32**
Bassey, Shirley **25**
Campbell, Naomi **1, 31**
Carby, Hazel **27**
Christie, Linford **8**
David, Craig **31**
Davidson, Jaye **5**
Henry, Lenny **9**
Jean-Baptiste, Marianne **17**
Jordan, Ronny **26**
Julien, Isaac **3**
King, Oona **27**
Lewis, Denise **33**
Lewis, Lennox **27**
Lindo, Delroy **18**
Newton, Thandie **26**
Pitt, David Thomas **10**
Seal **14**
Taylor, John (David Beckett) **16**

Burkinabé
Somé, Malidoma Patrice **10**

Burundian
Ndadaye, Melchior **7**
Ntaryamira, Cyprien **8**

Cameroonian
Biya, Paul **28**
Kotto, Yaphet **7**
Milla, Roger **2**

Canadian
Bell, Ralph S. **5**
Brand, Dionne **32**
Carnegie, Herbert **25**
Clarke, Austin **32**
Clarke, George **32**
Cox, Deborah **28**
Foster, Cecil **32**
Fox, Rick **27**
Fuhr, Grant **1**
Johnson, Ben **1**
McKegney, Tony **3**
O'Ree, Willie **5**
Philip, Marlene Nourbese **32**
Reuben, Gloria **15**
Richards, Lloyd **2**

Cape Verdean
Evora, Cesaria **12**
Pereira, Aristides **30**

Chadian
Déby, Idriss **30**
Habré, Hissène **6**

Congolese
Kabila, Joseph **30**
Lumumba, Patrice **33**

Costa Rican
McDonald, Erroll **1**

Cuban
León, Tania **13**
Quirot, Ana **13**

Dominican
Charles, Mary Eugenia **10**
Sosa, Sammy **21**

Dutch
Liberia-Peters, Maria Philomena **12**

Ethiopian
Haile Selassie **7**
Meles Zenawi **3**

French
Baker, Josephine **3**
Baldwin, James **1**
Bonaly, Surya **7**
Noah, Yannick **4**
Tanner, Henry Ossawa **1**

Gabonese
Bongo, Omar **1**

Gambian
Jammeh, Yahya **23**

German
Massaquoi, Hans J. **30**

Ghanaian
Annan, Kofi Atta **15**
DuBois, Shirley Graham **21**
Jawara, Sir Dawda Kairaba **11**
Nkrumah, Kwame **3**
Rawlings, Jerry **9**
Rawlings, Nana Konadu Agyeman **13**

Guinea-Bissauan
Vieira, Joao **14**

Guinean
Conté, Lansana **7**
Diallo, Amadou **27**
Touré, Sekou **6**

Guyanese
Beaton, Norman **14**
Jagan, Cheddi **16**
van Sertima, Ivan **25**

Haitian
Aristide, Jean-Bertrand **6**
Auguste, Rose-Anne **13**
Beauvais, Garcelle **29**
Charlemagne, Manno **11**
Christophe, Henri **9**
Danticat, Edwidge **15**
Jean, Wyclef **20**
Laferriere, Dany **33**
Pascal-Trouillot, Ertha **3**
Peck, Raoul **32**
Pierre, Andre **17**
Siméus, Dumas M. **25**

Irish
Mumba, Samantha **29**

Italian
Esposito, Giancarlo **9**

Cumulative Occupation Index

Volume numbers appear in **bold**

Art and design

Allen, Tina **22**
Alston, Charles **33**
Andrews, Benny **22**
Andrews, Bert **13**
Armstrong, Robb **15**
Bailey, Radcliffe **19**
Bailey, Xenobia **11**
Barboza, Anthony **10**
Barnes, Ernie **16**
Barthe, Richmond **15**
Basquiat, Jean-Michel **5**
Bearden, Romare **2**
Biggers, John **20, 33**
Blacknurn, Robert **28**
Brandon, Barbara **3**
Brown, Donald **19**
Burke, Selma **16**
Burroughs, Margaret Taylor **9**
Camp, Kimberly **19**
Campbell, E. Simms **13**
Catlett, Elizabeth **2**
Chase-Riboud, Barbara **20**
Cowans, Adger W. **20**
Crite, Alan Rohan **29**
Delaney, Beauford **19**
Delaney, Joseph **30**
Douglas, Aaron **7**
Driskell, David C. **7**
Edwards, Melvin **22**
Ewing, Patrick A.**17**
Feelings, Tom **11**
Freeman, Leonard **27**
Fuller, Meta Vaux Warrick **27**
Gantt, Harvey **1**
Gilliam, Sam **16**
Golden, Thelma **10**
Goodnight, Paul **32**
Guyton, Tyree **9**
Harkless, Necia Desiree **19**
Harrington, Oliver W. **9**
Hathaway, Isaac Scott **33**
Hayden, Palmer **13**
Hope, John **8**
Hudson, Cheryl **15**
Hudson, Wade **15**
Hunt, Richard **6**
Hutson, Jean Blackwell **16**
Jackson, Earl **31**
John, Daymond **23**
Johnson, William Henry **3**
Jones, Lois Mailou **13**

Kitt, Sandra **23**
Lawrence, Jacob **4, 28**
Lee, Annie Francis **22**
Lee-Smith, Hughie **5, 22**
Lewis, Edmonia **10**
Lewis, Samella **25**
Manley, Edna **26**
McGee, Charles **10**
McGruder, Aaron **28**
Mitchell, Corinne **8**
Moody, Ronald **30**
Morrison, Keith **13**
Motley, Jr., Archibald **30**
Moutoussamy-Ashe, Jeanne **7**
N'Namdi, George R. **17**
Pierre, Andre **17**
Pinkney, Jerry **15**
Pippin, Horace **9**
Porter, James A. **11**
Ringgold, Faith **4**
Saar, Alison **16**
Saint James, Synthia **12**
Sanders, Joseph R., Jr. **11**
Savage, Augusta **12**
Serrano, Andres **3**
Shabazz, Attallah **6**
Simpson, Lorna **4**
Sims, Lowery Stokes **27**
Sklarek, Norma Merrick **25**
Sleet, Moneta, Jr. **5**
Tanner, Henry Ossawa **1**
Thomas, Alma **14**
Tolliver, William **9**
VanDerZee, James **6**
Walker, A'lelia **14**
Walker, Kara **16**
Washington, Alonzo **29**
Wells, James Lesesne **10**
White, John H. **27**
Williams, Billy Dee **8**
Williams, O. S. **13**
Williams, Paul R. **9**
Williams, William T. **11**
Woodruff, Hale **9**

Business

Abbot, Robert Sengstacke **27**
Abdul-Jabbar, Kareem **8**
Ailey, Alvin **8**
Al-Amin, Jamil Abdullah **6**
Alexander, Archie Alphonso **14**
Allen, Byron **24**

Ames, Wilmer **27**
Amos, Wally **9**
Auguste, Donna **29**
Avant, Clarence **19**
Baemon, Bob **30**
Baker, Dusty **8**
Baker, Ella **5**
Baker, Gwendolyn Calvert **9**
Baker, Maxine **28**
Banks, Jeffrey **17**
Banks, William **11**
Barden, Don H. **9, 20**
Barrett, Andrew C. **12**
Bennett, Lerone, Jr. **5**
Bing, Dave **3**
Borders, James **9**
Boston, Kelvin E. **25**
Boston, Lloyd **24**
Boyd, John W., Jr. **20**
Boyd, T. B., III **6**
Brimmer, Andrew F. **2**
Bronner, Nathaniel H., Sr. **32**
Brown, Les **5**
Brown, Marie Dutton **12**
Brunson, Dorothy **1**
Bryant, John **26**
Burrell, Thomas J. **21**
Burroughs, Margaret Taylor **9**
Busby, Jheryl **3**
Cain, Herman **15**
CasSelle, Malcolm **11**
Chamberlain, Wilt **18**
Chapman, Jr., Nathan A. **21**
Chappell, Emma **18**
Chenault, Kenneth I. **4**
Chisholm, Samuel J. **32**
Clark, Celeste **15**
Clark, Patrick **14**
Clay, William Lacy **8**
Clayton, Xernona **3**
Cobbs, Price M. **9**
Colbert, Virgis William **17**
Coleman, Donald A. **24**
Connerly, Ward **14**
Conyers, Nathan G. **24**
Cooper, Barry **33**
Cornelius, Don **4**
Cosby, Bill **7, 26**
Cottrell, Comer **11**
Creagh, Milton **27**
Daniels-Carter, Valerie **23**
Dash, Darien **29**

Lewis, Delano **7**
Lewis, John **2**
Mallett, Conrad, Jr. **16**
Marsh, Henry, III **32**
Marshall, Bella **22**
Marshall, Thurgood **1**
Martin, Louis E. **16**
McCall, H. Carl **27**
McKinney, Cynthia Ann **11**
McKissick, Floyd B. **3**
Meek, Carrie **6**
Meeks, Gregory **25**
Meredith, James H. **11**
Metcalfe, Ralph **26**
Mfume, Kweisi **6**
Millender-McDonald, Juanita **21**
Morial, Ernest "Dutch" **26**
Morial, Marc **20**
Moses, Robert Parris **11**
Norton, Eleanor Holmes **7**
O'Leary, Hazel **6**
Owens, Major **6**
Page, Alan **7**
Paige, Rod **29**
Patrick, Deval **12**
Patterson, Louise **25**
Payne, Donald M. **2**
Perez, Anna **1**
Perkins, Edward **5**
Perry, Lowell **30**
Pinchback, P. B. S. **9**
Powell, Adam Clayton, Jr. **3**
Powell, Colin **1, 28**
Powell, Debra A. **23**
Powell, Michael **32**
Raines, Franklin Delano **14**
Randolph, A. Philip **3**
Rangel, Charles **3**
Reeves, Triette Lipsey **27**
Rice, Condoleezza **3, 28**
Rice, Norm **8**
Robinson, Randall **7**
Rogers, Joe **27**
Ross, Don **27**
Rush, Bobby **26**
Rustin, Bayard **4**
Sampson, Edith S. **4**
Satcher, David **7**
Sayles Belton, Sharon **9, 16**
Schmoke, Kurt **1**
Scott, Robert C. **23**
Sears-Collins, Leah J. **5**
Shakur, Assata **6**
Shavers, Cheryl **31**
Sharpton, Al **21**
Simpson, Carole **6, 30**
Sisulu, Sheila Violet Makate **24**
Slater, Rodney E. **15**
Stanton, Robert **20**
Staupers, Mabel K. **7**
Stokes, Carl B. **10**
Stokes, Louis **3**
Stone, Chuck **9**
Street, John F. **24**
Sullivan, Louis **8**
Thomas, Clarence **2**
Thompson, Bennie G. **26**
Towns, Edolphus **19**
Tribble, Israel, Jr. **8**
Trotter, Donne E. **28**
Tubbs Jones, Stephanie **24**
Tucker, C. DeLores **12**
Turner, Henry McNeal **5**
Usry, James L. **23**
Von Lipsey, Roderick K. **11**

Wallace, Phyllis A. **9**
Washington, Harold **6**
Washington, Val **12**
Waters, Maxine **3**
Watkins, Shirley R. **17**
Watt, Melvin **26**
Watts, J. C., Jr. **14**
Weaver, Robert C. **8**
Webb, Wellington **3**
Wharton, Clifton R., Jr. **7**
Wheat, Alan **14**
White, Jesse **22**
White, Michael R. **5**
Wilder, L. Douglas **3**
Wilkins, Roger **2**
Williams, Anthony **21**
Williams, George Washington **18**
Williams, Hosea Lorenzo **15, 31**
Williams, Maggie **7**
Wilson, Sunnie **7**
Wynn, Albert **25**
Young, Andrew **3**

Law

Alexander, Clifford **26**
Alexander, Joyce London **18**
Alexander, Sadie Tanner Mossell **22**
Archer, Dennis **7**
Arnwine, Barbara **28**
Banks, William **11**
Barrett, Andrew C. **12**
Barrett, Jacqueline **28**
Baugh, David **23**
Bell, Derrick **6**
Berry, Mary Frances **7**
Berry, Theodore M. **31**
Bishop Jr., Sanford D. **24**
Bolin, Jane **22**
Bolton, Terrell D. **25**
Bosley, Freeman, Jr. **7**
Boykin, Keith **24**
Bradley, Thomas **2**
Braun, Carol Moseley **4**
Brooke, Edward **8**
Brown, Cora **33**
Brown, Joe **29**
Brown, Lee Patrick **1, 24**
Brown, Ron **5**
Brown, Willie L., Jr. **7**
Bryant, Wayne R. **6**
Burris, Roland W. **25**
Butler, Paul D. **17**
Campbell, Bill **9**
Carter, Stephen L. **4**
Chambers, Julius **3**
Cleaver, Kathleen Neal **29**
Clendenon, Donn **26**
Cochran, Johnnie L., Jr. **11**
Conyers, John, Jr. **4**
Crockett, George, Jr. **10**
Darden, Christopher **13**
Days, Drew S., III **10**
Diggs-Taylor, Anna **20**
Dinkins, David **4**
Dixon, Sharon Pratt **1**
Edelman, Marian Wright **5**
Edley, Christopher **2**
Ellington, E. David **11**
Ephriam, Mablean **29**
Espy, Mike **6**
Fields, Cleo **13**
Frazier-Lyde, Jacqui **31**
Freeman, Charles **19**
Gary, Willie E. **12**
Gibson, Johnnie Mae **23**

Glover, Nathaniel, Jr. **12**
Gomez-Preston, Cheryl **9**
Graham, Lawrence Otis **12**
Grimké, Archibald H. **9**
Guinier, Lani **7, 30**
Haley, George Williford Boyce **21**
Hall, Elliott S. **24**
Harris, Patricia Roberts **2**
Harvard, Beverly **11**
Hastie, William H. **8**
Hastings, Alcee L. **16**
Hatchett, Glenda **32**
Hawkins, Steven **14**
Haywood, Margaret A. **24**
Higginbotham, A. Leon, Jr. **13, 25**
Hill, Anita **5**
Hillard, Terry **25**
Hills, Oliver W. **24**
Holder, Eric H., Jr. **9**
Hooks, Benjamin L. **2**
Houston, Charles Hamilton **4**
Hunter, Billy **22**
Jackson Lee, Sheila **20**
Jackson, Maynard **2**
Johnson, James Weldon **5**
Johnson, Norma L. Holloway **17**
Jones, Elaine R. **7**
Jones, Star **10, 27**
Jordan, Vernon E. **3**
Kearse, Amalya Lyle **12**
Keith, Damon J. **16**
Kennard, William Earl **18**
Kennedy, Florynce **12, 33**
King, Bernice **4**
Kirk, Ron **11**
Lafontant, Jewel Stradford **3**
Lewis, Delano **7**
Lewis, Reginald F. **6**
Mallett, Conrad, Jr. **16**
Mandela, Nelson **1, 14**
Marsh, Henry, III **32**
Marshall, Thurgood **1**
Mathis, Greg **26**
McDonald, Gabrielle Kirk **20**
McDougall, Gay J. **11**
McKinnon, Isaiah **9**
McKissick, Floyd B. **3**
McPhail, Sharon **2**
Meeks, Gregory **25**
Morial, Ernest "Dutch" **26**
Motley, Constance Baker **10**
Muhammad, Ava **31**
Napoleon, Benny N. **23**
Norton, Eleanor Holmes **7**
O'Leary, Hazel **6**
Ogletree, Charles, Jr. **12**
Page, Alan **7**
Paker, Kellis E. **30**
Parks, Bernard C. **17**
Parsons, James **14**
Parsons, Richard Dean **11, 33**
Pascal-Trouillot, Ertha **3**
Patrick, Deval **12**
Perry, Lowell **30**
Philip, Marlene Nourbese **32**
Powell, Michael **32**
Ramsey, Charles H. **21**
Redding, Louis L. **26**
Richie, Leroy C. **18**
Robinson, Randall **7**
Russell-McCloud, Patricia **17**
Sampson, Edith S. **4**
Schmoke, Kurt **1**
Sears-Collins, Leah J. **5**
Stokes, Carl B. **10**

Cumulative Subject Index

Volume numbers appear in **bold**

Bushi Designs
Rhymes, Busta **31**

Busing (anti-busing legislation)
Bosley, Freeman, Jr. **7**

BVA
See Beach Volleyball America

Cabinet
See U.S. Cabinet

Cable News Network (CNN)
Chideya, Farai **14**
Hickman, Fred **11**
Quarles, Norma **25**
Shaw, Bernard **2, 28**

California Angels baseball team
Baylor, Don **6**
Carew, Rod **20**
Robinson, Frank **9**
Winfield, Dave **5**

California State Assembly
Brown, Willie L., Jr. **7**
Dixon, Julian C. **24**
Lee, Barbara **25**
Millender-McDonald, Juanita **21**
Waters, Maxine **3**

Calypso
Belafonte, Harry **4**
Jean, Wyclef **20**

Cameroon National Union (CNU)
Biya, Paul **28**

Cameroon People's Democratic Movement (CPDM)
Biya, Paul **28**

Canadian Football League (CFL)
Gilliam, Frank **23**
Moon, Warren **8**
Weathers, Carl **10**

Cancer research
Chinn, May Edward **26**
Clark, Celeste **15**
Freeman, Harold P. **23**
Leffall, LaSalle, Jr. **3**

Capital punishment
Hawkins, Steven **14**

Cardiac research
Watkins, Levi, Jr. **9**

CARE
Gossett, Louis, Jr. **7**
Stone, Chuck **9**

Caribbean dance
Ailey, Alvin **8**
Dunham, Katherine **4**
Fagan, Garth **18**
Nichols, Nichelle **11**
Primus, Pearl **6**

Caroline Jones Advertising, Inc
Jones, Caroline R. **29**

Cartoonists
Armstrong, Robb **15**
Brandon, Barbara **3**
Campbell, E. Simms **13**
Harrington, Oliver W. **9**
McGruder, Aaron **28**

Catholicism
See Roman Catholic Church

CBEA
See Council for a Black Economic Agenda

CBC
See Congressional Black Caucus

CBS
See Columbia Broadcasting System

CBS Television Stations Division
Rodgers, Johnathan **6**

CDC
See Centers for Disease Control and Prevention

CDF
See Children's Defense Fund

CEDBA
See Council for the Economic Development of Black Americans

Celebrities for a Drug-Free America
Vereen, Ben **4**

Censorship
Butts, Calvin O., III **9**
Ice-T **6, 31**

Center of Hope Church
Reems, Ernestine Cleveland **27**

Centers for Disease Control and Prevention (CDC)
Gayle, Helene D. **3**
Satcher, David **7**

CFL
See Canadian Football League

CHA
See Chicago Housing Authority

Challenger
McNair, Ronald **3**

Chama cha Mapinduzi (Tanzania; Revolutionary Party)
Mkapa, Benjamin **16**
Mongella, Gertrude **11**
Nyerere, Julius **5**

Chamber of Deputies (Brazil)
da Silva, Benedita **5**

Chanteuses
Baker, Josephine **3**
Dandridge, Dorothy **3**
Horne, Lena **5**
Kitt, Eartha **16**

Moore, Melba **21**
Moten, Etta **18**
Reese, Della **6, 20**

Charlotte Hornets basketball team
Bryant, Kobe **15, 31**

Che-Lumumba Club
Davis, Angela **5**

Chemistry
Hall, Lloyd A. **8**
Humphries, Frederick **20**
Julian, Percy Lavon **6**
Massie, Jr., Samuel Proctor **29**

Chemurgy
Carver, George Washington **4**

Chesapeake and Potomac Telephone Company
Lewis, Delano **7**

Chess
Ashley, Maurice **15**

Chicago Bears football team
Page, Alan **7**
Payton, Walter **11, 25**
Sayers, Gale **28**
Singletary, Mike **4**

Chicago Bulls basketball team
Brand, Elton **31**
Jordan, Michael **6, 21**
Pippen, Scottie **15**
Rodman, Dennis **12**

Chicago city government
Metcalfe, Ralph **26**
Washington, Harold **6**

Chicago Cubs baseball team
Banks, Ernie **33**
Carter, Joe **30**
Sosa, Sammy **21**

Chicago Defender
Abbott, Robert Sengstacke **27**
Payne, Ethel L. **28**

Chicago Defender Charities
Joyner, Marjorie Stewart **26**

Chicago Eight
Seale, Bobby **3**

Chicago Housing Authority (CHA)
Lane, Vincent **5**

Chicago Library Board
Williams, Fannie Barrier **27**

Chicago Negro Chamber of Commerce
Fuller, S. B. **13**

Chicago Police Department
Hillard, Terry **25**

Chicago Reporter
Washington, Laura S. **18**

Chinn, May Edward **26**
Christian-Green, Donna M. **17**
Comer, James P. **6**
Cooper, Edward S. **6**
Dickens, Helen Octavia **14**
Drew, Charles Richard **7**
Elders, Joycelyn **6**
Fisher, Rudolph **17**
Foster, Henry W., Jr. **26**
Freeman, Harold P. **23**
Fuller, Solomon Carter, Jr. **15**
Gayle, Helene D. **3**
Gibson, William F. **6**
Hinton, William Augustus **8**
Jemison, Mae C. **1**
Kountz, Samuel L. **10**
Lawless, Theodore K. **8**
Leffall, LaSalle, Jr. **3**
Logan, Onnie Lee **14**
Pitt, David Thomas **10**
Poussaint, Alvin F. **5**
Satcher, David **7**
Sullivan, Louis **8**
Thomas, Vivien **9**
Watkins, Levi, Jr. **9**
Welsing, Frances Cress **5**
Williams, Daniel Hale **2**
Witt, Edwin T. **26**
Wright, Louis Tompkins **4**

Meharry Medical College
Foster, Henry W., Jr. **26**
Lyttle, Hulda Margaret **14**

Melanin theory of racism
See also Cress Theory of Color Confrontation and Racism

Men's movement
Somé, Malidoma Patrice **10**

Merce Cunningham Dance Company
Dove, Ulysses **5**

MESBICs
See Minority Enterprise Small Business Investment Corporations

Metropolitan Applied Research Center (MARC Corp.)
Clark, Kenneth B. **5**

Metropolitan Opera
Anderson, Marian **2, 33**
Collins, Janet **33**
Shirley, George **33**

MFDP
See Mississippi Freedom Democratic Party

Miami Dolphins football team
Greene, Joe **10**

Michael Jordan Foundation
Jordan, Michael **6, 21**

Michigan House of Representatives
Collins, Barbara-Rose **7**
Kilpatrick, Carolyn Cheeks **16**
Reeves, Triette Lipsey **27**

Michigan state government
Brown, Cora **33**

Michigan State Supreme Court
Archer, Dennis **7**
Mallett, Conrad, Jr. **16**

Michigan State University
Wharton, Clifton R., Jr. **7**

Microsoft Corporation
Millines Dziko, Trish **28**

Midwifery
Logan, Onnie Lee **14**
Robinson, Sharon **22**

Military police
Cadoria, Sherian Grace **14**

Miller Brewing Company
Colbert, Virgis William **17**

Millinery
Bailey, Xenobia **11**

Million Man March
Farrakhan, Louis **15**
Hawkins, La-Van **17**
Worrill, Conrad **12**

Milwaukee Braves baseball team
Aaron, Hank **5**

Milwaukee Brewers baseball team
Aaron, Hank **5**
Baylor, Don **6**
Sheffield, Gary **16**

Milwaukee Bucks basketball team
Abdul-Jabbar, Kareem **8**
Lucas, John **7**
Robertson, Oscar **26**

Mingo-Jones Advertising
Chisholm, Samuel J. **32**
Jones, Caroline R. **29**
Mingo, Frank **32**

Minneapolis City Council
Sayles Belton, Sharon **9, 16**

Minneapolis city government
Sayles Belton, Sharon **9, 16**

Minnesota State Supreme Court
Page, Alan **7**

Minnesota Timberwolves basketball team
Garnett, Kevin **14**

Minnesota Twins baseball team
Baylor, Don **6**
Carew, Rod **20**
Puckett, Kirby **4**
Winfield, Dave **5**

Minnesota Vikings football team
Carter, Cris **21**
Culpepper, Daunte **32**
Cunningham, Randall **23**
Dungy, Tony **17**

Gilliam, Frank **23**
Green, Dennis **5**
Moon, Warren **8**
Moss, Randy **23**
Page, Alan **7**
Rashad, Ahmad **18**
Walker, Herschel **1**

Minority Business Resource Center
Hill, Jessie, Jr. **13**

Minority Enterprise Small Business Investment
Lewis, Reginald F. **6**

Minstrel shows
McDaniel, Hattie **5**

Miss America
Vincent, Marjorie Judith **2**
Williams, Vanessa L. **4, 17**

Mississippi Freedom Democratic Party (MFDP)
Baker, Ella **5**
Blackwell, Unita **17**
Hamer, Fannie Lou **6**
Henry, Aaron **19**
Norton, Eleanor Holmes **7**

Mississippi state government
Hamer, Fannie Lou **6**

Miss USA
Gist, Carole **1**

MLA
See Modern Language Association of America

MNSD
See National Movement for the Development of Society

Model Inner City Community Organization (MICCO)
Fauntroy, Walter E. **11**

Modeling
Banks, Tyra **11**
Beckford, Tyson **11**
Berry, Halle **4, 19**
Campbell, Naomi **1, 31**
Hardison, Bethann **12**
Hounsou, Djimon **19**
Houston, Whitney **7, 28**
Iman **4, 33**
Johnson, Beverly **2**
Langhart, Janet **19**
Leslie, Lisa **16**
LisaRaye **27**
Michele, Michael **31**
Powell, Maxine **8**
Rochon, Lela **16**
Sims, Naomi **29**
Smith, Barbara **11**
Tamia **24**
Tyrese **27**
Tyson, Cicely **7**
Webb, Veronica **10**
Wek, Alek **18**

Cumulative Name Index

Volume numbers appear in **bold**

Fox, Ulrich Alexander
  See Fox, Rick
Fox, Vivica A. 1964— **15**
Foxx, Jamie 1967— **15**
Foxx, Redd 1922-1991 **2**
Franklin, Aretha 1942— **11**
Franklin, Carl 1949— **11**
Franklin, Hardy R. 1929— **9**
Franklin, John Hope 1915— **5**
Franklin, Kirk 1970— **15**
Franklin, Robert M(ichael) 1954— **13**
Franks, Gary 1954(?)— **2**
Frazier, Edward Franklin 1894-1962 **10**
Frazier, Joe 1944— **19**
Frazier-Lyde, Jacqui 1961— **31**
Freelon, Nnenna 1954— **32**
Freeman, Al(bert Cornelius), Jr. 1934— **11**
Freeman, Cathy 1973— **29**
Freeman, Charles Eldridge 1933— **19**
Freeman, Harold P. 1933— **23**
Freeman, Leonard 1950— **27**
Freeman, Marianna 1957— **23**
Freeman, Morgan 1937— **2, 20**
Freeman, Yvette **27**
French, Albert 1943— **18**
Fresh Prince, The
  See Smith, Will
Friday, Jeff 1964(?)— **24**
Fudge, Ann (Marie) 1951(?)— **11**
Fuhr, Grant 1962— **1**
Fulani, Lenora (Branch) 1950— **11**
Fuller, Arthur 1972— **27**
Fuller, Charles (Henry) 1939— **8**
Fuller, Meta Vaux Warrick 1877-1968 **27**
Fuller, S. B. 1895-1988 **13**
Fuller, Solomon Carter, Jr. 1872-1953 **15**
Fuller, Vivian 1954— **33**
Futch, Eddie 1911-2001 **33**
Gaines, Ernest J(ames) 1933— **7**
Gaither, Jake 1903-1994 **14**
Gantt, Harvey (Bernard) 1943— **1**
Garnett, Kevin 1976— **14**
Garrison, Zina 1963— **2**
Garvey, Marcus 1887-1940 **1**
Gary, Willie Edward 1947— **12**
Gaston, Arthur G(eorge) 1892— **4**
Gates, Henry Louis, Jr. 1950— **3**
Gates, Sylvester James, Jr. 1950— **15**
Gay, Marvin Pentz, Jr.
  See Gaye, Marvin
Gaye, Marvin 1939-1984 **2**
Gayle, Helene D(oris) 1955— **3**
Gentry, Alvin 1954— **23**
George, Nelson 1957— **12**
Gibson, Althea 1927— **8**
Gibson, Bob 1935— **33**
Gibson, Johnnie Mae 1949— **23**
Gibson, Josh 1911-1947 **22**
Gibson, Kenneth Allen 1932— **6**
Gibson, Tyrese
  See Tyrese
Gibson, William F(rank) 1933— **6**
Giddings, Paula (Jane) 1947— **11**
Gillespie, Dizzy 1917-1993 **1**
Gillespie, John Birks
  See Gillespie, Dizzy
Gilliam, Frank 1934(?)— **23**
Gilliam, Joe, Jr. 1950-2000 **31**
Gilliam, Sam 1933— **16**
Giovanni, Nikki 1943— **9**
Giovanni, Yolande Cornelia, Jr.
  See Giovanni, Nikki
Gist, Carole 1970(?)— **1**
Givens, Robin 1965— **4, 25**
Glover, Danny 1948— **1, 24**

Glover, Nathaniel, Jr. 1943— **12**
Glover, Savion 1974— **14**
Goines, Donald 1937(?)-1974 **19**
Goldberg, Whoopi 1955— **4, 33**
Golden, Marita 1950— **19**
Golden, Thelma 1965— **10**
Goldsberry, Ronald 1942— **18**
Gomes, Peter J(ohn) 1942— **15**
Gomez, Jewelle 1948— **30**
Gomez-Preston, Cheryl 1954— **9**
Goode, Mal(vin Russell) 1908-1995 **13**
Goode, W(oodrow) Wilson 1938— **4**
Gooden, Dwight 1964— **20**
Gooden, Lolita
  See Roxanne Shante
Gooding, Cuba, Jr. 1968— **16**
Goodnight, Paul 1946— **32**
Gordon, Dexter 1923-1990 **25**
Gordon, Ed(ward Lansing, III) 1960— **10**
Gordon, Pamela 1955— **17**
Gordone, Charles 1925-1995 **15**
Gordy, Berry, Jr. 1929— **1**
Goreed, Joseph
  See Williams, Joe
Goss, Tom 1946— **23**
Gossett, Louis, Jr. 1936— **7**
Gourdine, Meredith 1929-1998 **33**
Gourdine, Simon (Peter) 1940— **11**
Graham, Lawrence Otis 1962— **12**
Graham, Stedman 1951(?)— **13**
Grandmaster Flash 1958— **33**
Grant, Gwendolyn Goldsby 19(?)(?)— **28**
Gravely, Samuel L(ee), Jr. 1922— **5**
Graves, Denyce Antoinette 1964— **19**
Graves, Earl G(ilbert) 1935— **1**
Gray, F. Gary 1969— **14**
Gray, Frizzell
  See Mfume, Kweisi
Gray, Macy 1970— **29**
Gray, William H., III 1941— **3**
Greely, M. Gasby 1946— **27**
Greely, Margaret Gasby
  See Greely, M. Gasby
Green, A. C. 1963— **32**
Green, Albert 1946— **13**
Green, Dennis 1949— **5**
Greene, Joe 1946— **10**
Greene, Maurice 1974— **27**
Greenfield, Eloise 1929— **9**
Gregg, Eric 1951— **16**
Gregory, Dick 1932— **1**
Gregory, Frederick D(rew) 1941— **8**
Grier, David Alan 1955— **28**
Grier, Pam(ala Suzette) 1949— **9, 31**
Grier, Roosevelt (Rosey) 1932— **13**
Griffey, George Kenneth, Jr. 1969— **12**
Griffith, Mark Winston 1963— **8**
Griffith, Yolanda 1970— **25**
Griffith-Joyner, Florence 1959-1998 **28**
Griffiths, Marcia 1948(?)— **29**
Grimké, Archibald H(enry) 1849-1930 **9**
Guarionex
  See Schomburg, Arthur Alfonso
Guillaume, Robert 1927— **3**
Guinier, (Carol) Lani 1950— **7, 30**
Gumbel, Bryant Charles 1948— **14**
Gumbel, Greg 1946— **8**
Gunn, Moses 1929-1993 **10**
Guy, (George) Buddy 1936— **31**
Guy, Jasmine 1964(?)— **2**
Guy, Rosa 1925(?)— **5**
Guy-Sheftall, Beverly 1946— **13**
Guyton, Tyree 1955— **9**
Gwynn, Anthony Keith 1960— **18**
Habré, Hissène 1942— **6**

Habyarimana, Juvenal 1937-1994 **8**
Haile Selassie 1892-1975 **7**
Hailey, JoJo 1971— **22**
Hailey, K-Ci 1969— **22**
Hale, Clara 1902-1992 **16**
Hale, Lorraine 1926(?)— **8**
Haley, Alex (Palmer) 1921-1992 **4**
Haley, George Williford Boyce 1925— **21**
Hall, Elliott S. 1938(?)— **24**
Hall, Lloyd A(ugustus) 1894-1971 **8**
Hamblin, Ken 1940— **10**
Hamer, Fannie Lou (Townsend) 1917-
  1977 **6**
Hamilton, Virginia 1936— **10**
Hammer
  See Hammer, M. C.
Hammer, M. C. 1963— **20**
Hammond, Fred 1960— **23**
Hampton, Fred 1948-1969 **18**
Hampton, Henry (Eugene, Jr.) 1940— **6**
Hampton, Lionel 1908(?)— **17**
Hancock, Herbie Jeffrey 1940— **20**
Handy, W(illiam) C(hristopher) 1873-
  1937 **8**
Hani, Chris 1942-1993 **6**
Hani, Martin Thembisile
  See Hani, Chris
Hannah, Marc (Regis) 1956— **10**
Hansberry, Lorraine (Vivian) 1930-1965 **6**
Hansberry, William Leo 1894-1965 **11**
Hardaway, Anfernee (Deon)
  See Hardaway, Anfernee (Penny)
Hardaway, Anfernee (Penny) 1971— **13**
Hardaway, Penny
  See Hardaway, Anfernee (Penny)
Hardison, Bethann 19??— **12**
Hardison, Kadeem 1966— **22**
Harkless, Necia Desiree 1920— **19**
Harmon, Clarence 1940(?)— **26**
Harper, Frances E(llen) W(atkins) 1825-
  1911 **11**
Harper, Frank
  See Harper, Hill
Harper, Hill 1973— **32**
Harrell, Andre (O'Neal) 1962(?)— **9, 30**
Harrington, Oliver W(endell) 1912— **9**
Harris, "Sweet" Alice
  See Harris, Alice
Harris, Alice 1934— **7**
Harris, Barbara 1930— **12**
Harris, E. Lynn 1957— **12, 33**
Harris, Eddy L. 1956— **18**
Harris, James, III
  See Jimmy Jam
Harris, Jay **19**
Harris, Leslie 1961— **6**
Harris, Marcelite Jordan 1943— **16**
Harris, Mary Styles 1949— **31**
Harris, Monica 1968— **18**
Harris, Patricia Roberts 1924-1985 **2**
Harris, Robin 1953-1990 **7**
Harrison, Alvin 1974— **28**
Harrison, Calvin 1974— **28**
Harsh, Vivian Gordon 1890-1960 **14**
Harvard, Beverly (Joyce Bailey) 1950— **11**
Harvey, Steve 1957— **18**
Haskins, Clem 1943— **23**
Hastie, William H(enry) 1904-1976 **8**
Hastings, Alcee Lamar 1936— **16**
Hatchett, Glenda 1951(?)— **32**
Hathaway, Donny 1945-1979 **18**
Hathaway, Isaac Scott 1874-1967 **33**
Haughton, Aaliyah
  See Aaliyah